WAITING FOR THE OTHER SHOE TO DROP...

WAITING FOR THE OTHER SHOE TO DROP...

MORE CARTOONS BY PAT OLIPHANT

Andrews and McMeel
A Universal Press Syndicate Company
Kansas City

Oliphant® is distributed internationally by Universal Press Syndicate.

ISBN: 0-8362-1765-9

Library of Congress Catalog Card Number: 94-77996

July 29, 1993

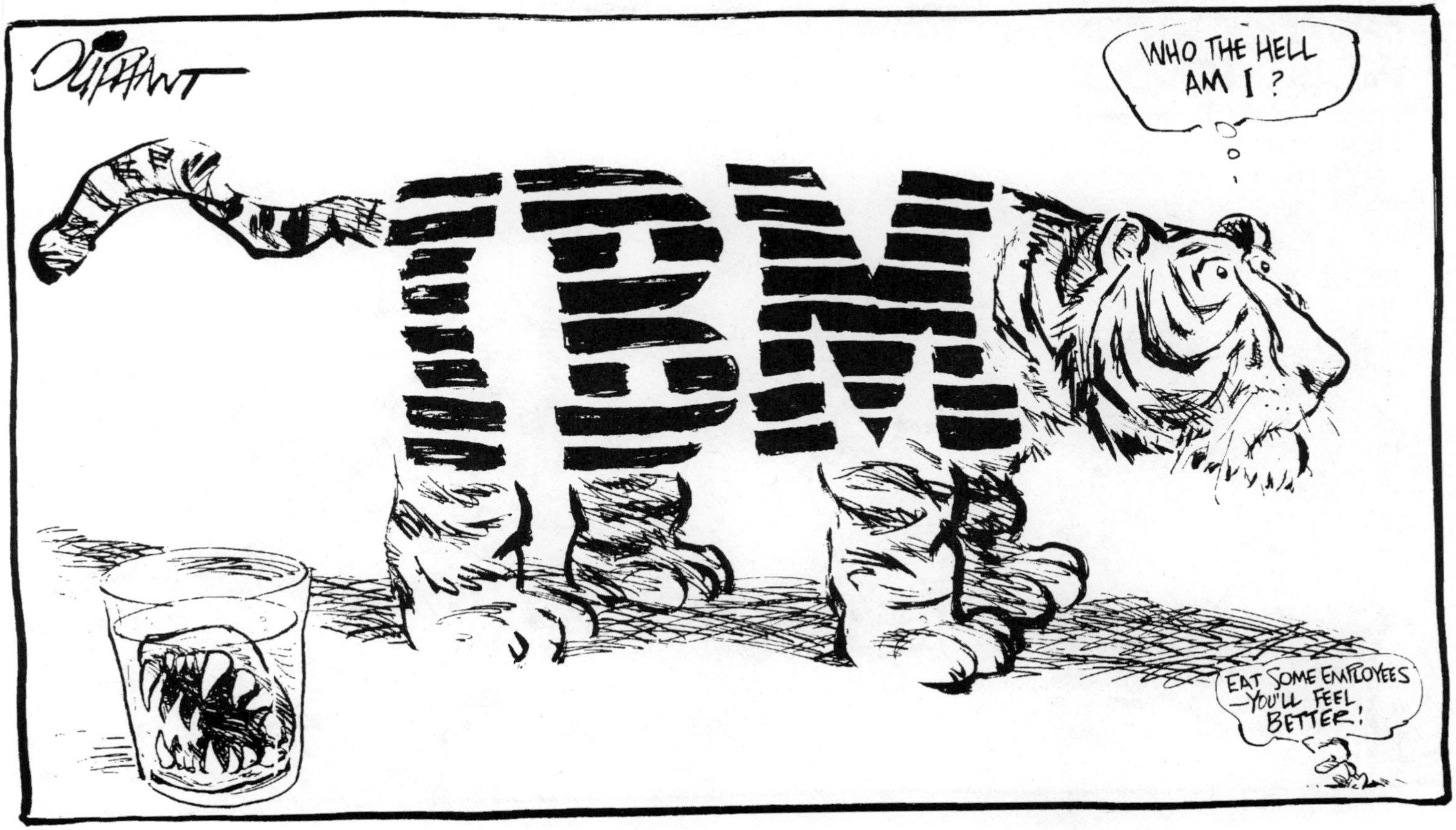
OLIPHANT
WHO THE HELL AM I?
IBM
EAT SOME EMPLOYEES —YOU'LL FEEL BETTER!

July 30, 1993

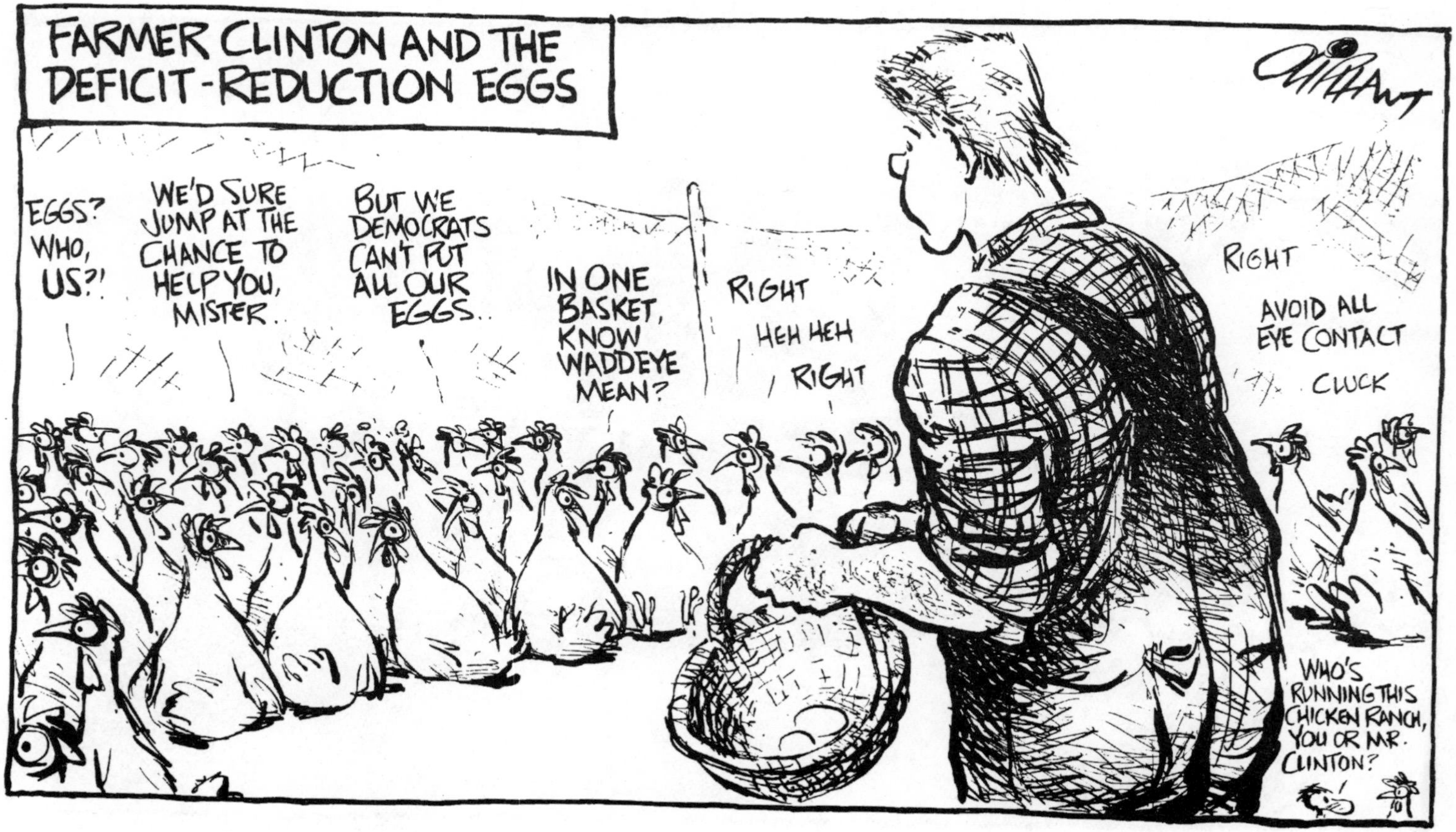
FARMER CLINTON AND THE DEFICIT-REDUCTION EGGS
EGGS? WHO, US?!
WE'D SURE JUMP AT THE CHANCE TO HELP YOU, MISTER..
BUT WE DEMOCRATS CAN'T PUT ALL OUR EGGS..
IN ONE BASKET, KNOW WADDEYE MEAN?
RIGHT
HEH HEH
RIGHT
RIGHT
AVOID ALL EYE CONTACT
CLUCK
WHO'S RUNNING THIS CHICKEN RANCH, YOU OR MR. CLINTON?

August 4, 1993

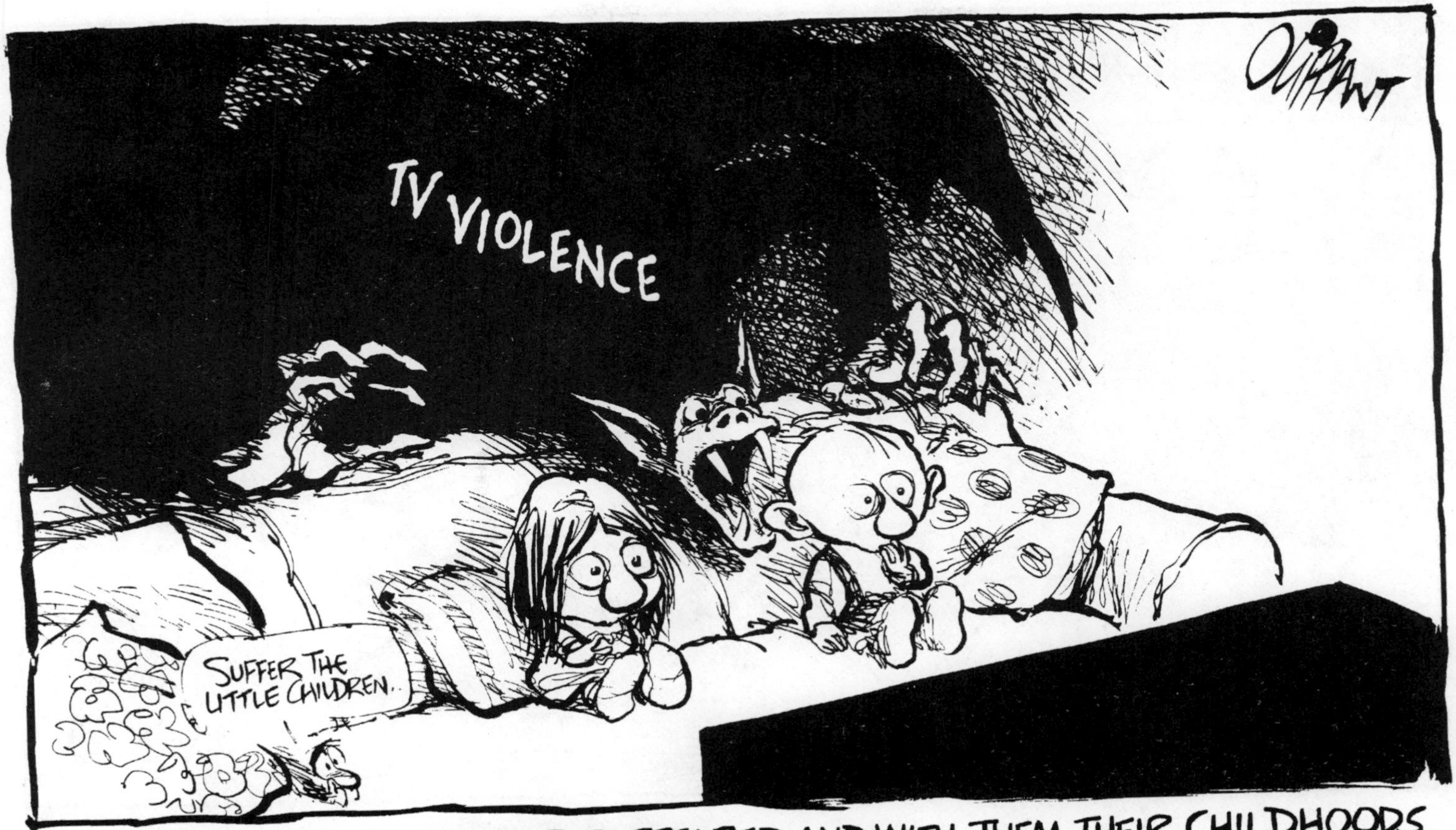
OLIPHANT
TV VIOLENCE
SUFFER THE LITTLE CHILDREN.

ONE BY ONE THE CHILDREN DISAPPEARED, AND WITH THEM THEIR CHILDHOODS.

August 5, 1993

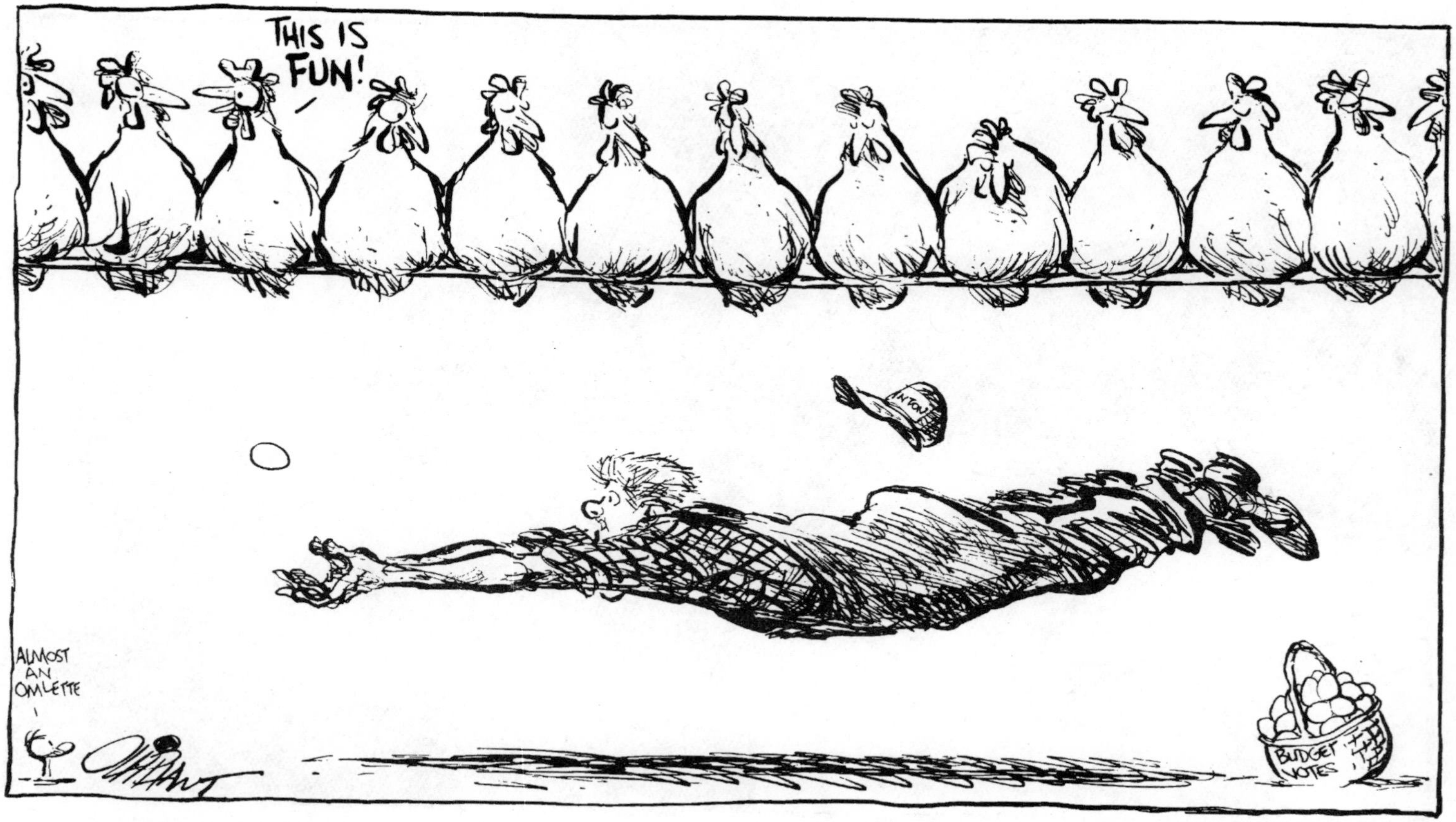
THIS IS FUN!
BUDGET VOTES
ALMOST AN OMLETTE

August 6, 1993

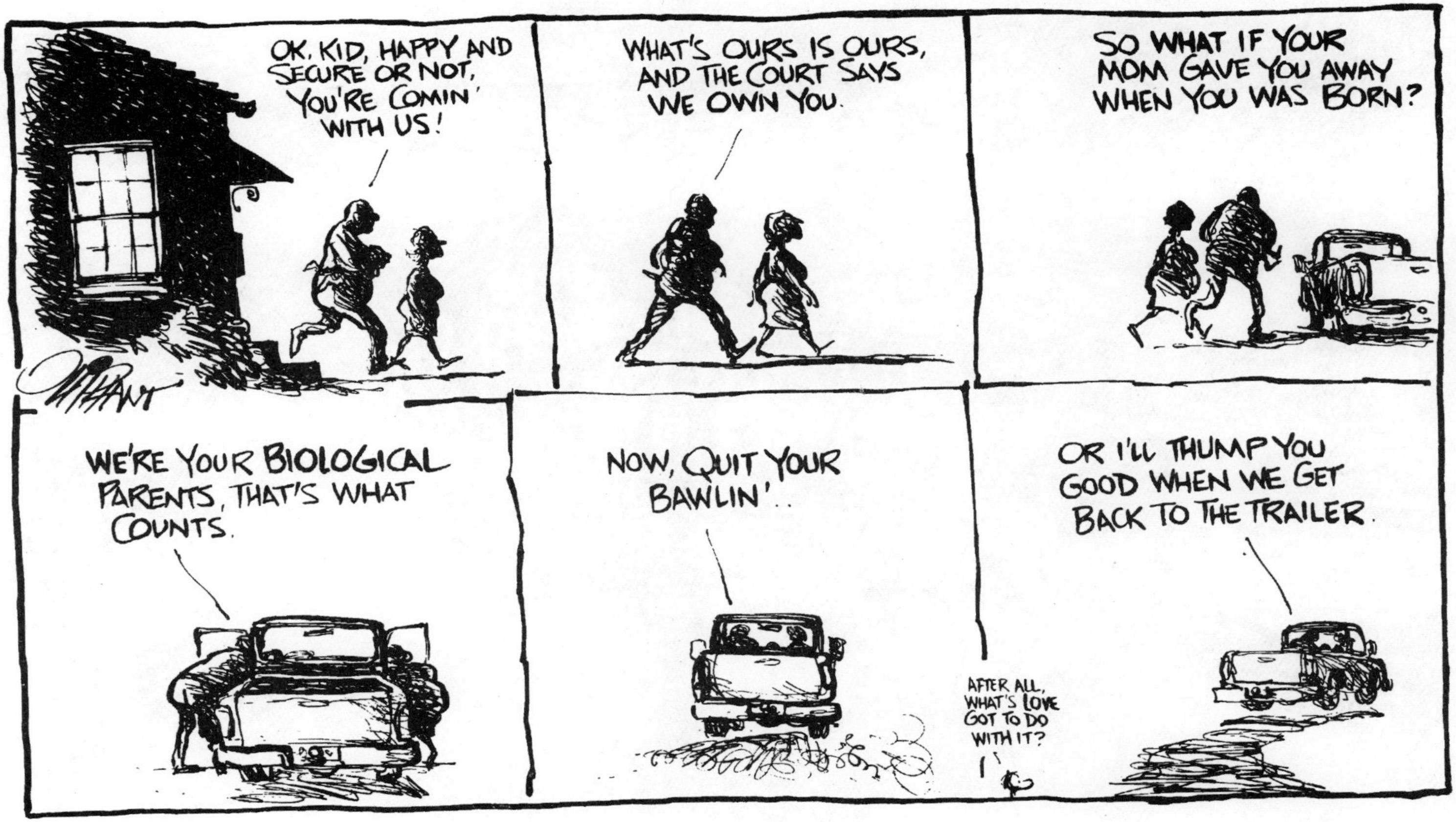

OK. KID, HAPPY AND SECURE OR NOT, YOU'RE COMIN' WITH US!
WHAT'S OURS IS OURS, AND THE COURT SAYS WE OWN YOU.
SO WHAT IF YOUR MOM GAVE YOU AWAY WHEN YOU WAS BORN?
WE'RE YOUR BIOLOGICAL PARENTS, THAT'S WHAT COUNTS.
NOW, QUIT YOUR BAWLIN'...
AFTER ALL, WHAT'S LOVE GOT TO DO WITH IT?
OR I'LL THUMP YOU GOOD WHEN WE GET BACK TO THE TRAILER.

August 25, 1993

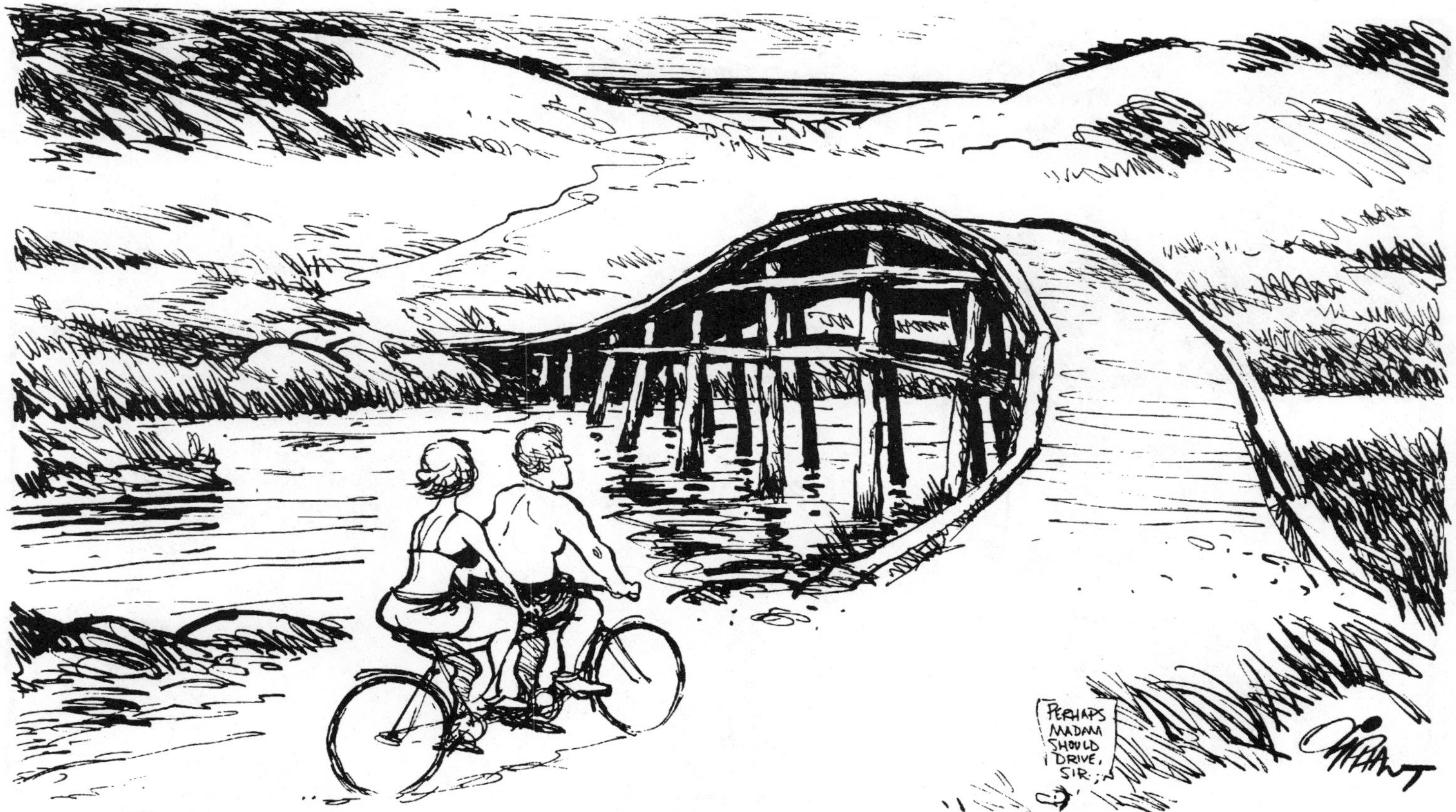
PERHAPS MADAM SHOULD DRIVE, SIR.

THE QUEST ETERNAL FOR THE KENNEDY COMPARISON — MARTHA'S VINEYARD.

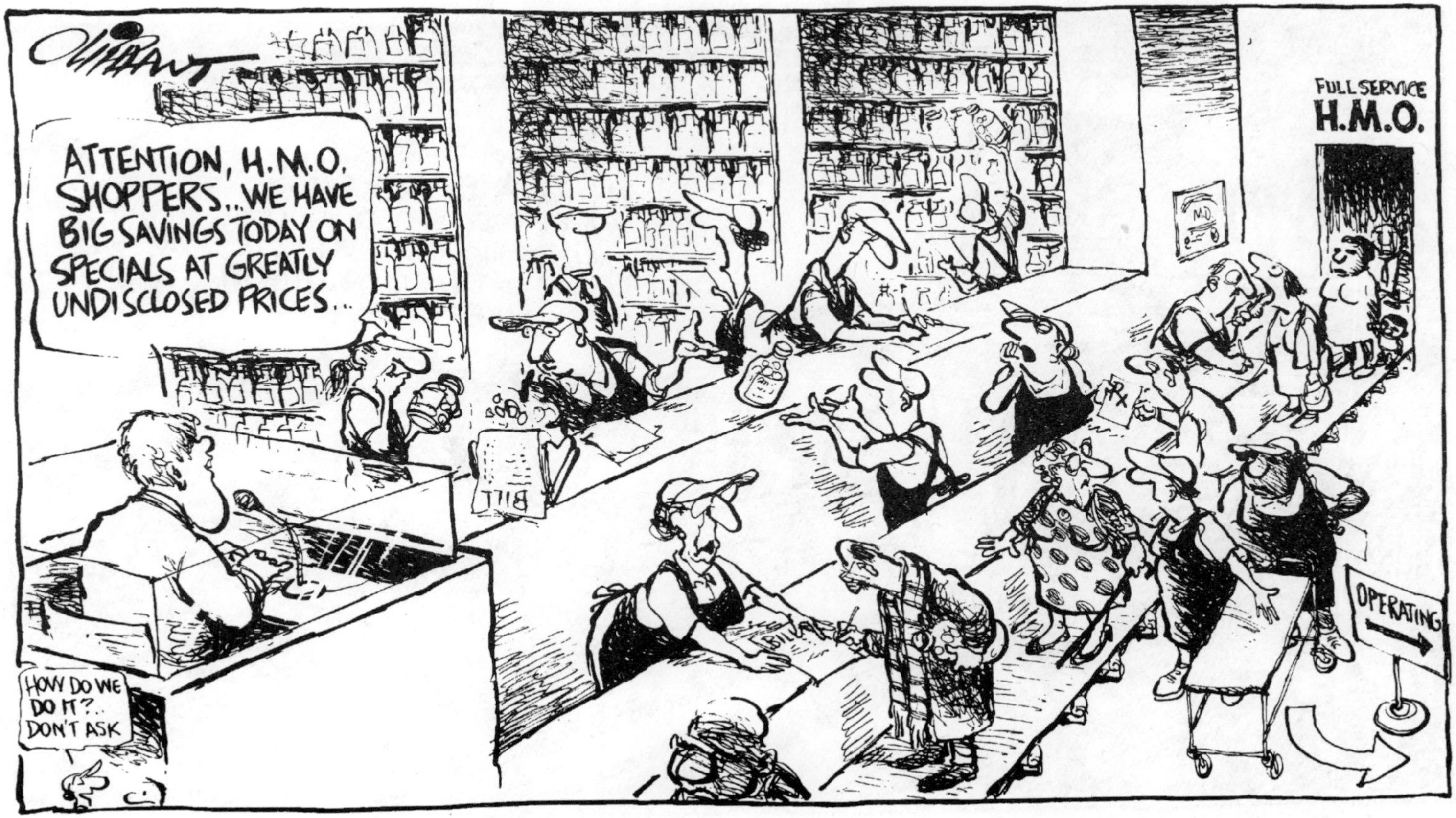
ATTENTION, H.M.O. SHOPPERS...WE HAVE BIG SAVINGS TODAY ON SPECIALS AT GREATLY UNDISCLOSED PRICES...
FULL SERVICE H.M.O.
BILL
OPERATING
HOW DO WE DO IT?.. DON'T ASK

September 1, 1993

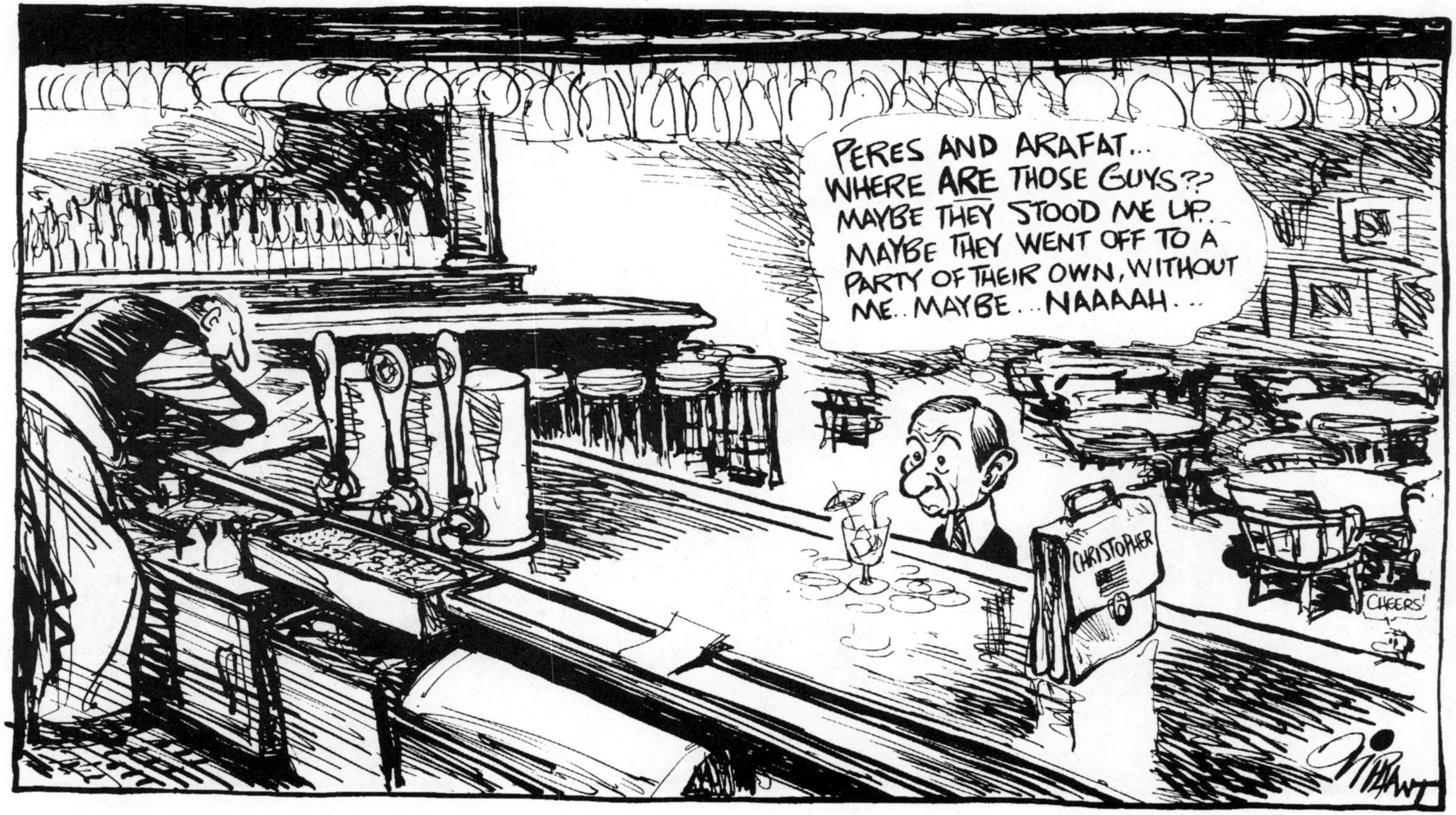
PERES AND ARAFAT...
WHERE ARE THOSE GUYS??
MAYBE THEY STOOD ME UP..
MAYBE THEY WENT OFF TO A
PARTY OF THEIR OWN, WITHOUT
ME.. MAYBE...NAAAAH...
CHRISTOPHER
CHEERS!

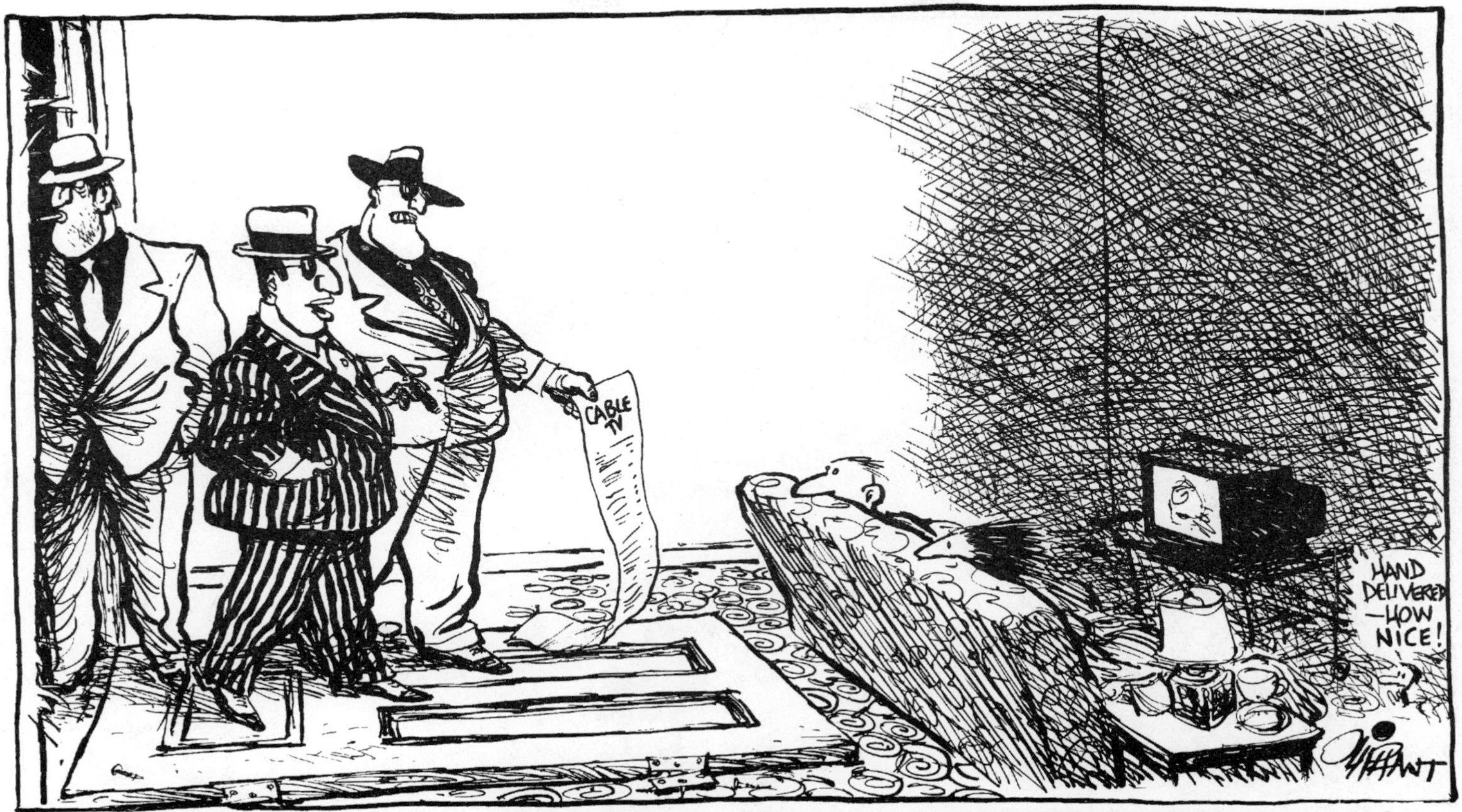
CABLE TV
HAND DELIVERED —HOW NICE!
OLIPHANT

'GREETINGS FROM YOUR LOCAL CABLE COMPANY. THE FCC HAS JUST MADE EXTORTION LEGAL. HERE IS YOUR NEW BILL.'

September 3, 1993

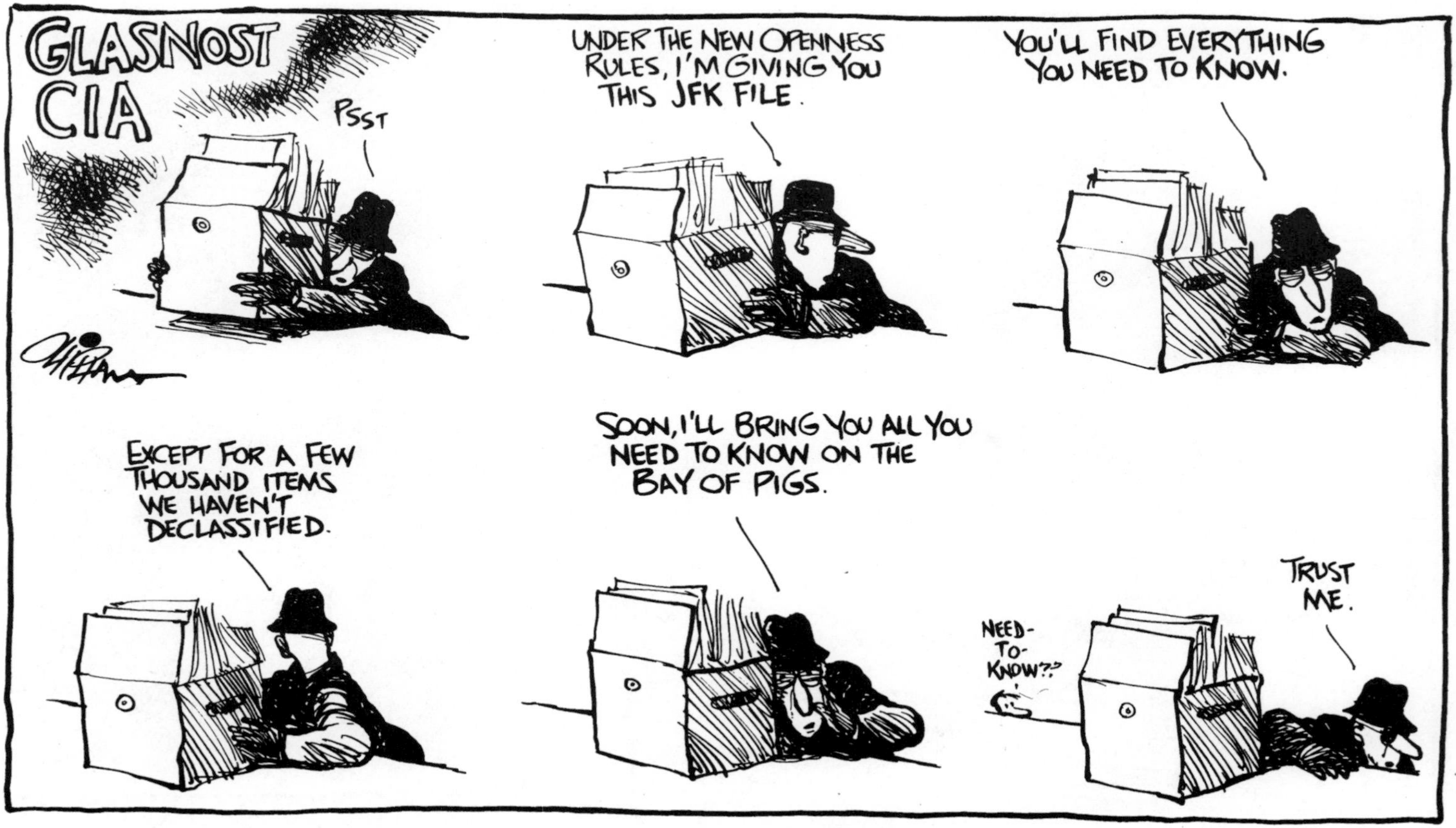
GLASNOST CIA
PSST
UNDER THE NEW OPENNESS RULES, I'M GIVING YOU THIS JFK FILE.
YOU'LL FIND EVERYTHING YOU NEED TO KNOW.
EXCEPT FOR A FEW THOUSAND ITEMS WE HAVEN'T DECLASSIFIED.
SOON, I'LL BRING YOU ALL YOU NEED TO KNOW ON THE BAY OF PIGS.
NEED-TO-KNOW??
TRUST ME.

September 8, 1993

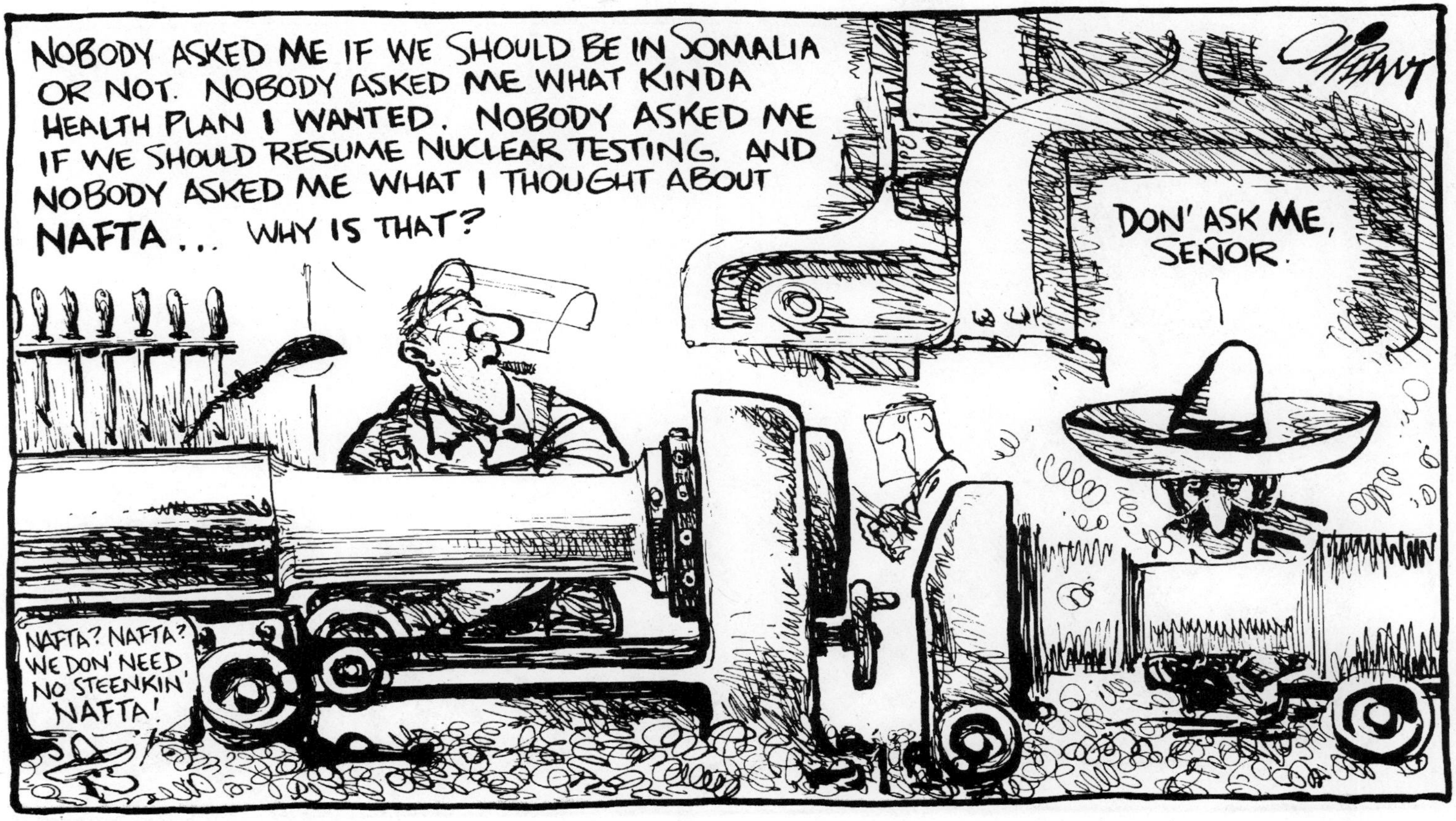
NOBODY ASKED ME IF WE SHOULD BE IN SOMALIA OR NOT. NOBODY ASKED ME WHAT KINDA HEALTH PLAN I WANTED. NOBODY ASKED ME IF WE SHOULD RESUME NUCLEAR TESTING. AND NOBODY ASKED ME WHAT I THOUGHT ABOUT NAFTA... WHY IS THAT?
DON' ASK ME, SEÑOR.
NAFTA? NAFTA? WE DON' NEED NO STEENKIN' NAFTA!
OLIPHANT

September 14, 1993

September 15, 1993

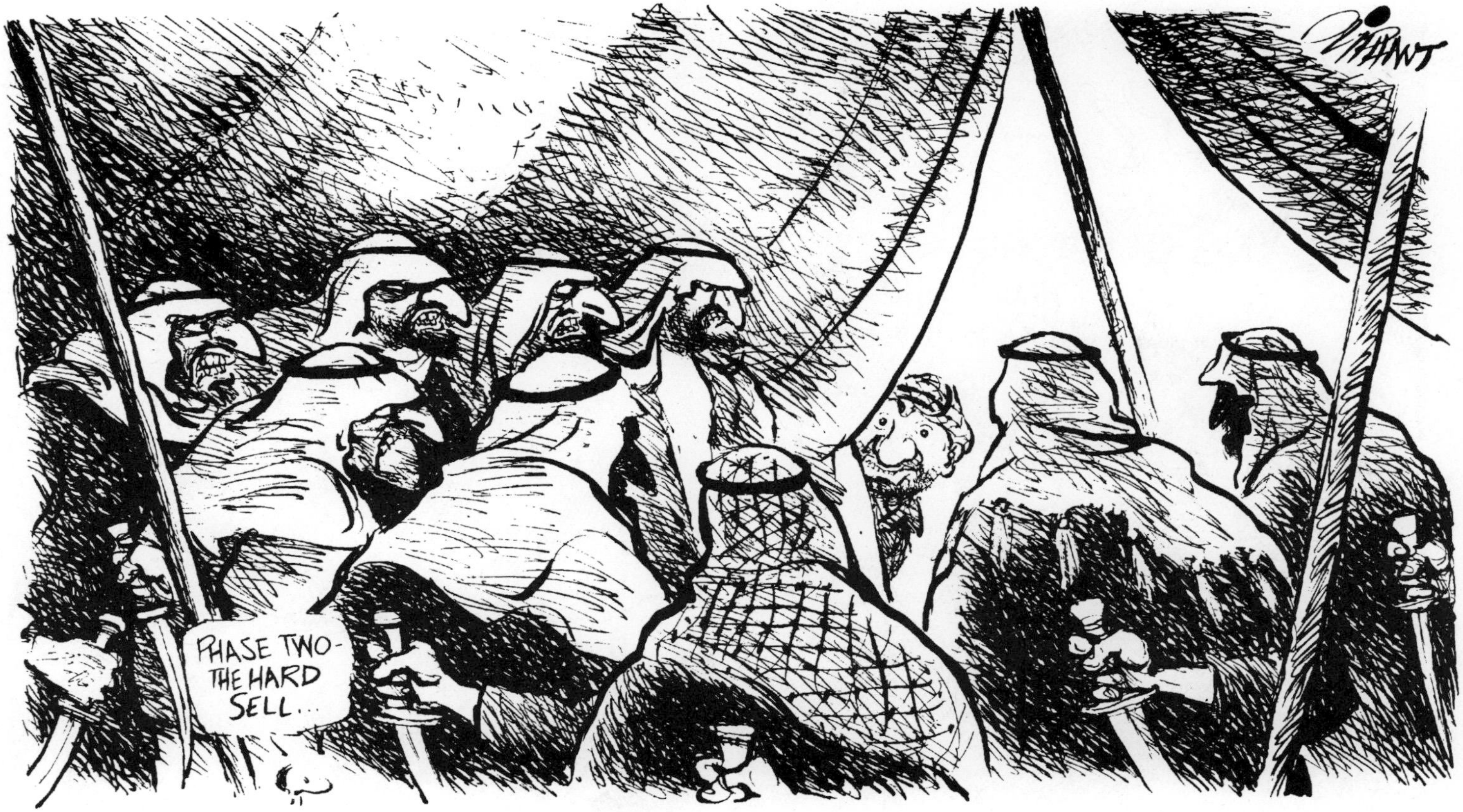
PHASE TWO-
THE HARD
SELL...

September 16, 1993

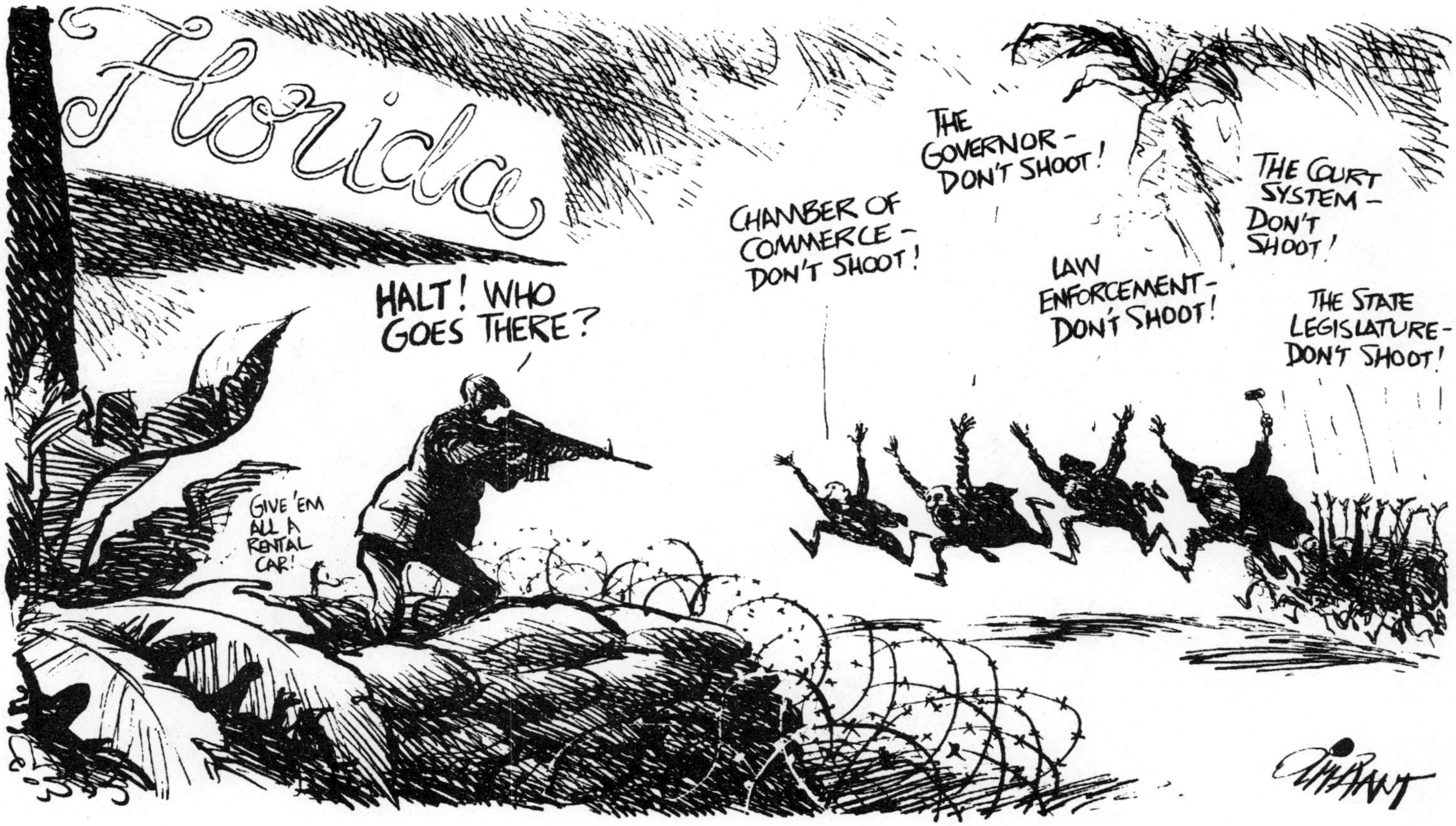
Florida
HALT! WHO GOES THERE?
GIVE 'EM ALL A RENTAL CAR!
CHAMBER OF COMMERCE - DON'T SHOOT!
THE GOVERNOR - DON'T SHOOT!
LAW ENFORCEMENT - DON'T SHOOT!
THE COURT SYSTEM - DON'T SHOOT!
THE STATE LEGISLATURE - DON'T SHOOT!

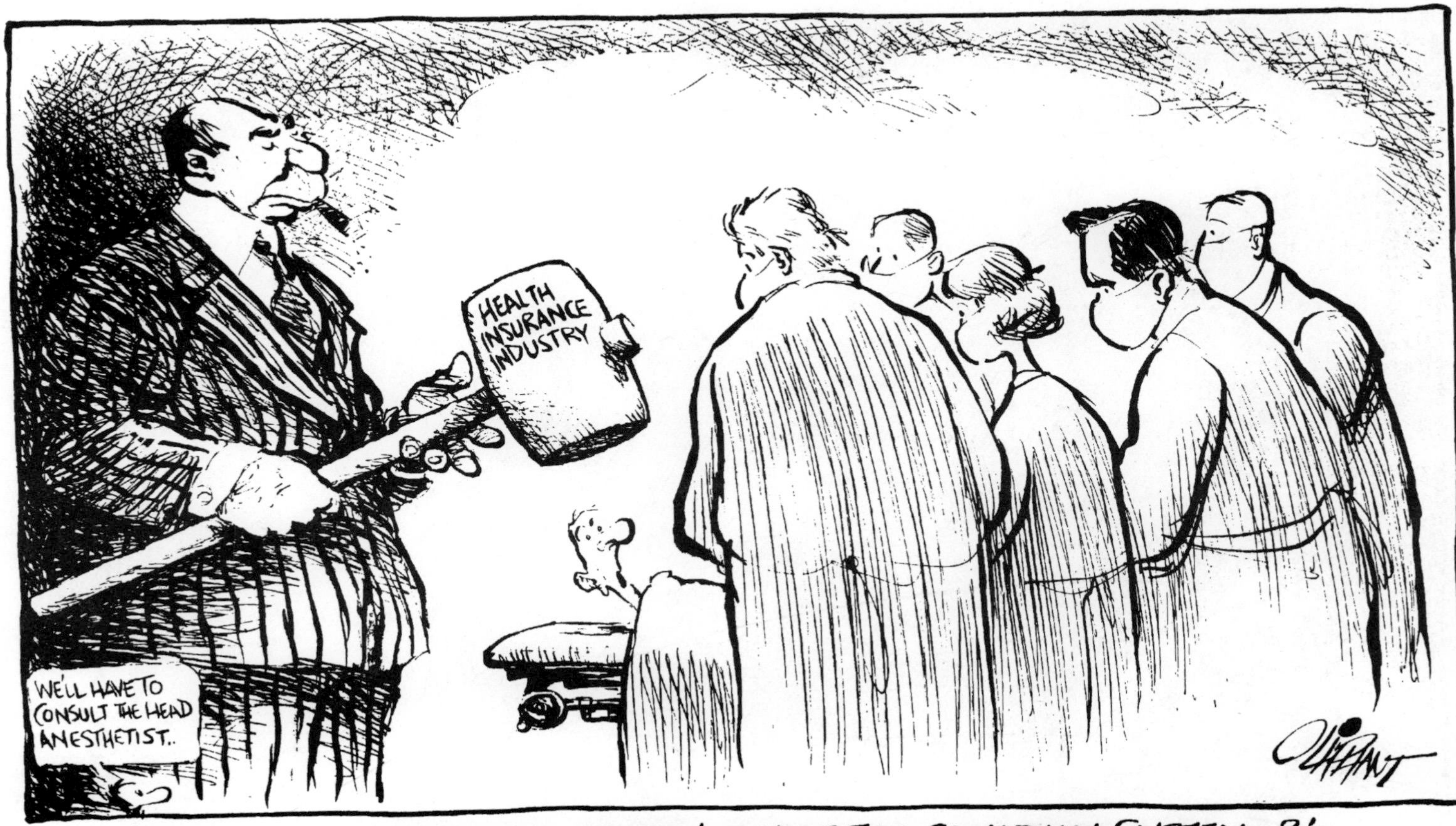
HEALTH INSURANCE INDUSTRY
WE'LL HAVE TO CONSULT THE HEAD ANESTHETIST..
OLIPHANT

'COULD WE JUST TAKE ONE MORE LOOK AT THE CANADIAN SYSTEM..?'

September 21, 1993

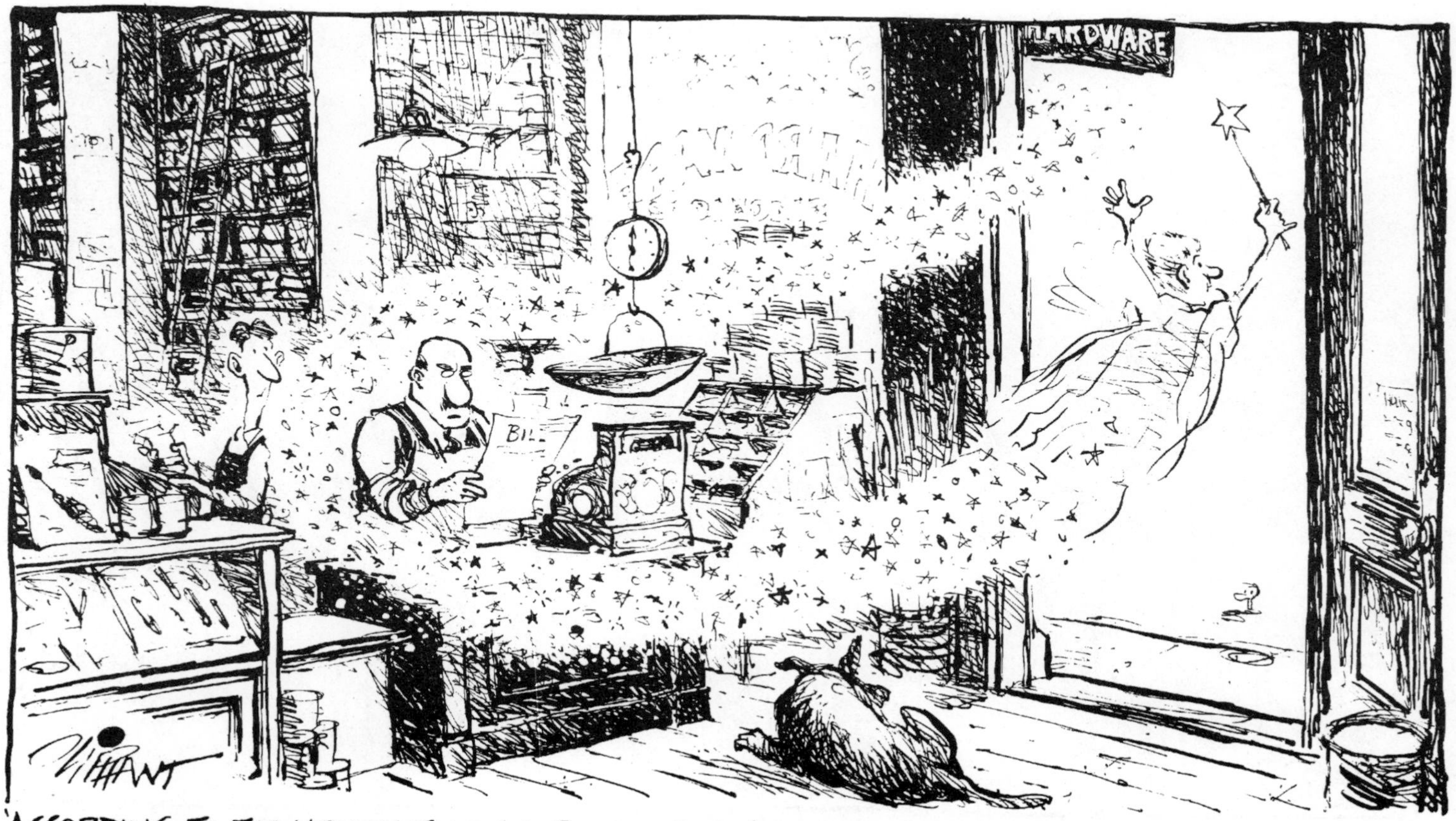

'ACCORDING TO THE HEALTH FAIRY, I GET TO PAY YOUR HEALTH CARE PREMIUMS. YOU'RE FIRED.'

September 22, 1993

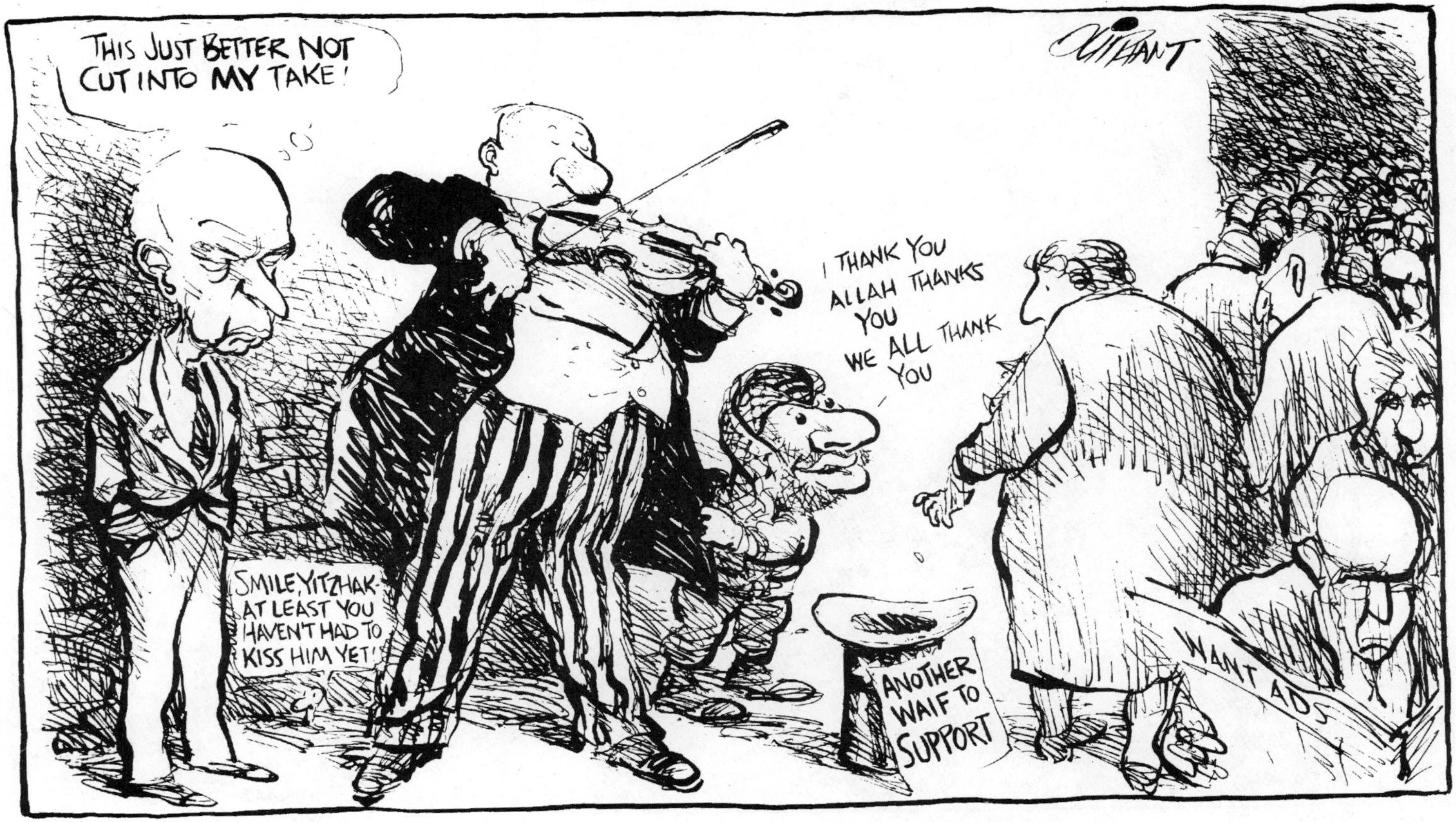
THIS JUST BETTER NOT CUT INTO MY TAKE!
I THANK YOU
ALLAH THANKS YOU
WE ALL THANK YOU
SMILE, YITZHAK - AT LEAST YOU HAVEN'T HAD TO KISS HIM YET!
ANOTHER WAIF TO SUPPORT
WANT ADS
OLIPHANT

September 24, 1993

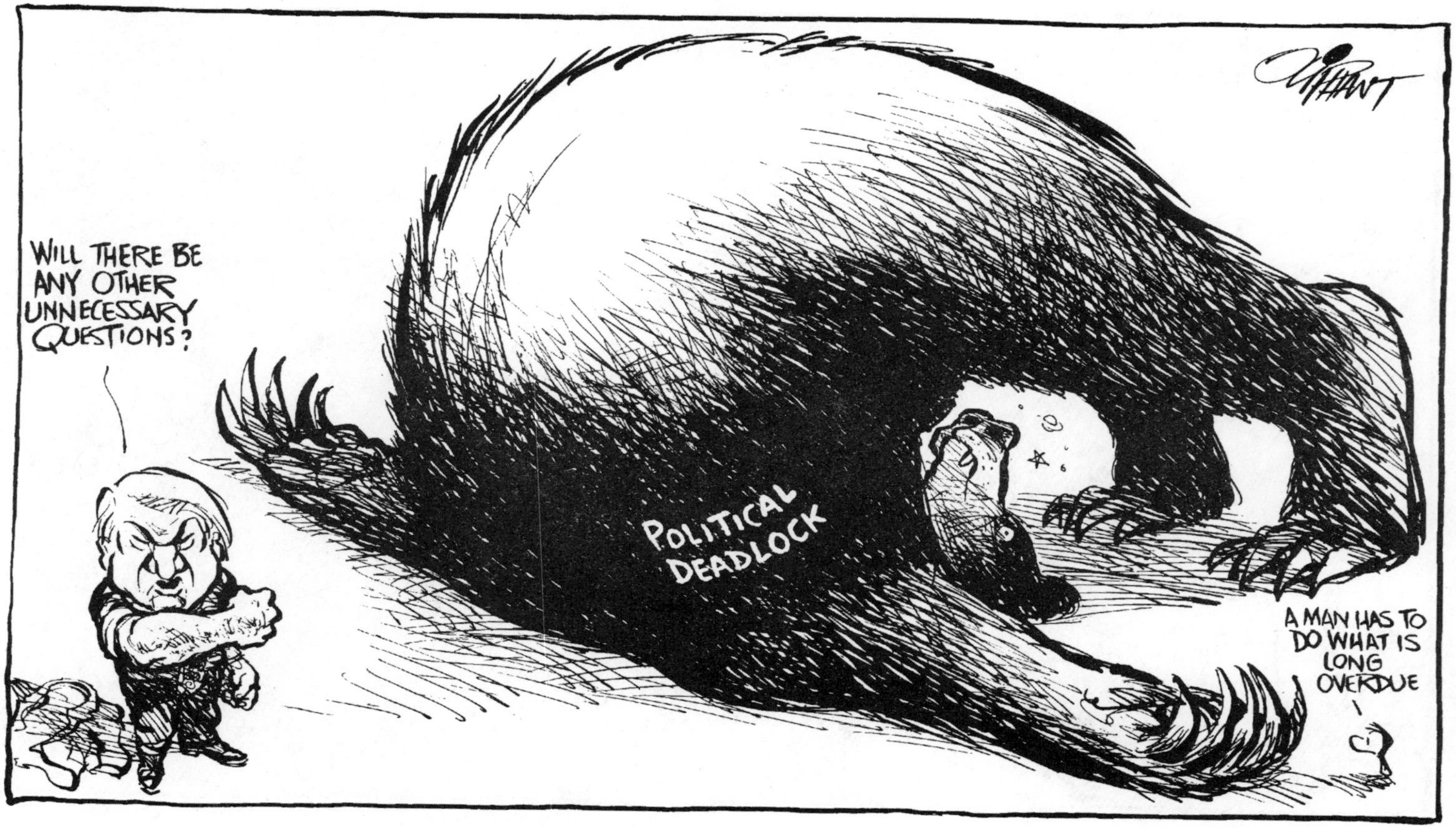

WILL THERE BE ANY OTHER UNNECESSARY QUESTIONS?
POLITICAL DEADLOCK
A MAN HAS TO DO WHAT IS LONG OVERDUE

September 27, 1993

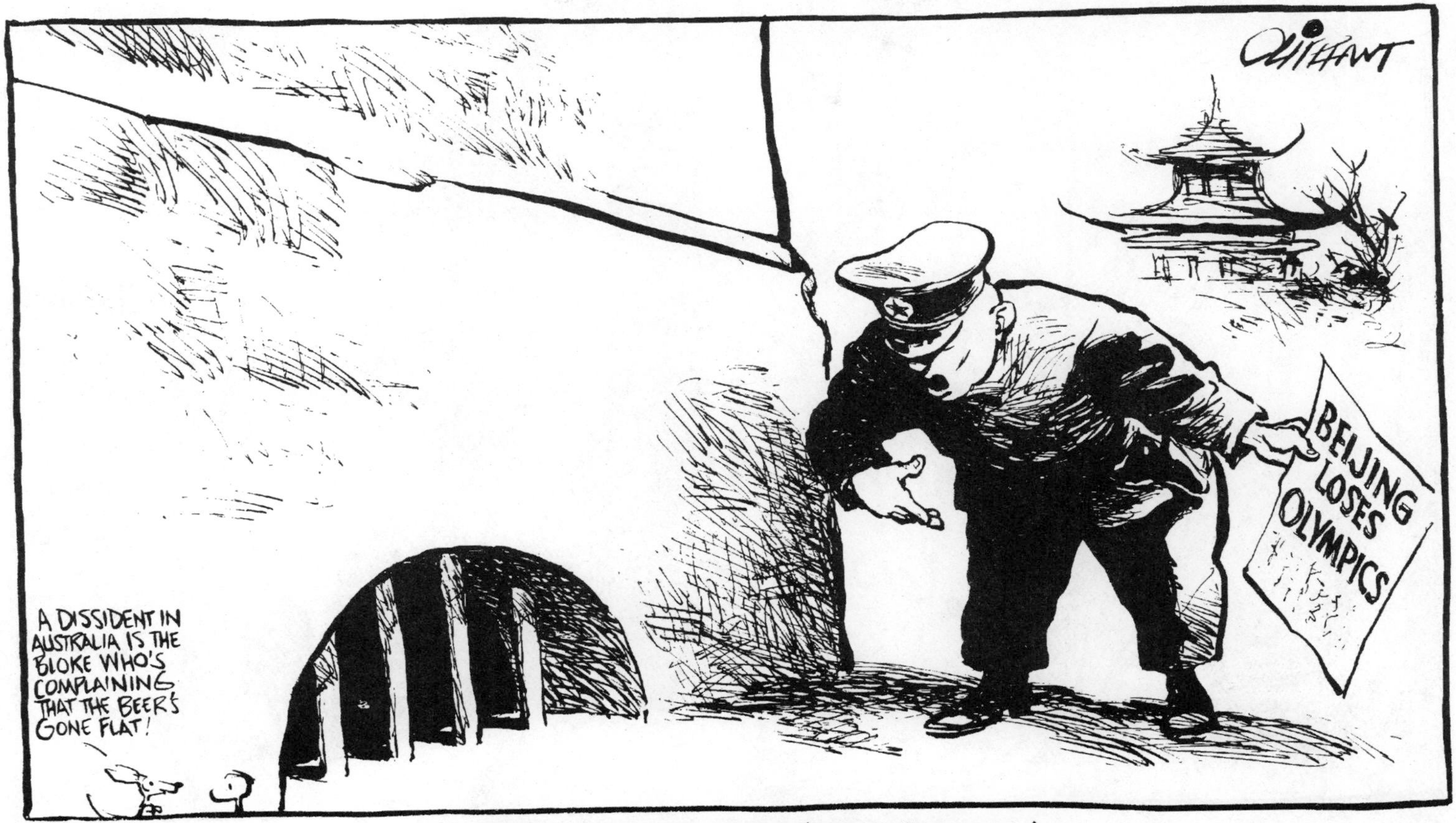
OLIPHANT
BEIJING LOSES OLYMPICS
A DISSIDENT IN AUSTRALIA IS THE BLOKE WHO'S COMPLAINING THAT THE BEER'S GONE FLAT!

'NOW LOOK WHAT YOU'VE DONE!'

September 30, 1993

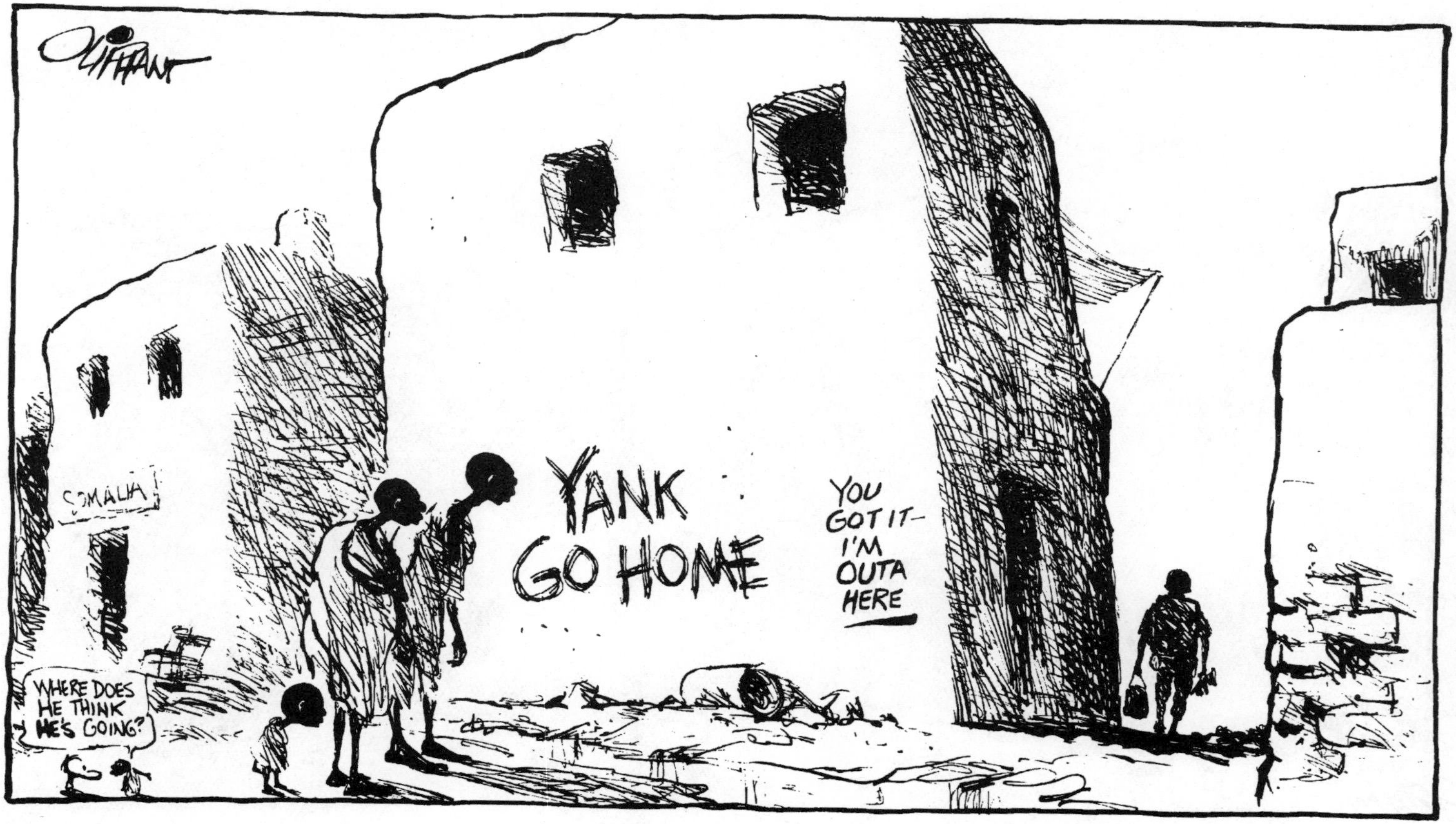
OLIPHANT
SOMALIA
YANK GO HOME
YOU GOT IT- I'M OUTA HERE
WHERE DOES HE THINK HE'S GOING?

September 30, 1993

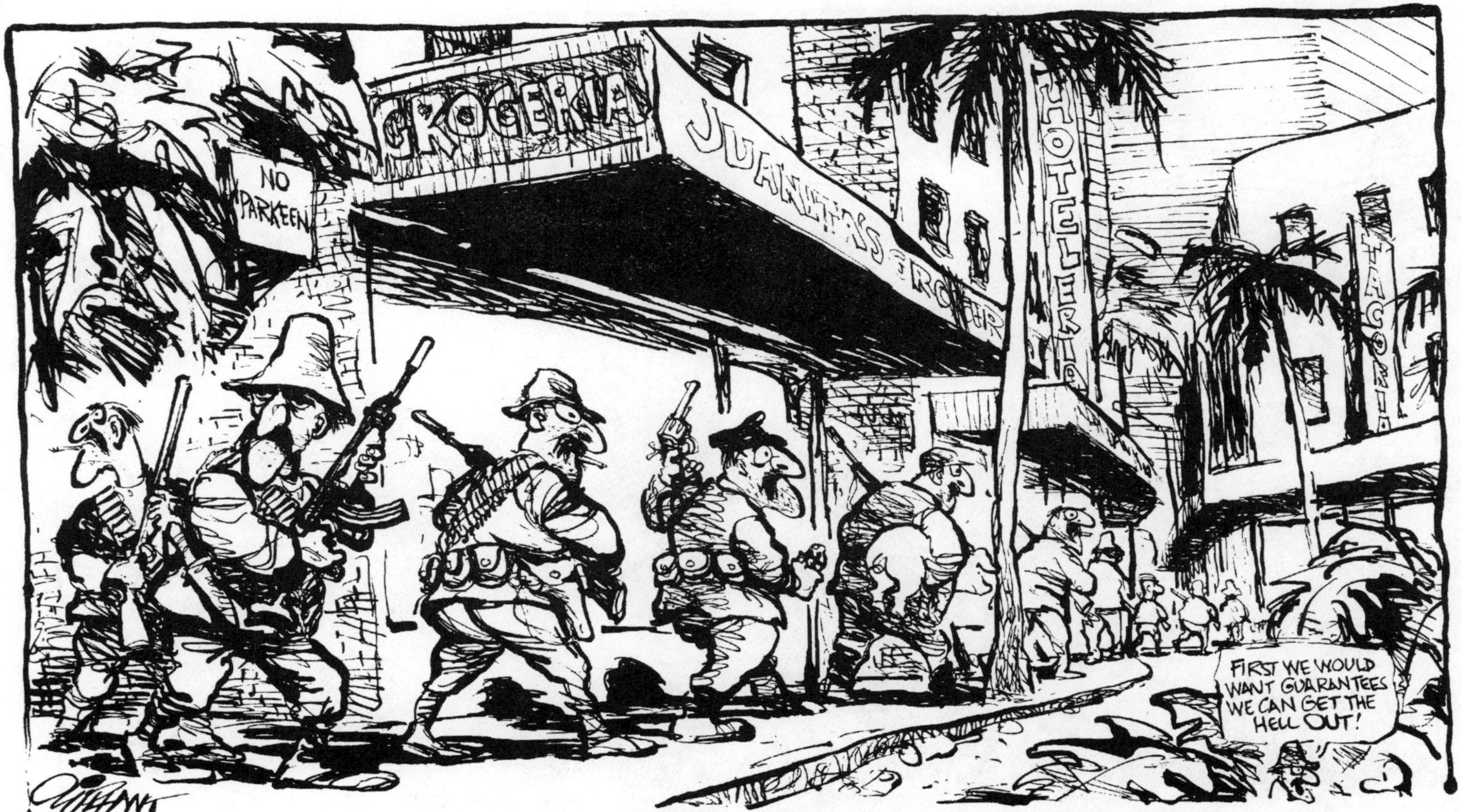
GROCERIA
NO PARKEEN
JUANITA'S GROCERIA
HOTELERIA
TACORIA
FIRST WE WOULD WANT GUARANTEES WE CAN GET THE HELL OUT!

SHOULD BOSNIA SEND A PEACE-KEEPING FORCE TO MIAMI?

October 1, 1993

IN
DID YOU KNOW OBESITY RESTRICTS YOU SOCIALLY AND ECONOMICALLY?
WRITE ME A REPORT

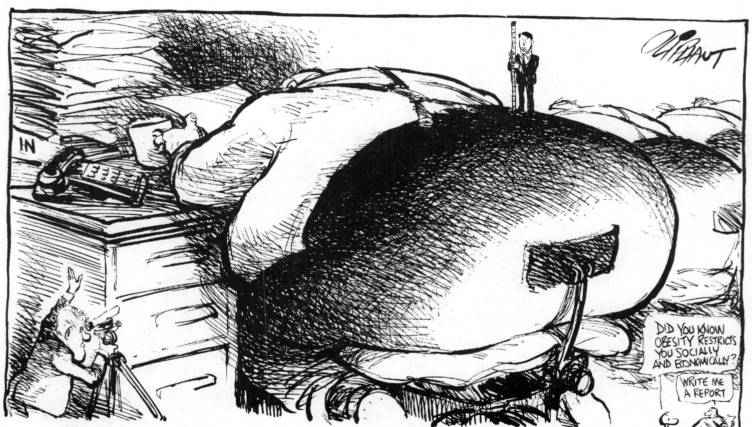

TO REDESIGN GOVERNMENT, FIRST SURVEY THE PROBLEM AREAS.

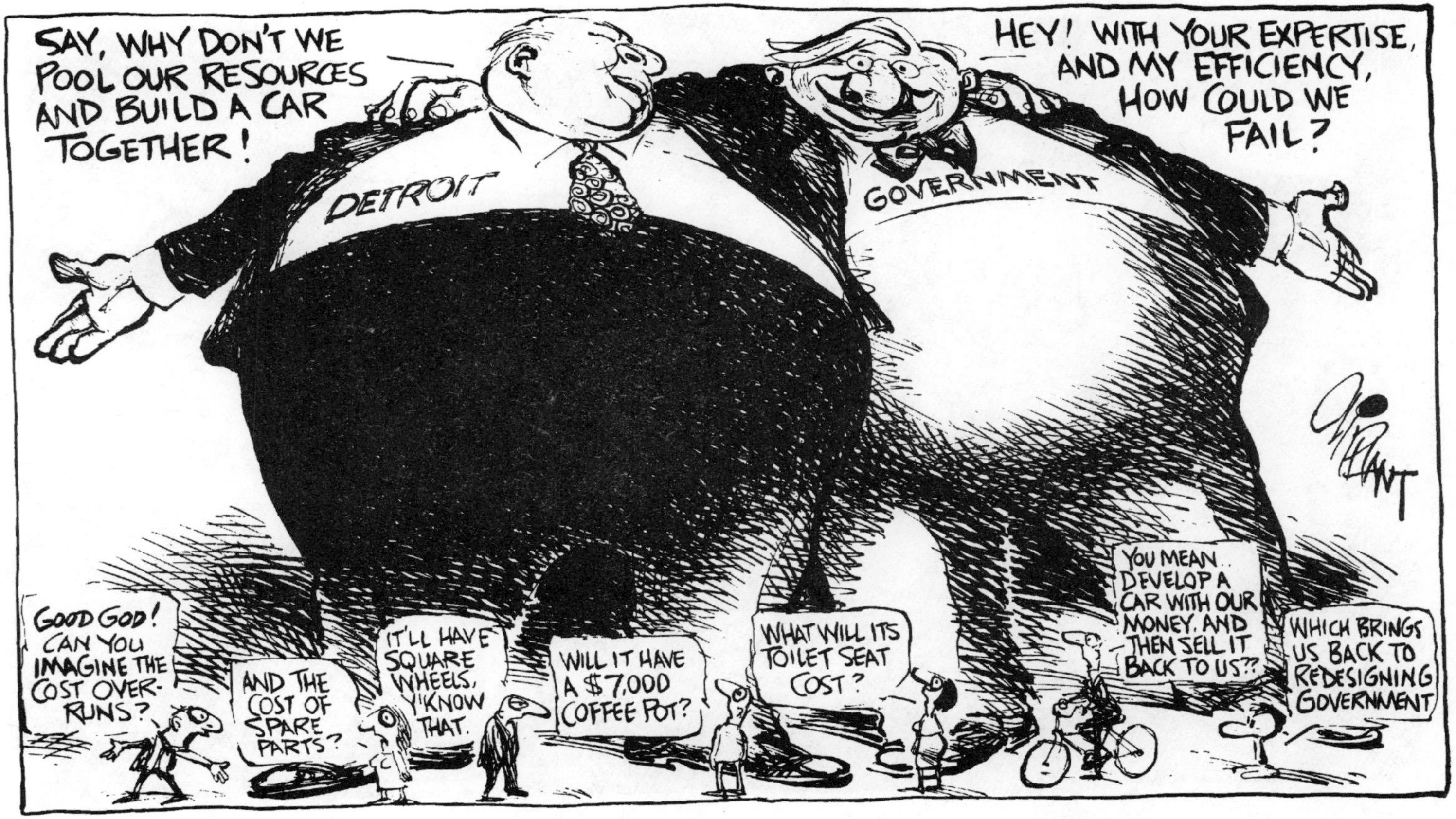
SAY, WHY DON'T WE POOL OUR RESOURCES AND BUILD A CAR TOGETHER!
HEY! WITH YOUR EXPERTISE, AND MY EFFICIENCY, HOW COULD WE FAIL?
DETROIT
GOVERNMENT
GOOD GOD! CAN YOU IMAGINE THE COST OVER-RUNS?
AND THE COST OF SPARE PARTS?
IT'LL HAVE SQUARE WHEELS, Y'KNOW THAT.
WILL IT HAVE A $7,000 COFFEE POT?
WHAT WILL ITS TOILET SEAT COST?
YOU MEAN.. DEVELOP A CAR WITH OUR MONEY, AND THEN SELL IT BACK TO US??
WHICH BRINGS US BACK TO REDESIGNING GOVERNMENT
OLIPHANT

October 6, 1993

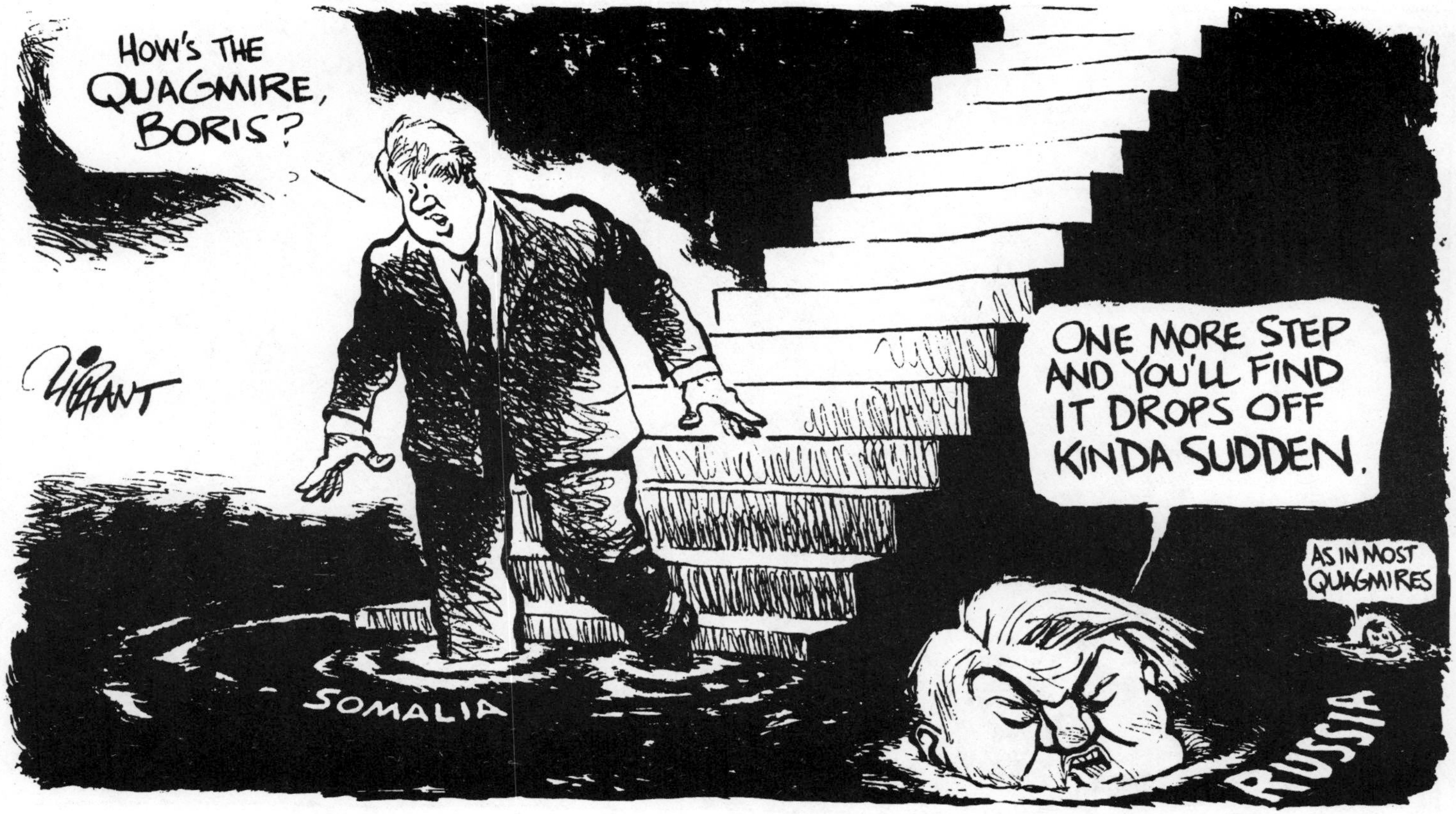
HOW'S THE QUAGMIRE, BORIS?
ONE MORE STEP AND YOU'LL FIND IT DROPS OFF KINDA SUDDEN.
AS IN MOST QUAGMIRES
SOMALIA
RUSSIA

October 7, 1993

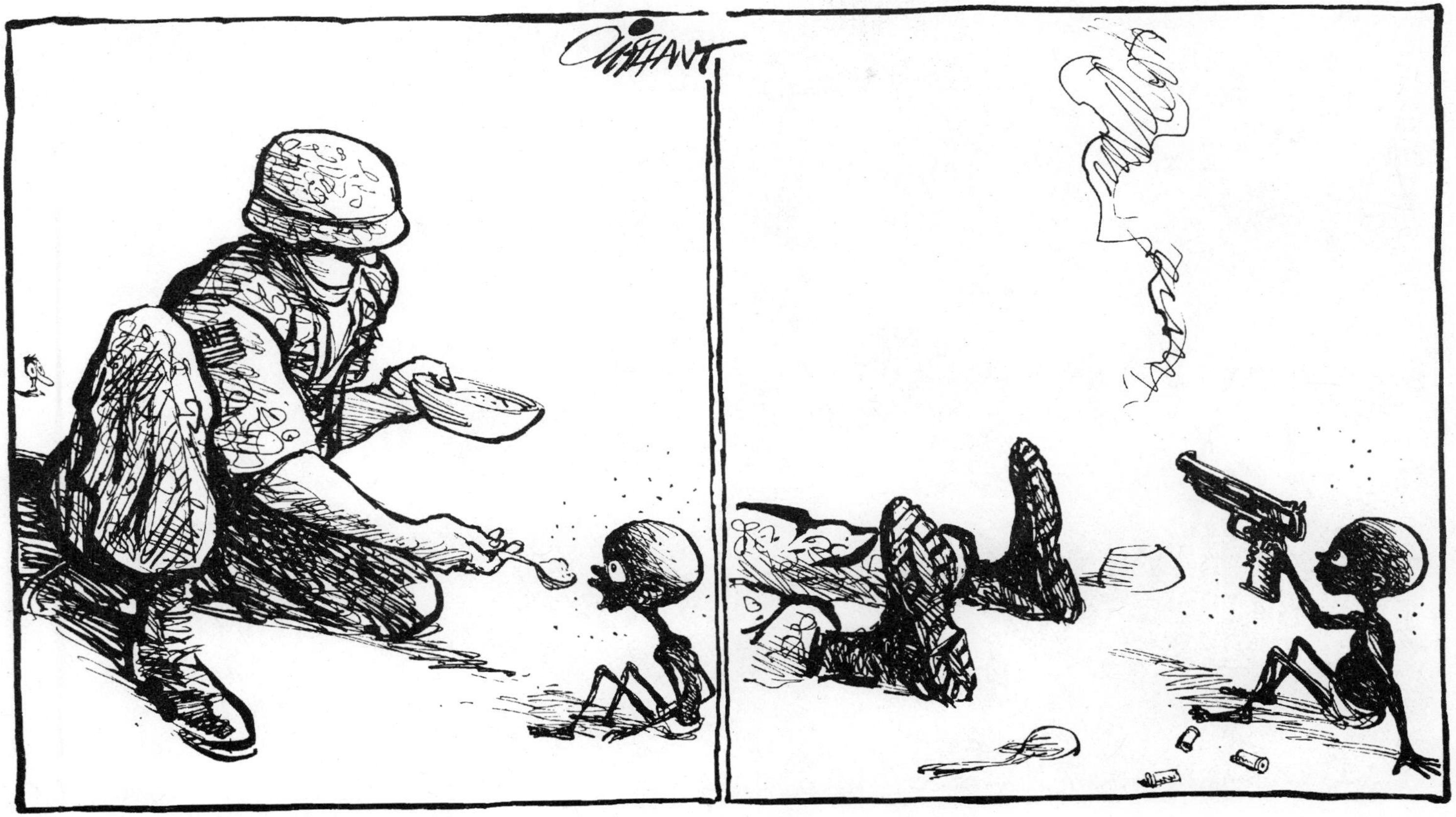
OLIPHANT

October 11, 1993

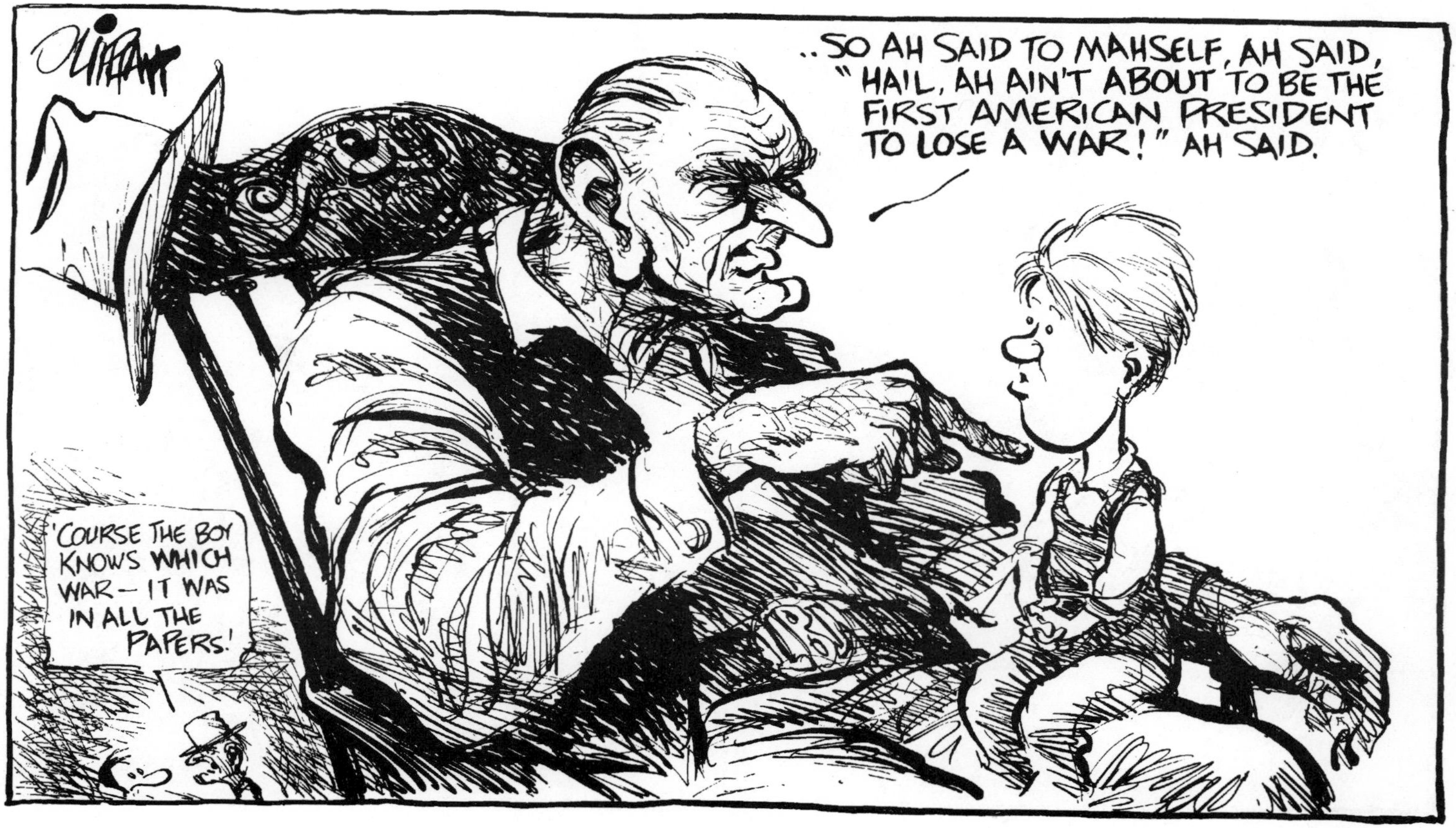
OLIPHANT
..SO AH SAID TO MAHSELF, AH SAID, "HAIL, AH AIN'T ABOUT TO BE THE FIRST AMERICAN PRESIDENT TO LOSE A WAR!" AH SAID.
'COURSE THE BOY KNOWS WHICH WAR – IT WAS IN ALL THE PAPERS!
LBJ

October 13, 1993

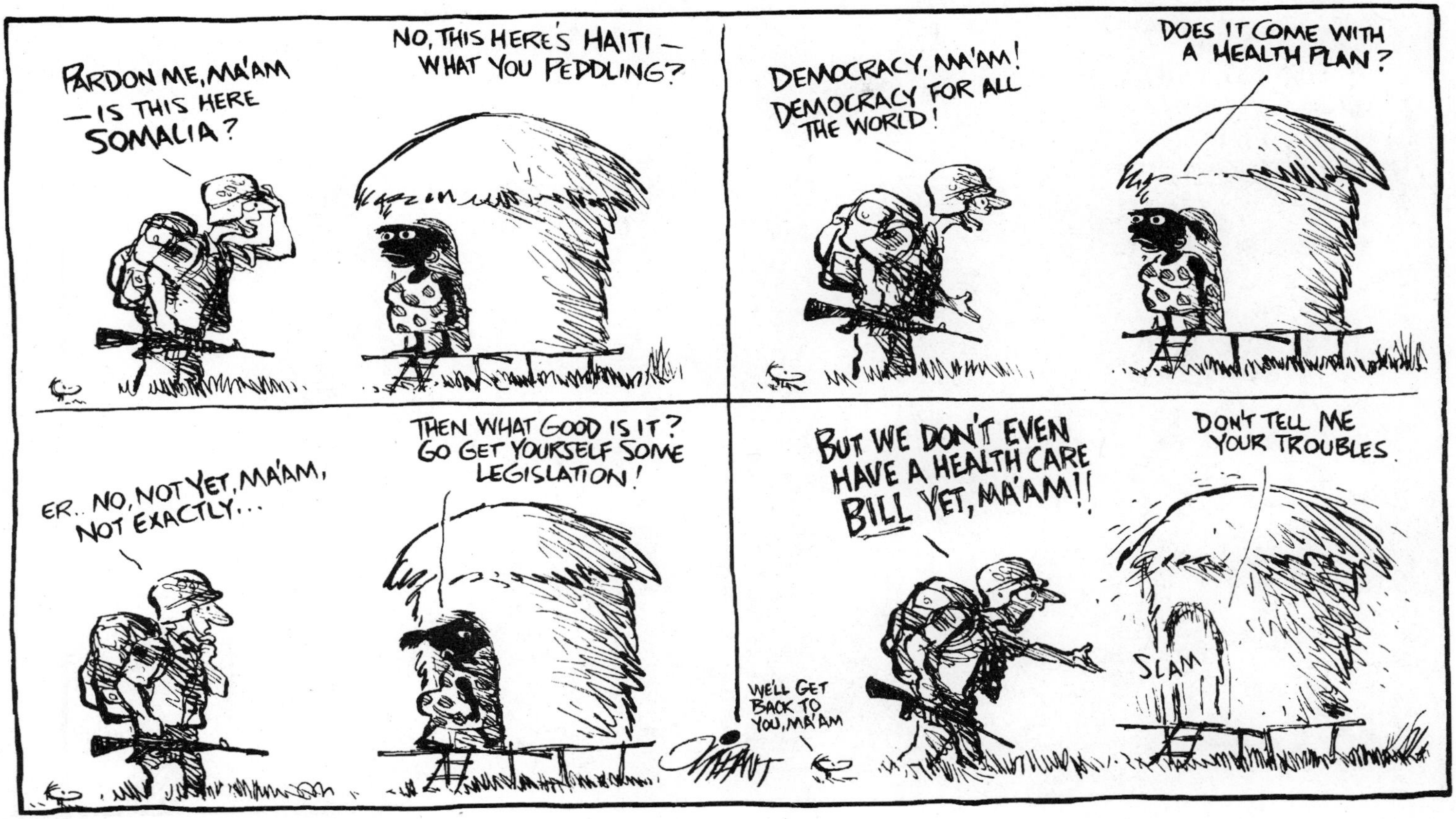
PARDON ME, MA'AM —IS THIS HERE SOMALIA?
NO, THIS HERE'S HAITI — WHAT YOU PEDDLING?
DEMOCRACY, MA'AM! DEMOCRACY FOR ALL THE WORLD!
DOES IT COME WITH A HEALTH PLAN?
ER.. NO, NOT YET, MA'AM, NOT EXACTLY...
THEN WHAT GOOD IS IT? GO GET YOURSELF SOME LEGISLATION!
BUT WE DON'T EVEN HAVE A HEALTH CARE BILL YET, MA'AM!!
DON'T TELL ME YOUR TROUBLES
SLAM
WE'LL GET BACK TO YOU, MA'AM

October 14, 1993

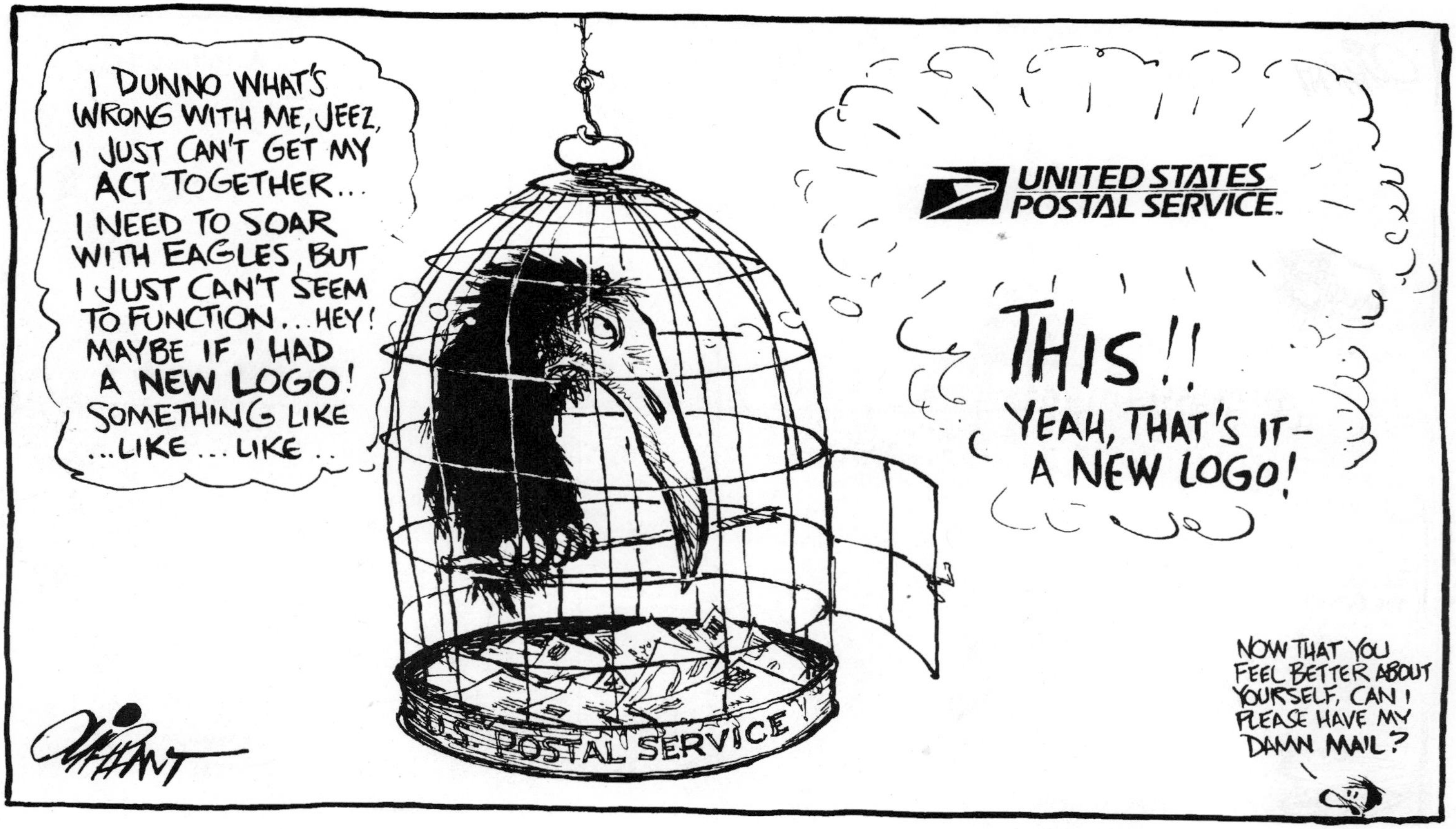
I DUNNO WHAT'S WRONG WITH ME, JEEZ, I JUST CAN'T GET MY ACT TOGETHER... I NEED TO SOAR WITH EAGLES, BUT I JUST CAN'T SEEM TO FUNCTION... HEY! MAYBE IF I HAD A NEW LOGO! SOMETHING LIKE ...LIKE ... LIKE ..
UNITED STATES POSTAL SERVICE
THIS!! YEAH, THAT'S IT- A NEW LOGO!
U.S. POSTAL SERVICE
NOW THAT YOU FEEL BETTER ABOUT YOURSELF, CAN I PLEASE HAVE MY DAMN MAIL?
OLIPHANT

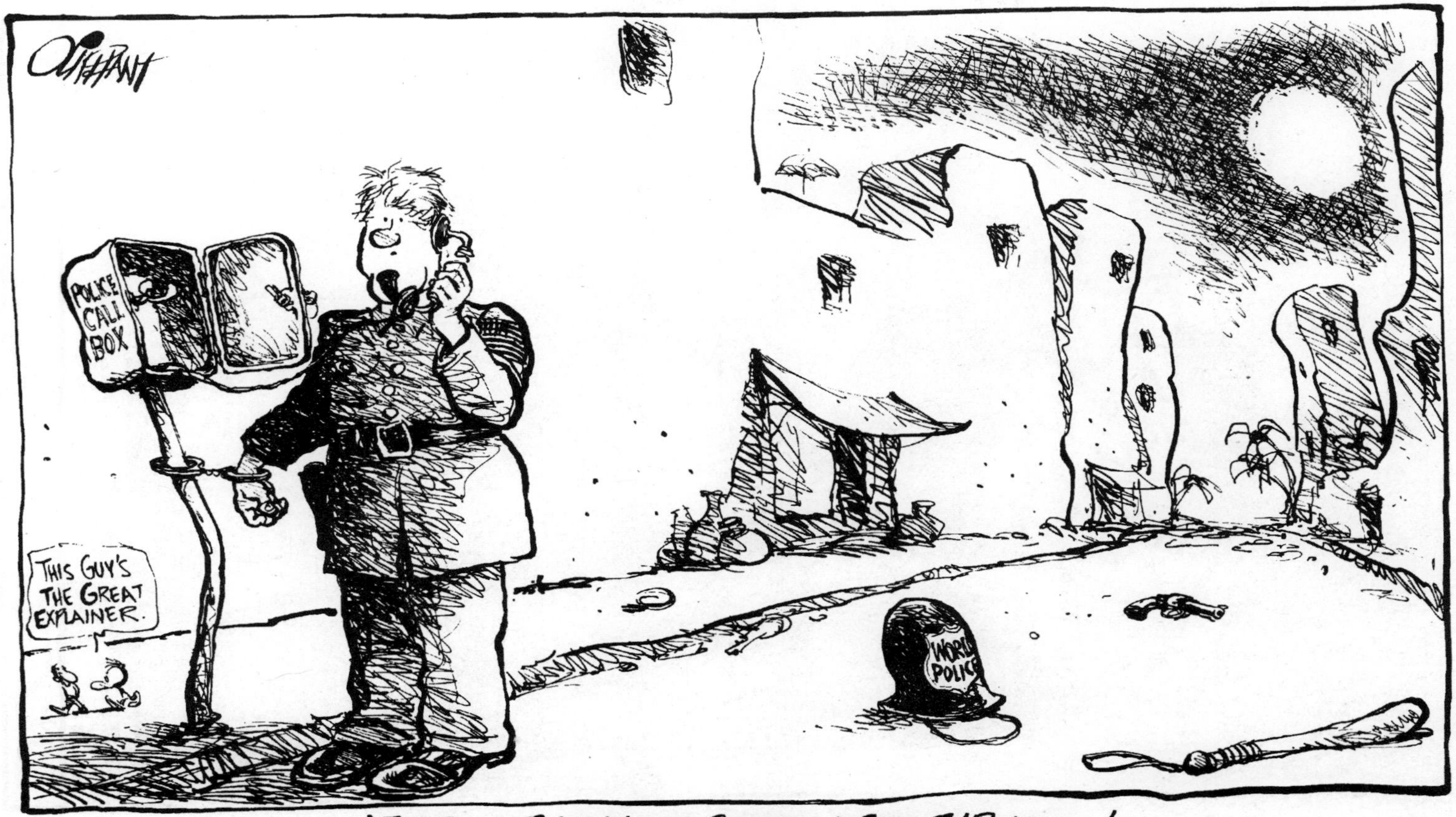
OLIPHANT
POLICE CALL BOX
WORLD POLICE
THIS GUY'S THE GREAT EXPLAINER.

'EXPLAIN? WHY, OF COURSE I CAN EXPLAIN...'

October 19, 1993

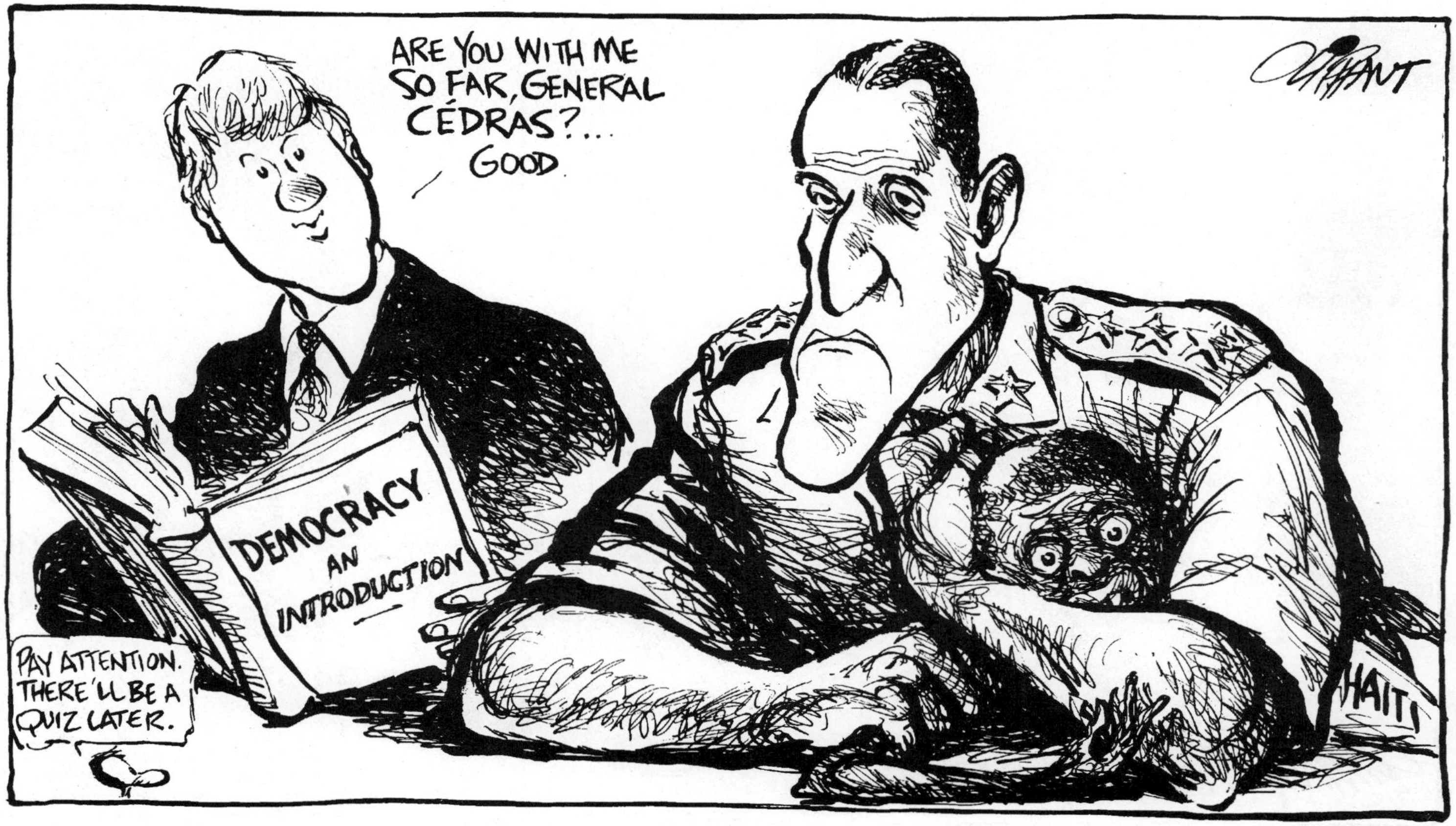
ARE YOU WITH ME SO FAR, GENERAL CÉDRAS?... GOOD.
DEMOCRACY AN INTRODUCTION
HAITI
PAY ATTENTION. THERE'LL BE A QUIZ LATER.
OLIPHANT

October 21, 1993

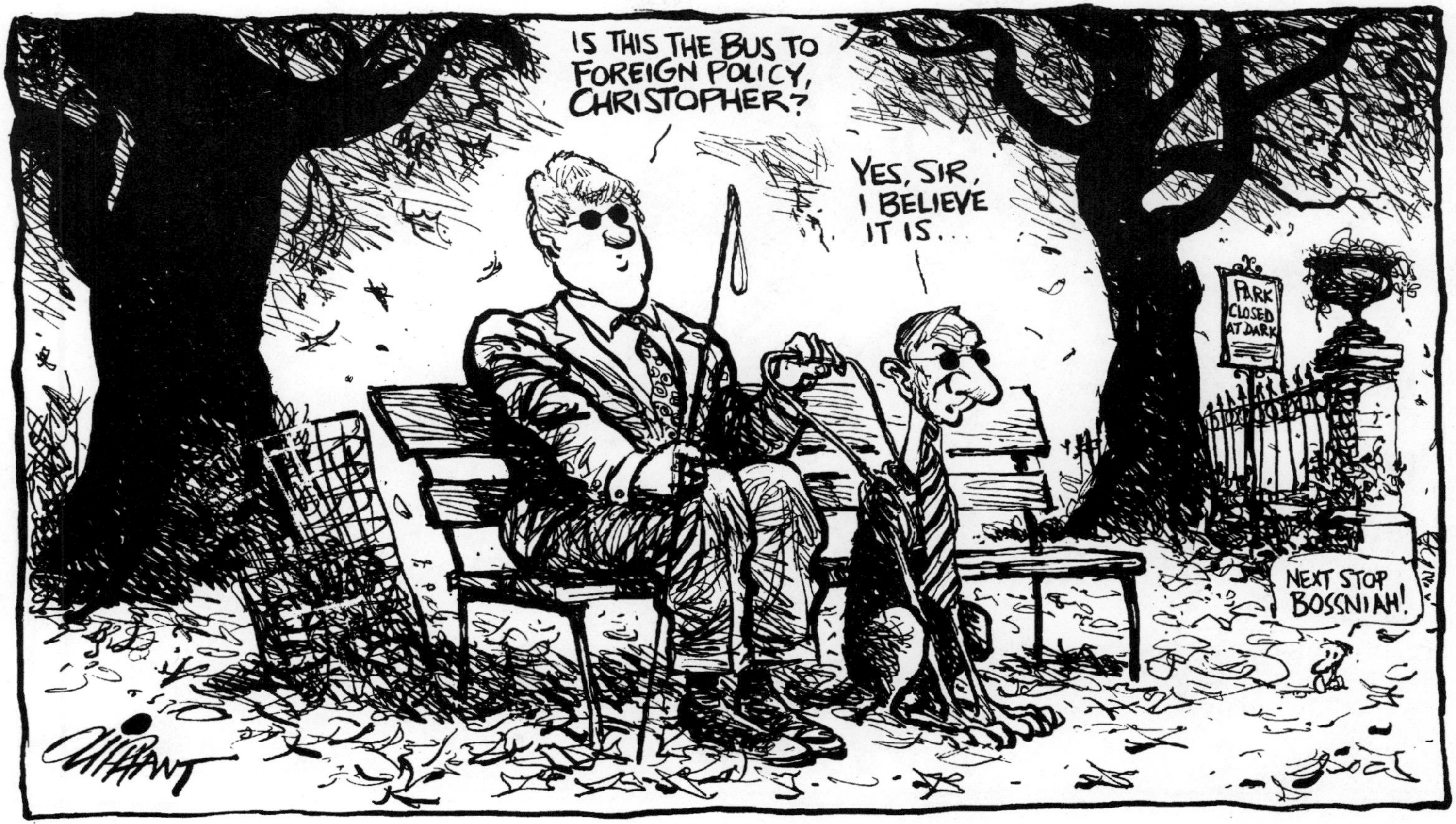

IS THIS THE BUS TO FOREIGN POLICY, CHRISTOPHER?
YES, SIR, I BELIEVE IT IS...
PARK CLOSED AT DARK
NEXT STOP BOSSNIAH!
OLIPHANT

October 22, 1993

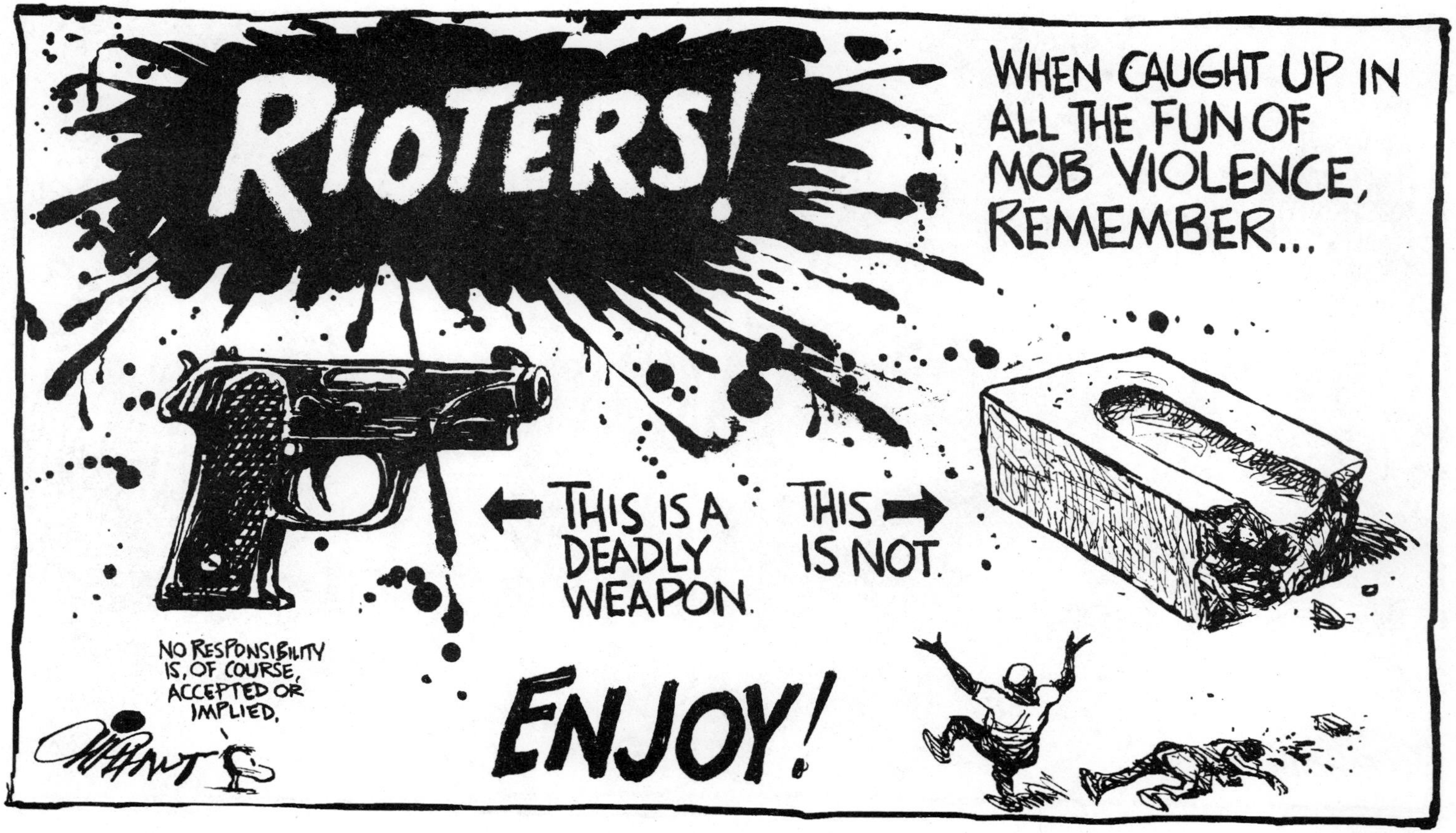
RIOTERS!
WHEN CAUGHT UP IN ALL THE FUN OF MOB VIOLENCE, REMEMBER...
THIS IS A DEADLY WEAPON.
THIS IS NOT.
NO RESPONSIBILITY IS, OF COURSE, ACCEPTED OR IMPLIED.
ENJOY!

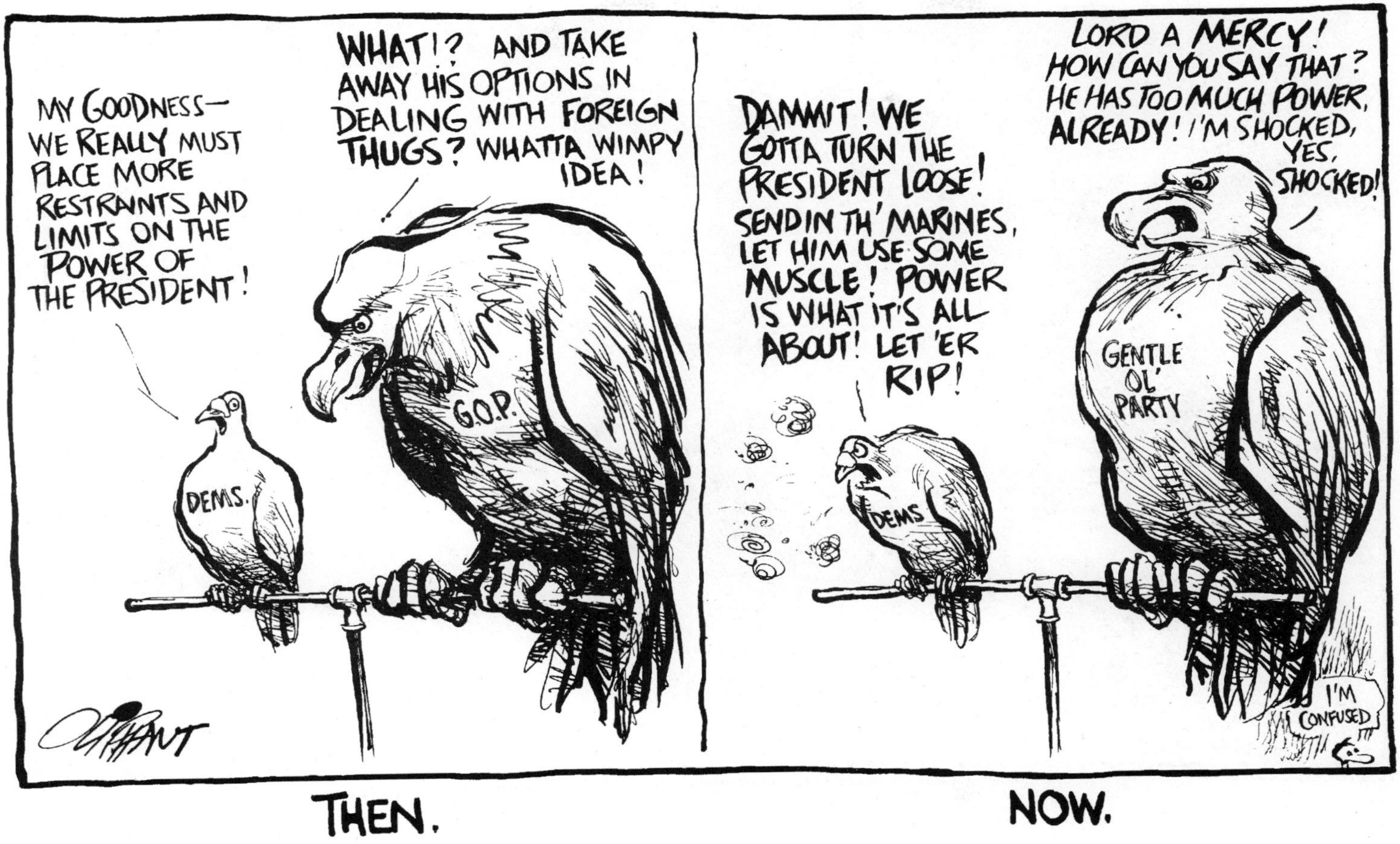
MY GOODNESS— WE REALLY MUST PLACE MORE RESTRAINTS AND LIMITS ON THE POWER OF THE PRESIDENT!
WHAT!? AND TAKE AWAY HIS OPTIONS IN DEALING WITH FOREIGN THUGS? WHATTA WIMPY IDEA!
DEMS.
G.O.P.
OLIPHANT
DAMMIT! WE GOTTA TURN THE PRESIDENT LOOSE! SEND IN TH' MARINES, LET HIM USE SOME MUSCLE! POWER IS WHAT IT'S ALL ABOUT! LET 'ER RIP!
LORD A MERCY! HOW CAN YOU SAY THAT? HE HAS TOO MUCH POWER, ALREADY! I'M SHOCKED, YES, SHOCKED!
DEMS
GENTLE OL' PARTY
I'M CONFUSED
THEN.
NOW.

October 28, 1993

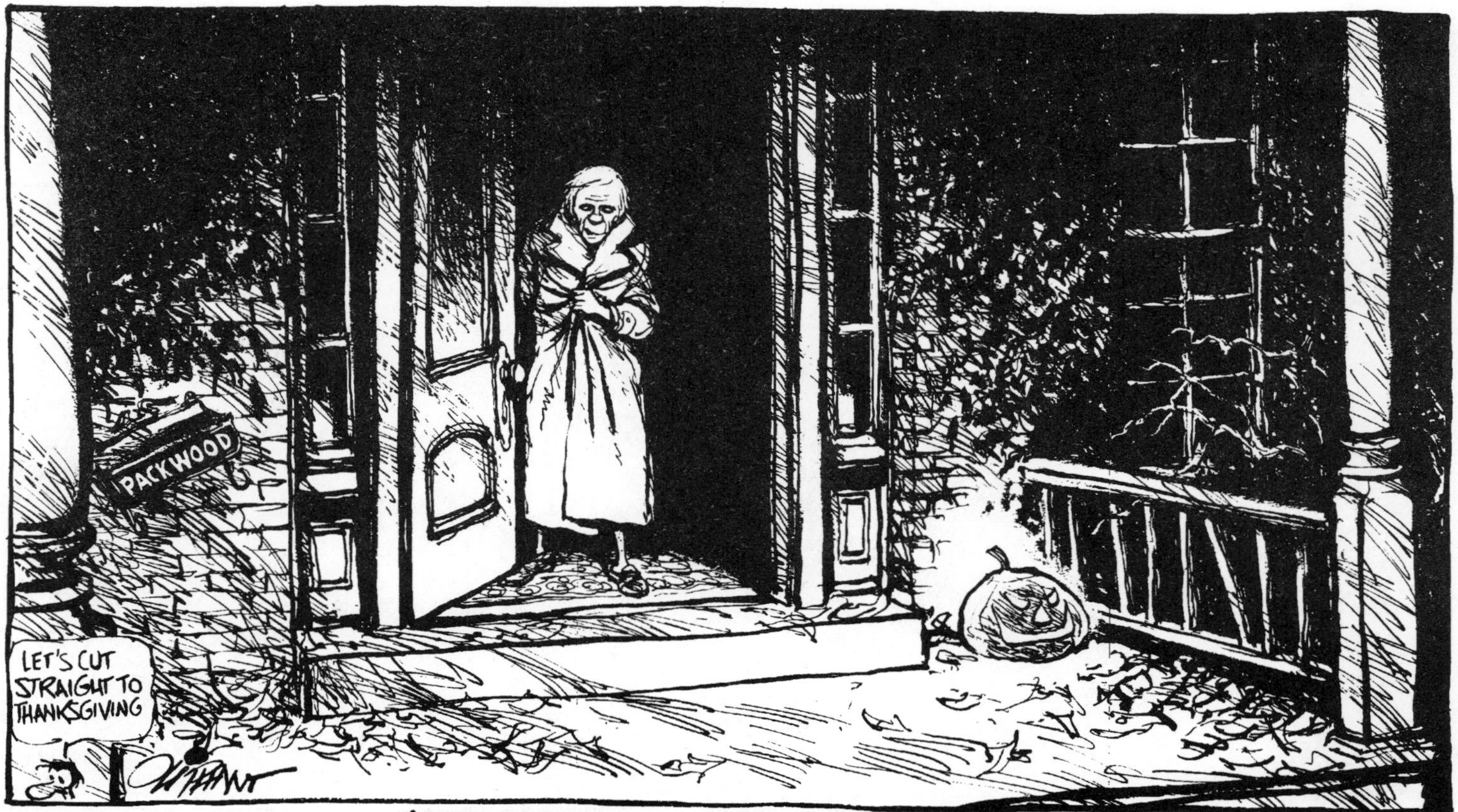
PACKWOOD
LET'S CUT STRAIGHT TO THANKSGIVING

'WANNA SEE MY DIARIES?'

October 29, 1993

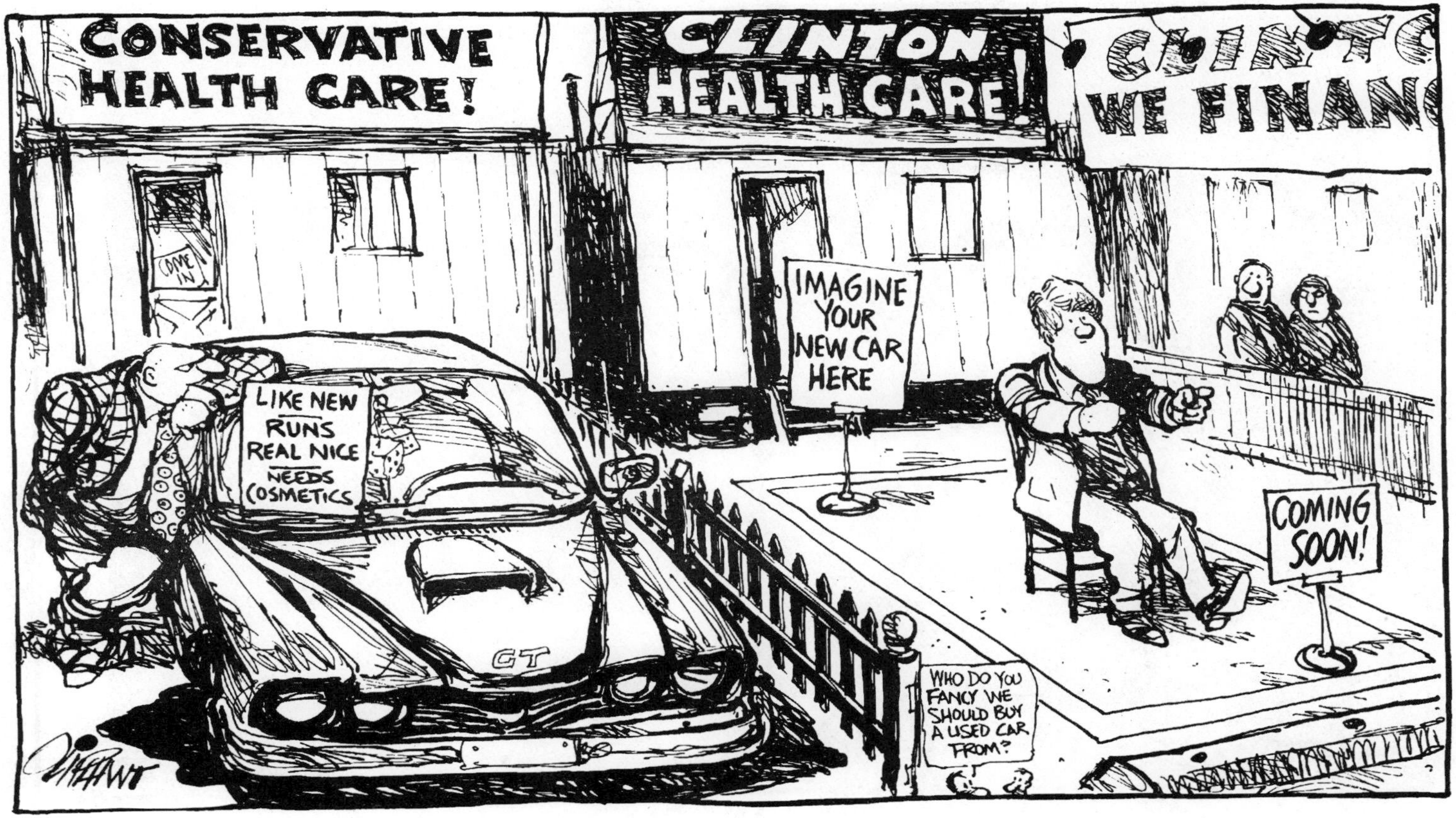

CONSERVATIVE HEALTH CARE!
CLINTON HEALTH CARE!
WE FINAN
COME IN
LIKE NEW
RUNS REAL NICE
NEEDS COSMETICS
IMAGINE YOUR NEW CAR HERE
COMING SOON!
GT
WHO DO YOU FANCY WE SHOULD BUY A USED CAR FROM?

October 30, 1993

WHEN AM I GOING HOME?
I'M READY TO GO HOME NOW.
AM I GOING HOME YET?
I'LL GET YOUR HAT.
OLIPHANT

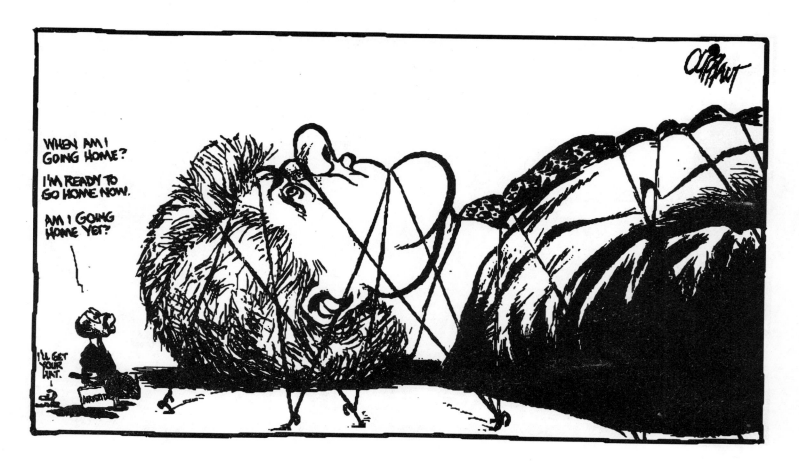

November 3, 1993

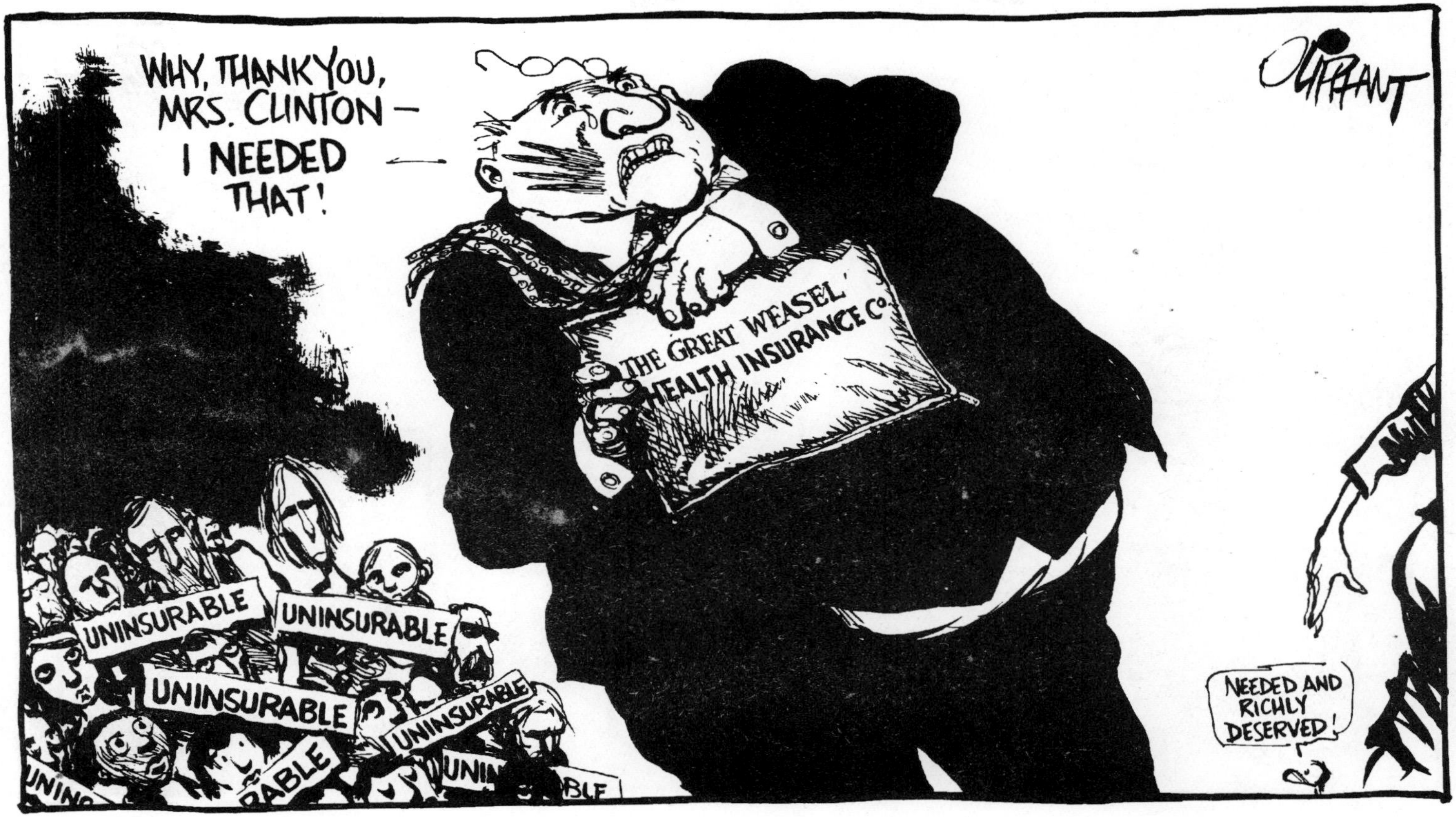
WHY, THANK YOU, MRS. CLINTON – I NEEDED THAT!
OLIPHANT
THE GREAT WEASEL HEALTH INSURANCE Co.
UNINSURABLE
UNINSURABLE
UNINSURABLE
UNINSURABLE
NEEDED AND RICHLY DESERVED!

November 4, 1993

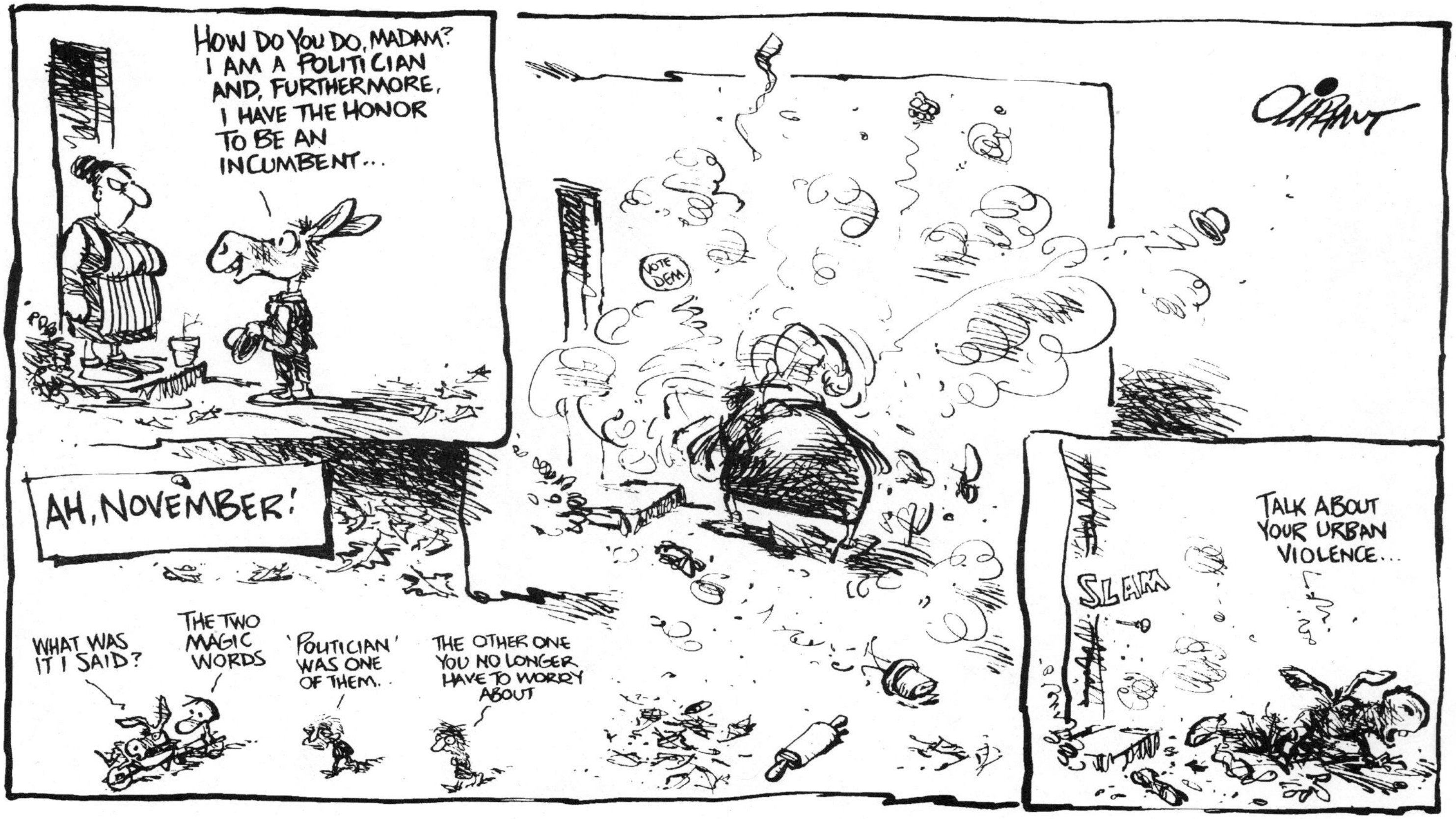
HOW DO YOU DO, MADAM? I AM A POLITICIAN AND, FURTHERMORE, I HAVE THE HONOR TO BE AN INCUMBENT...
AH, NOVEMBER!
VOTE DEM
SLAM
TALK ABOUT YOUR URBAN VIOLENCE...
WHAT WAS IT I SAID?
THE TWO MAGIC WORDS
'POLITICIAN' WAS ONE OF THEM.
THE OTHER ONE YOU NO LONGER HAVE TO WORRY ABOUT

November 8, 1993

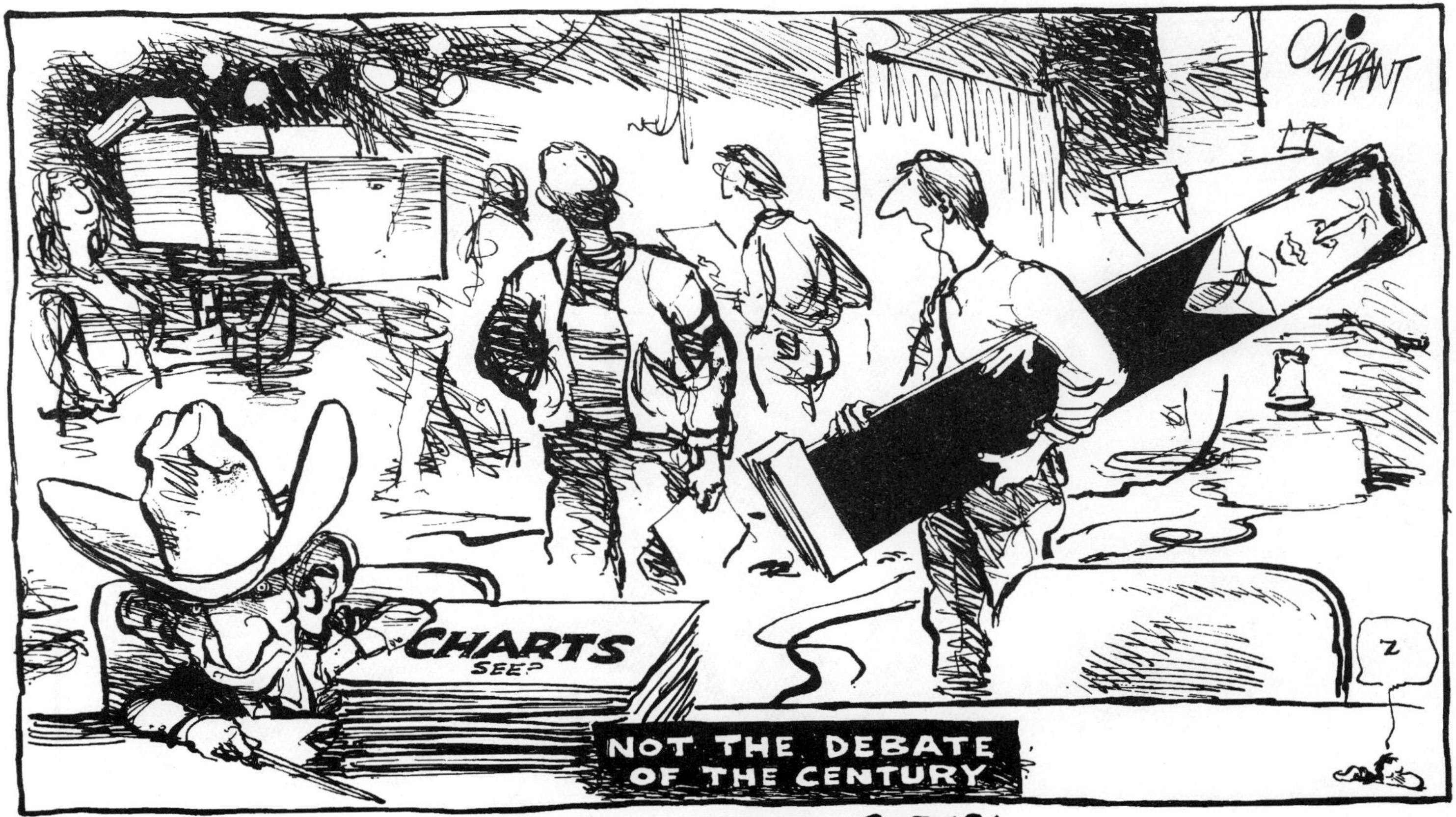
OLIPHANT
CHARTS
SEE?
Z
NOT THE DEBATE
OF THE CENTURY

'WHERE DO WE PUT MR. GORE?'

November 11, 1993

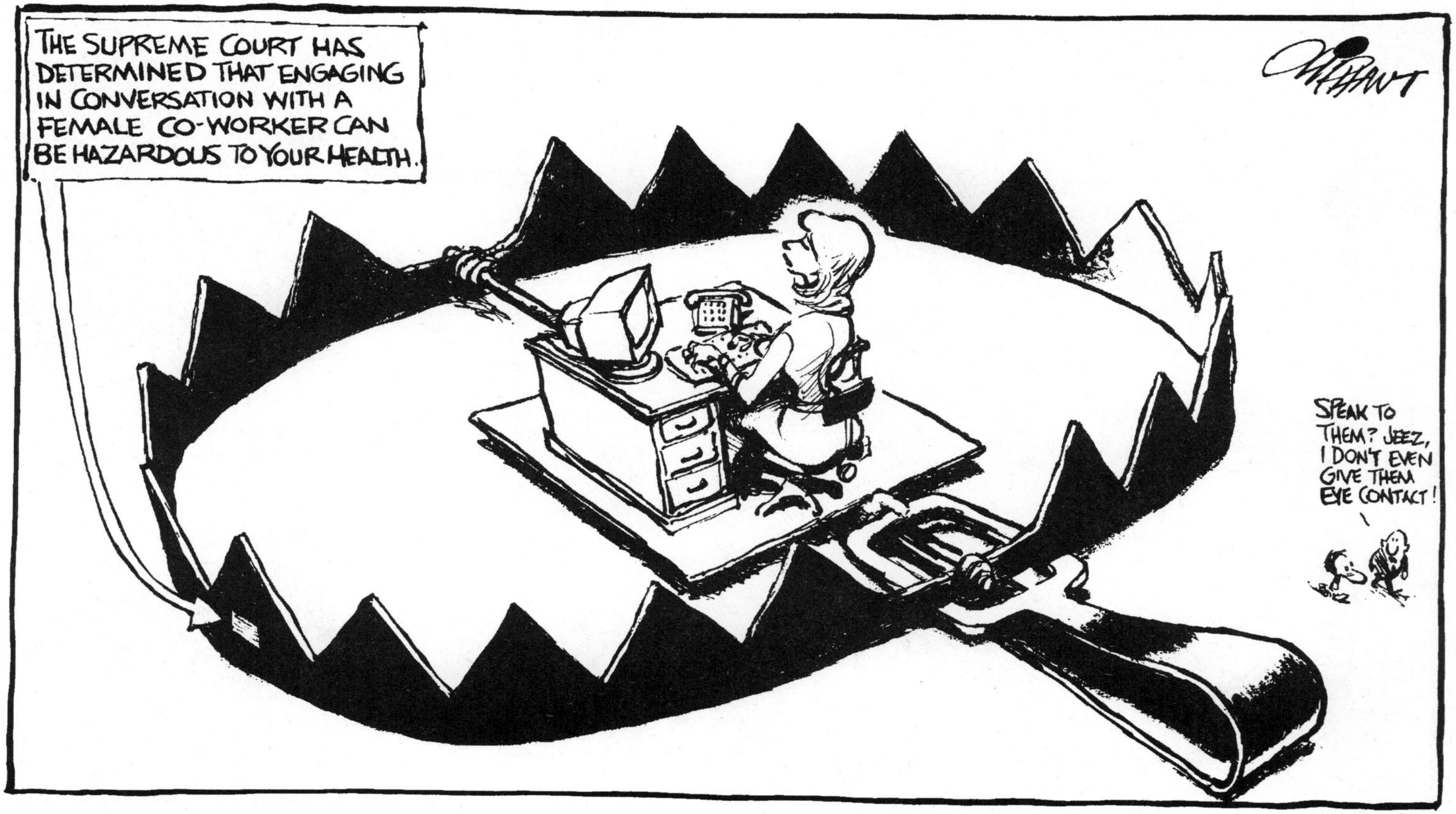
THE SUPREME COURT HAS DETERMINED THAT ENGAGING IN CONVERSATION WITH A FEMALE CO-WORKER CAN BE HAZARDOUS TO YOUR HEALTH.
SPEAK TO THEM? JEEZ, I DON'T EVEN GIVE THEM EYE CONTACT!

November 13, 1993

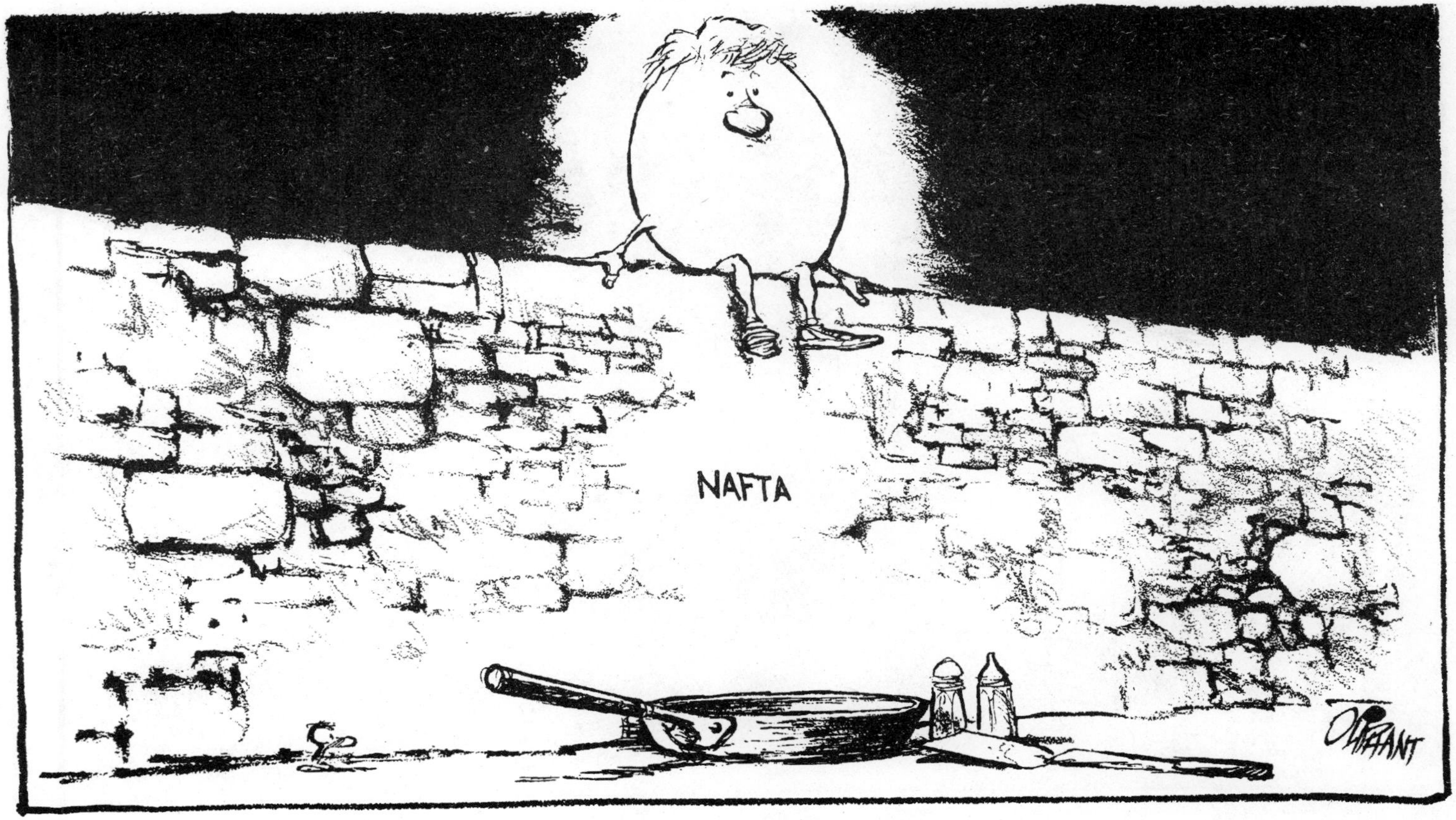
NAFTA
OLIPHANT

November 17, 1993

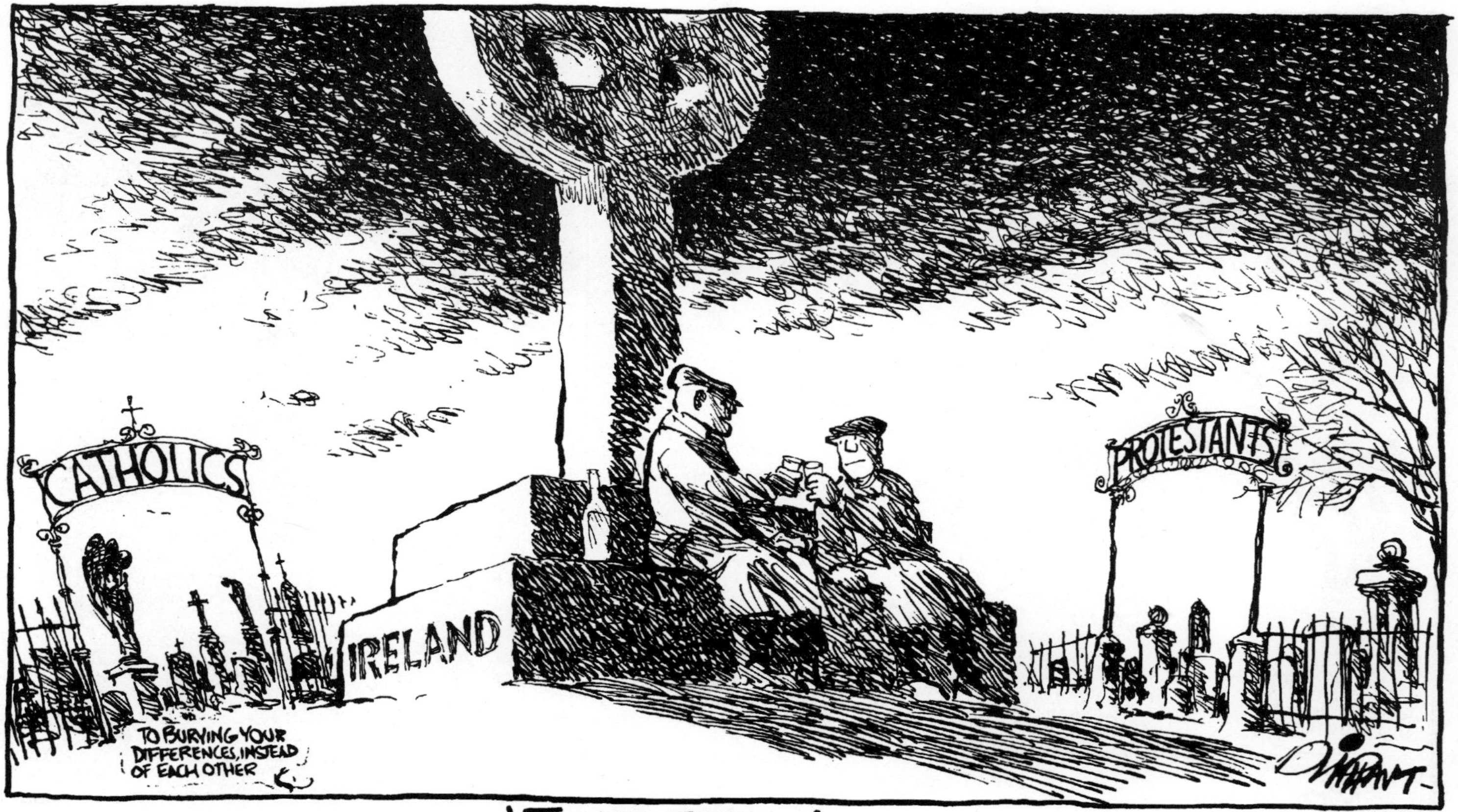
CATHOLICS
IRELAND
PROTESTANTS
TO BURYING YOUR DIFFERENCES, INSTEAD OF EACH OTHER
OLIPHANT

'TO US, THEN...'

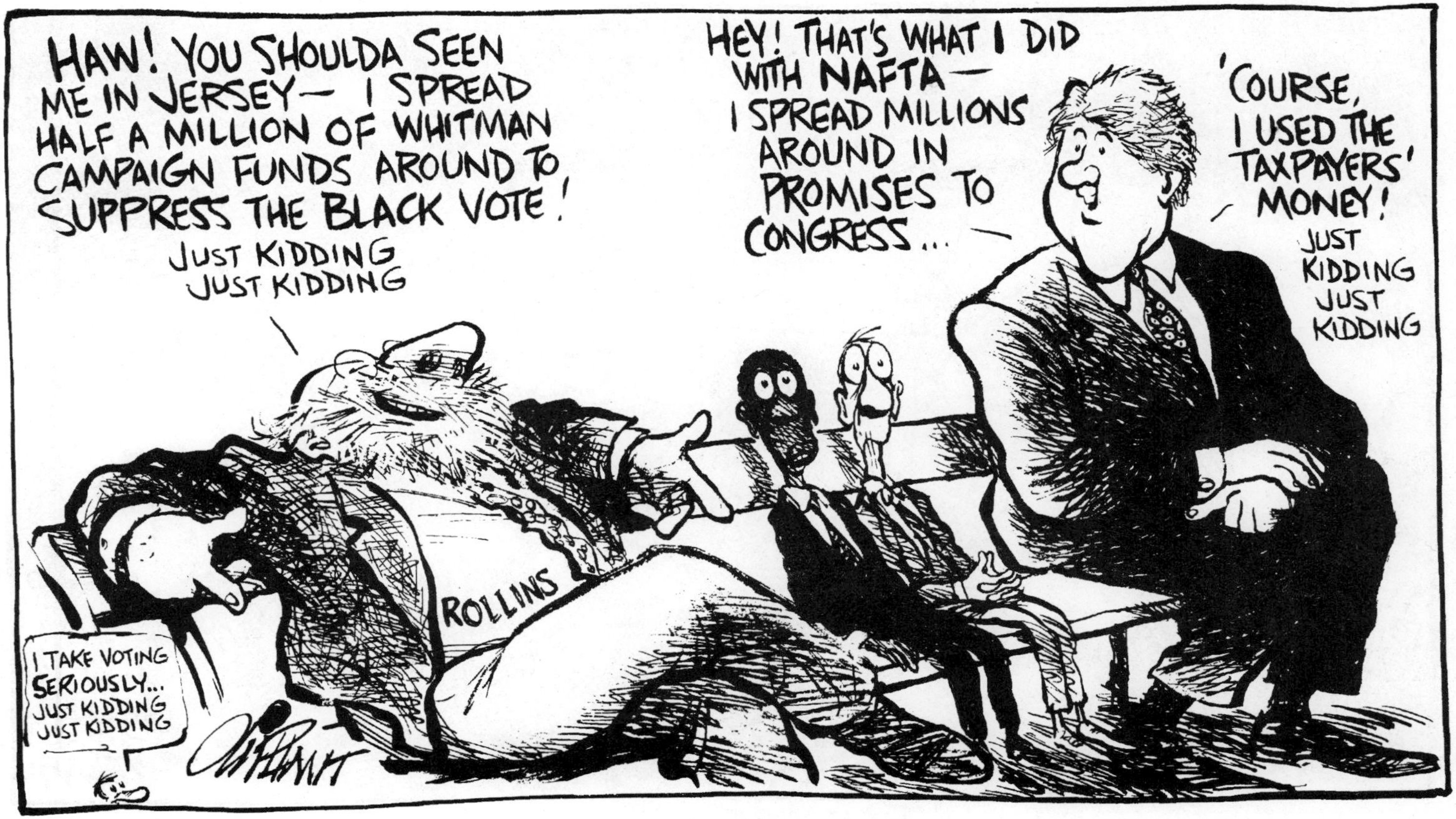
HAW! YOU SHOULDA SEEN ME IN JERSEY— I SPREAD HALF A MILLION OF WHITMAN CAMPAIGN FUNDS AROUND TO SUPPRESS THE BLACK VOTE!
JUST KIDDING JUST KIDDING
HEY! THAT'S WHAT I DID WITH NAFTA— I SPREAD MILLIONS AROUND IN PROMISES TO CONGRESS...
'COURSE, I USED THE TAXPAYERS' MONEY!
JUST KIDDING JUST KIDDING
ROLLINS
I TAKE VOTING SERIOUSLY... JUST KIDDING JUST KIDDING

November 18, 1993

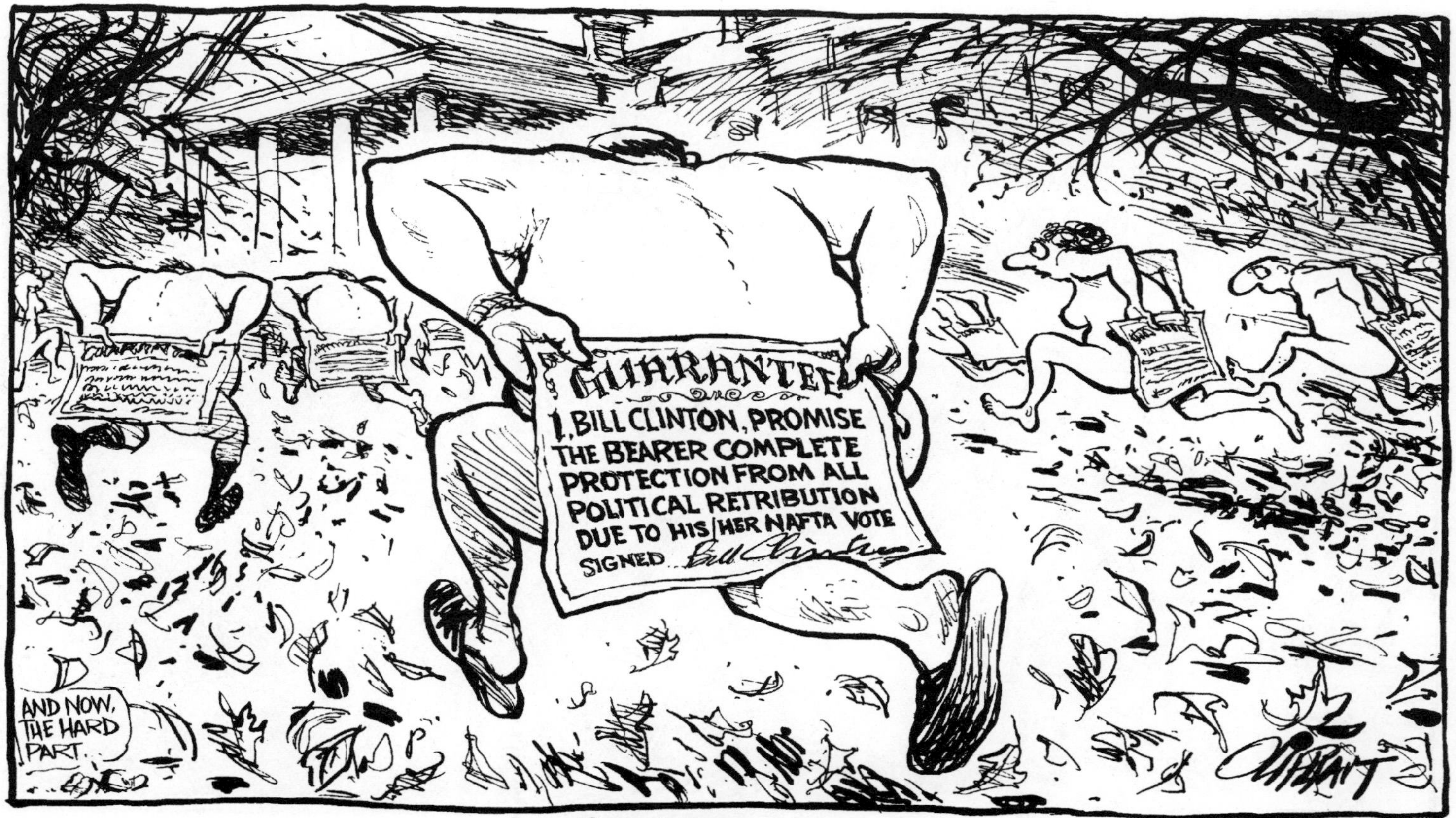
GUARANTEE
I, BILL CLINTON, PROMISE THE BEARER COMPLETE PROTECTION FROM ALL POLITICAL RETRIBUTION DUE TO HIS/HER NAFTA VOTE
SIGNED Bill Clinton
AND NOW, THE HARD PART.
OLIPHANT

COVERED.

November 19, 1993

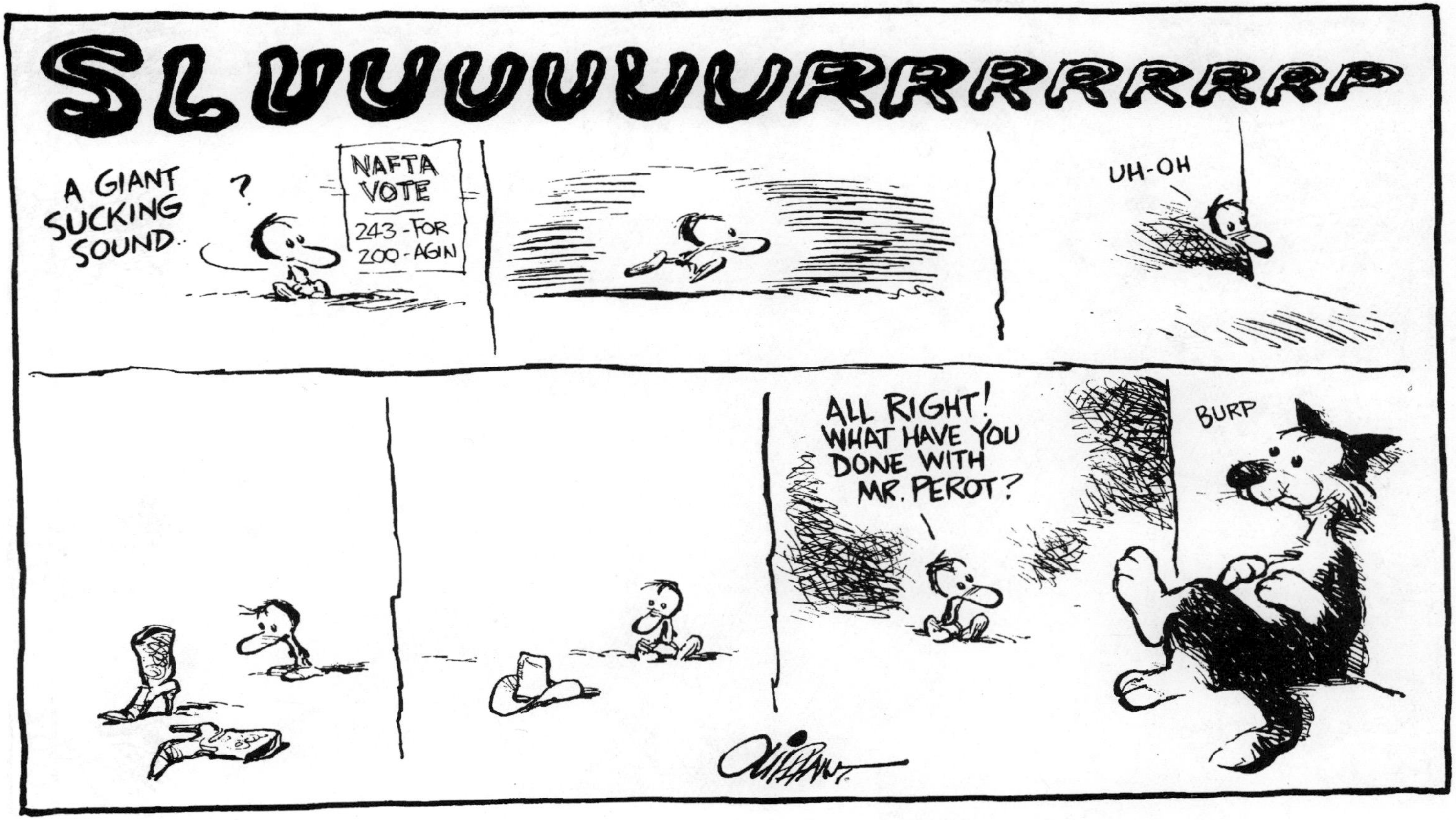
SLUUUUURRRRRRP
A GIANT SUCKING SOUND..
?
NAFTA VOTE
243 - FOR
200 - AGIN
UH-OH
ALL RIGHT! WHAT HAVE YOU DONE WITH MR. PEROT?
BURP

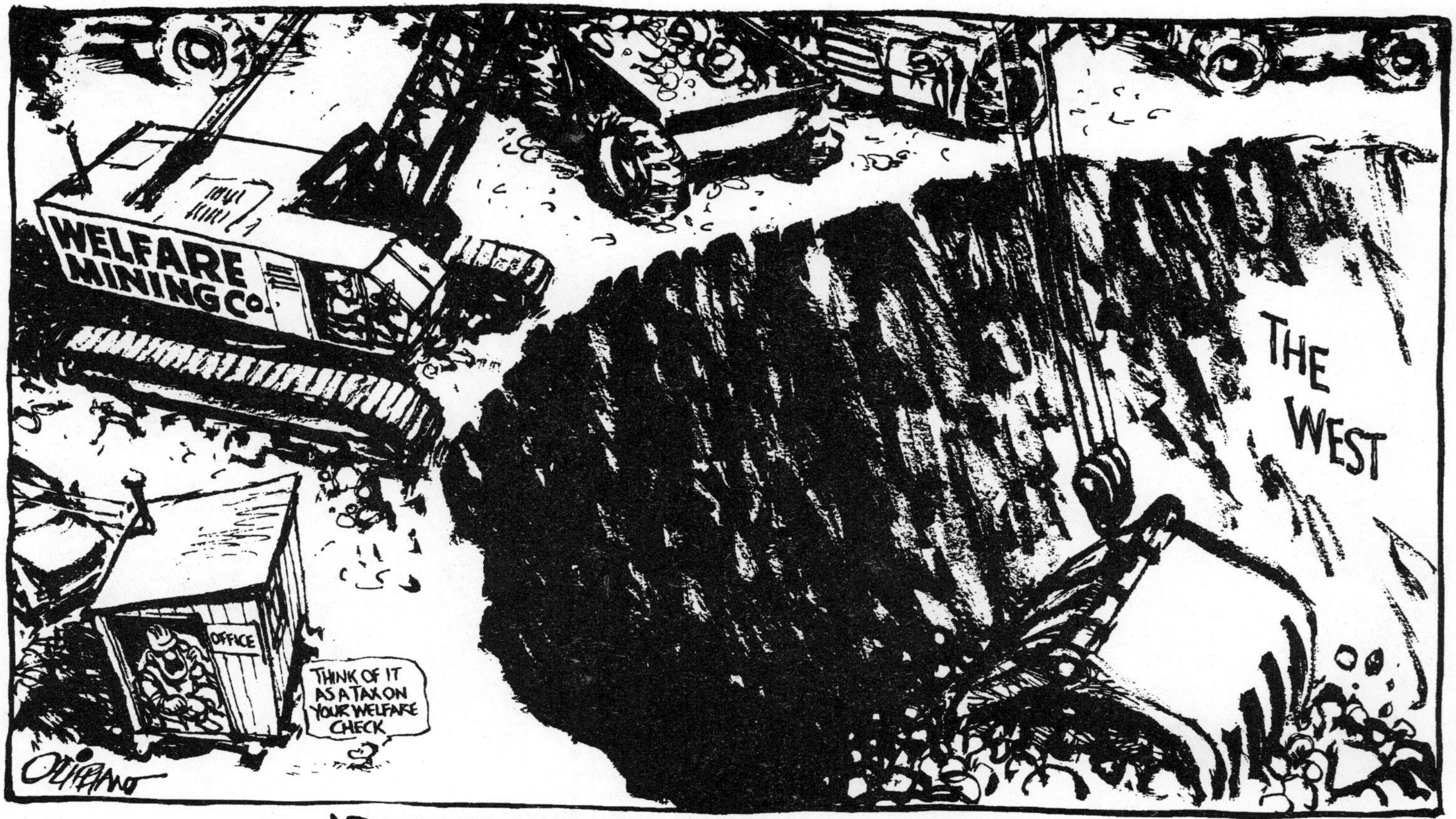
WELFARE MINING Co.
OFFICE
THINK OF IT AS A TAX ON YOUR WELFARE CHECK
THE WEST
OLIPHANT

'ROYALTIES? WHAT TH' HELL ARE ROYALTIES?'

November 24, 1993

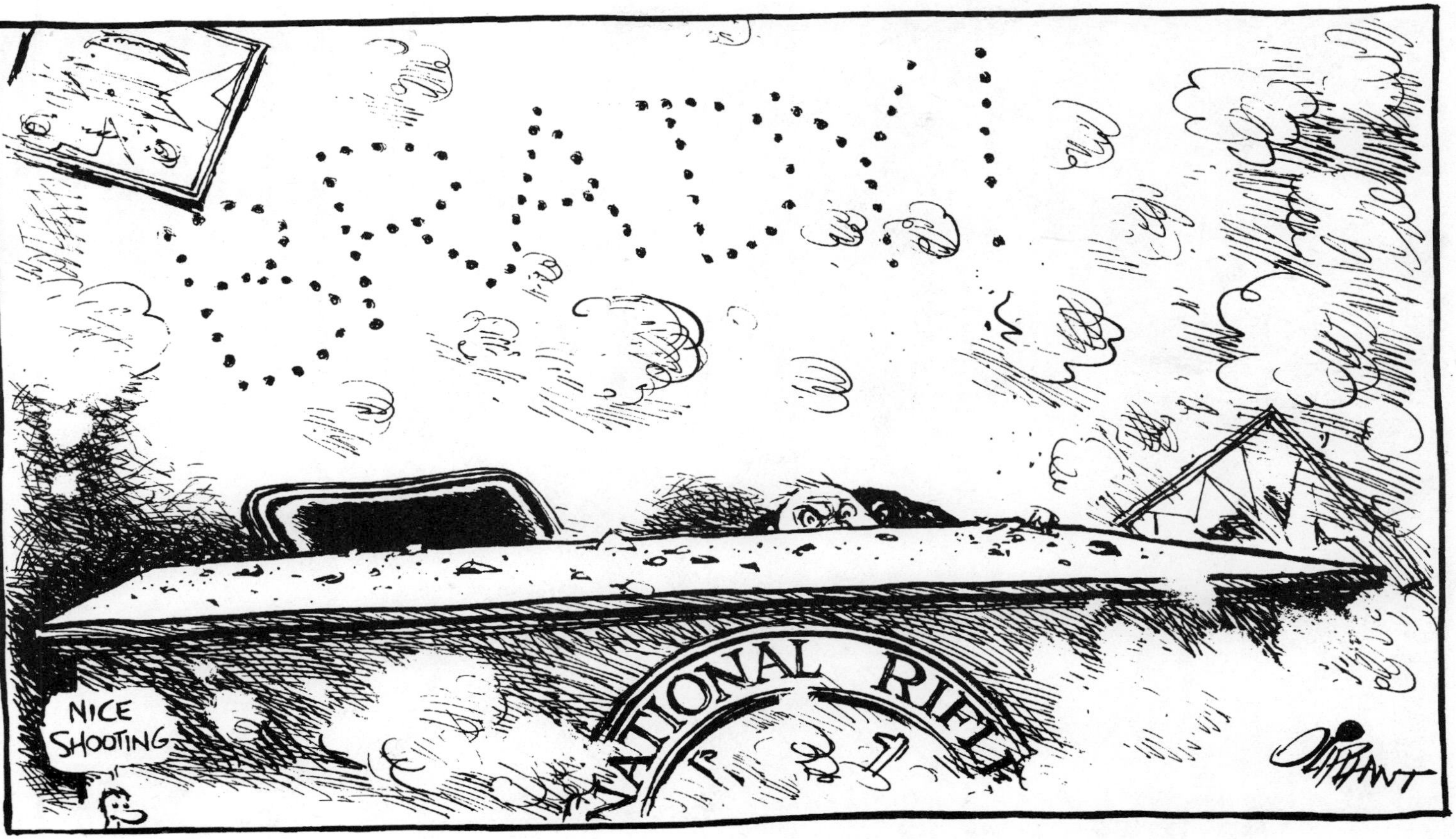
BRADY!
NATIONAL RIFLE
NICE SHOOTING
OLIPHANT

November 25, 1993

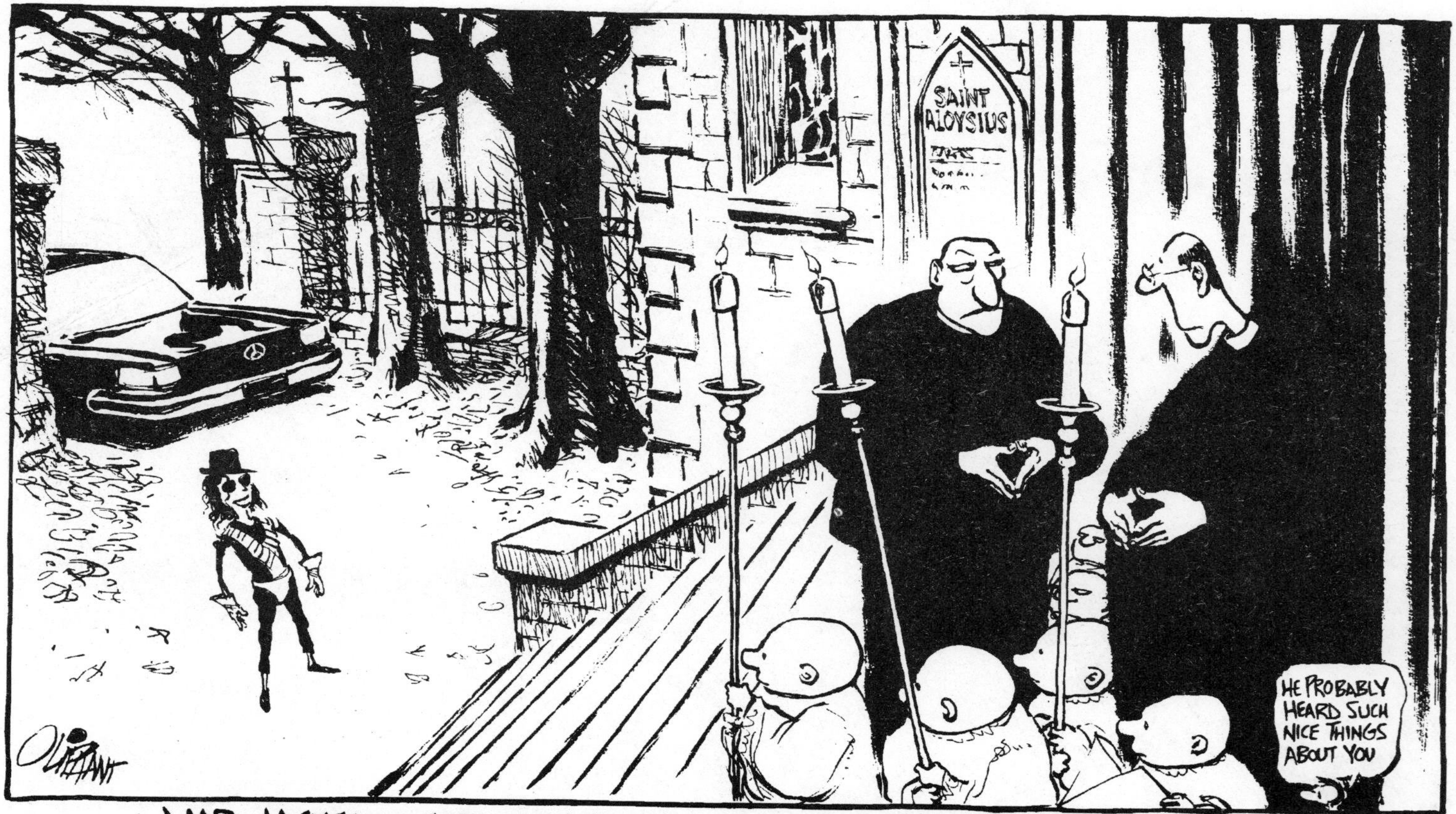
SAINT ALOYSIUS
HE PROBABLY HEARD SUCH NICE THINGS ABOUT YOU
OLIPHANT

'MR. JACKSON, IT SEEMS, WOULD LIKE TO JOIN THE PRIESTHOOD.'

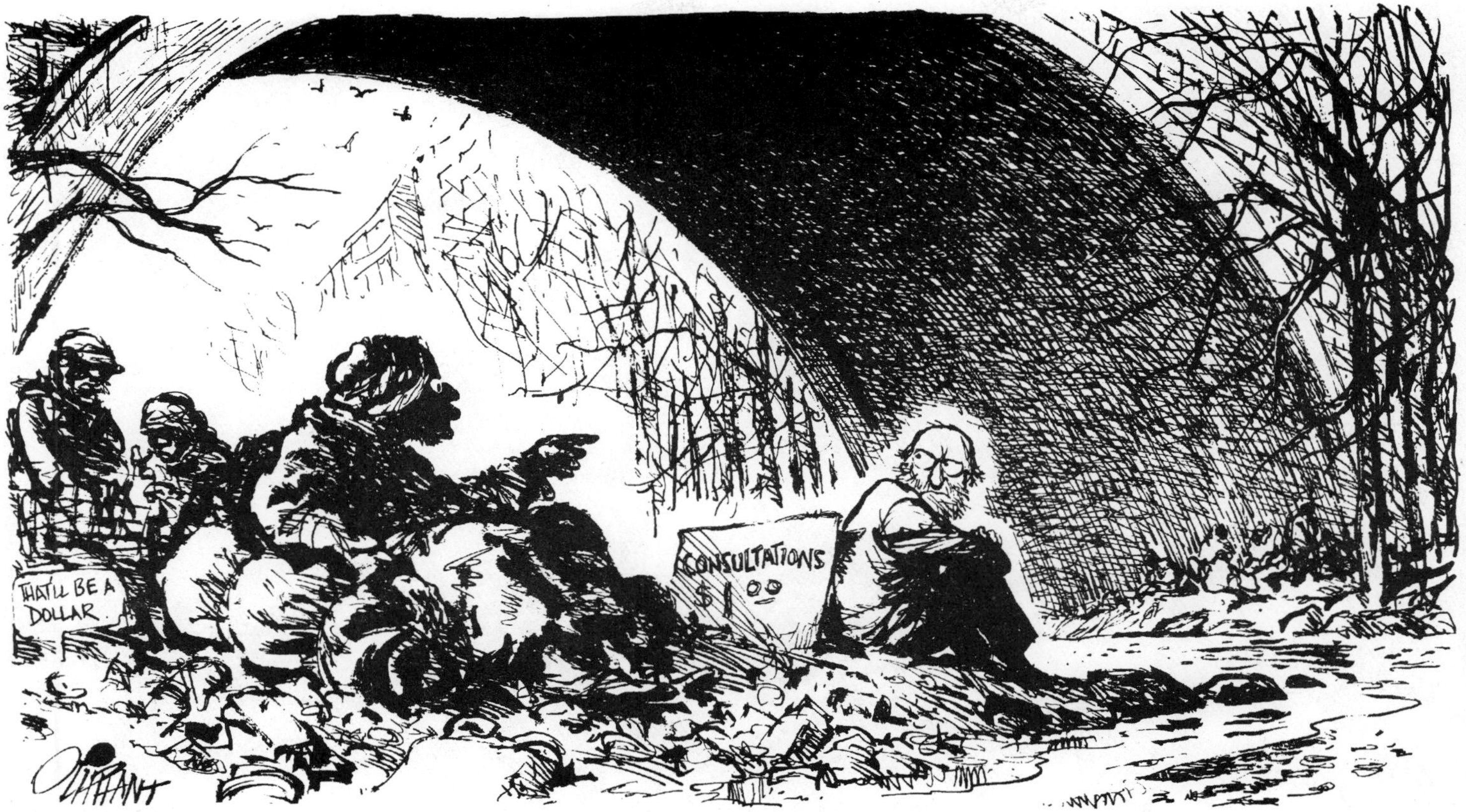
THAT'LL BE A DOLLAR
CONSULTATIONS $1.00
OLIPHANT

'HEY, MAN... DIDN'T YOU USED TO BE ED ROLLINS?'

December 2, 1993

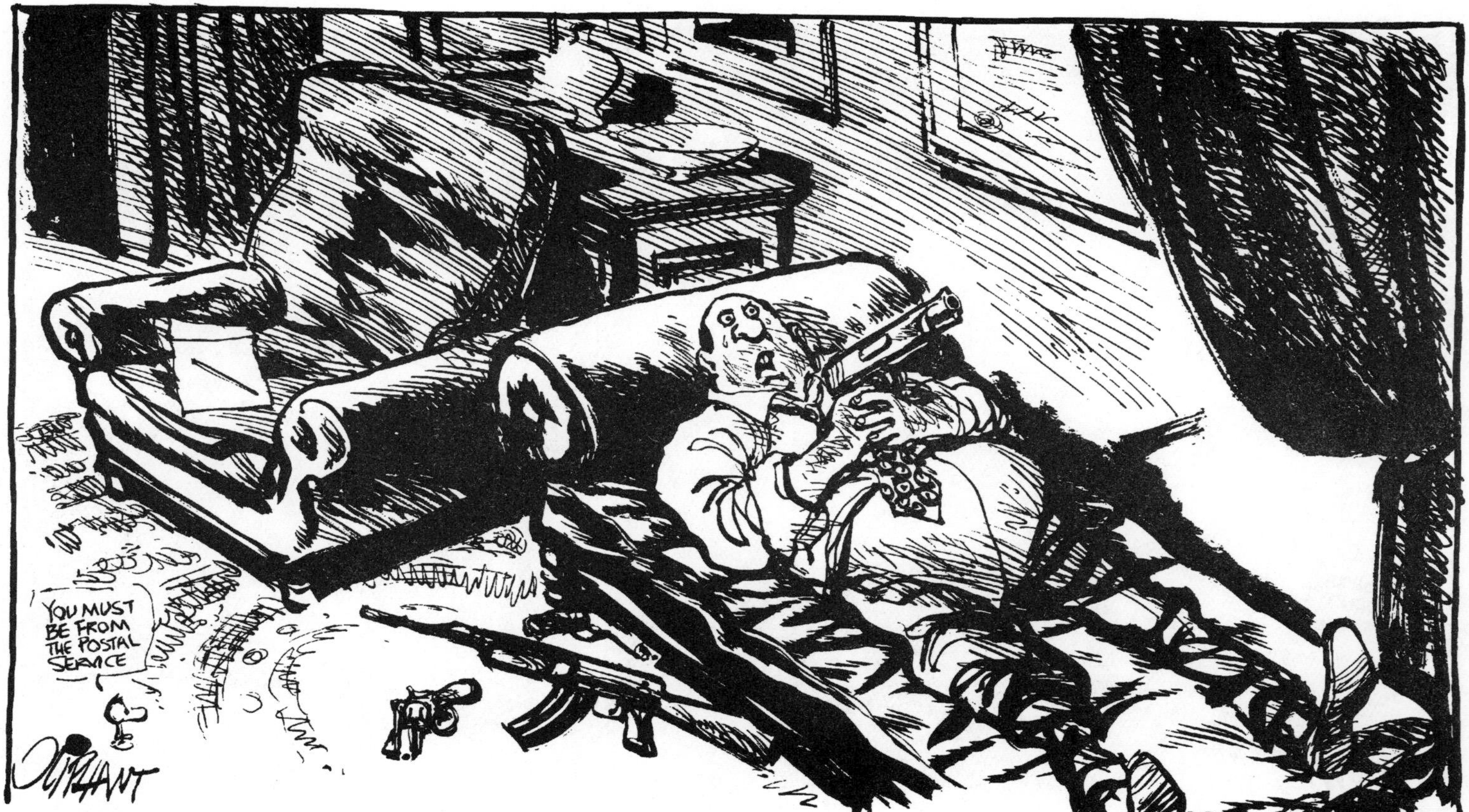
YOU MUST BE FROM THE POSTAL SERVICE
OLIPHANT

"...BUT ENOUGH ABOUT WHAT I THINK. WHAT DO YOU THINK OF THE BRADY BILL, DOC?"

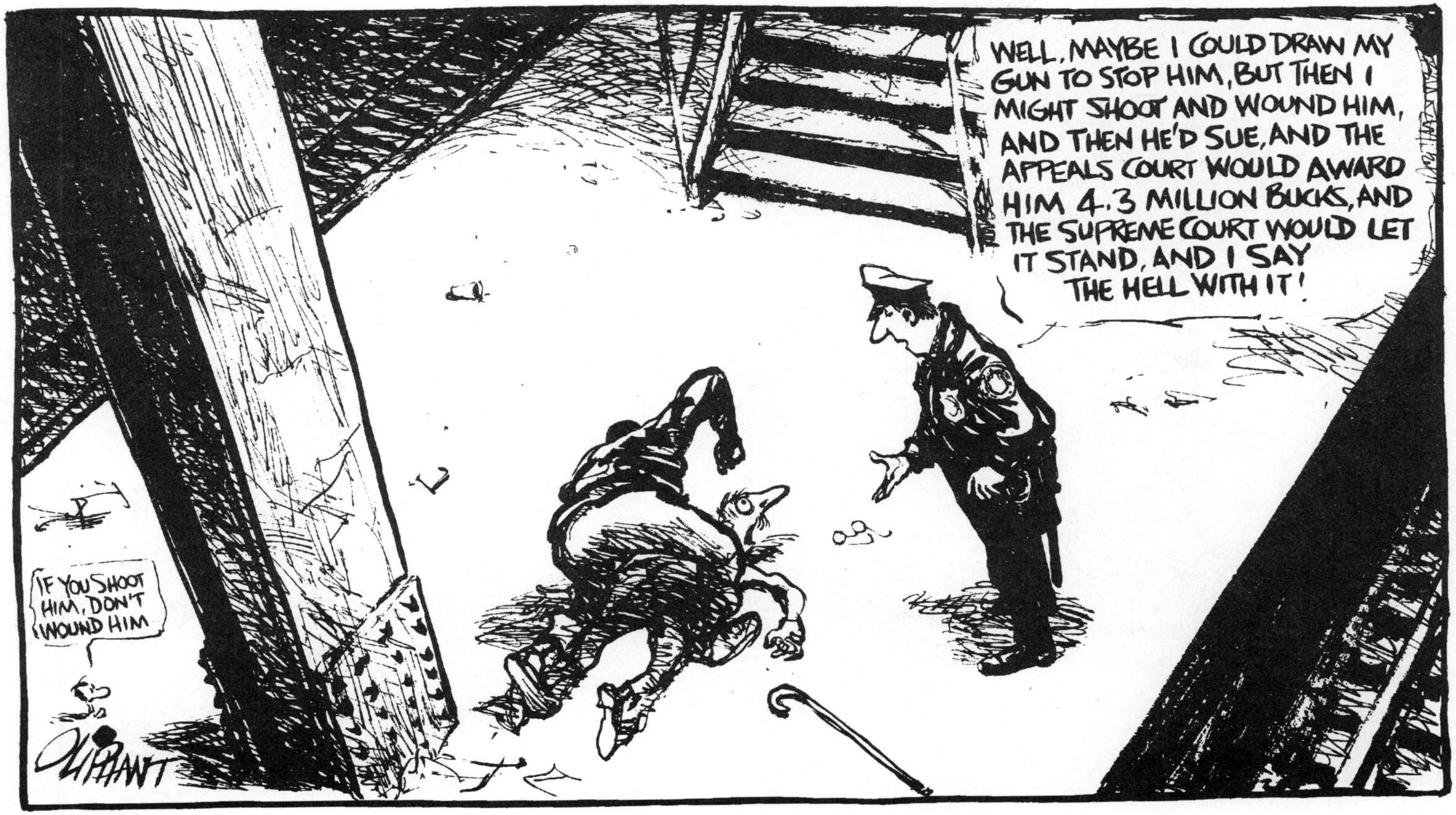
WELL, MAYBE I COULD DRAW MY GUN TO STOP HIM, BUT THEN I MIGHT SHOOT AND WOUND HIM, AND THEN HE'D SUE, AND THE APPEALS COURT WOULD AWARD HIM 4.3 MILLION BUCKS, AND THE SUPREME COURT WOULD LET IT STAND, AND I SAY THE HELL WITH IT!
IF YOU SHOOT HIM, DON'T WOUND HIM
OLIPHANT

December 8, 1993

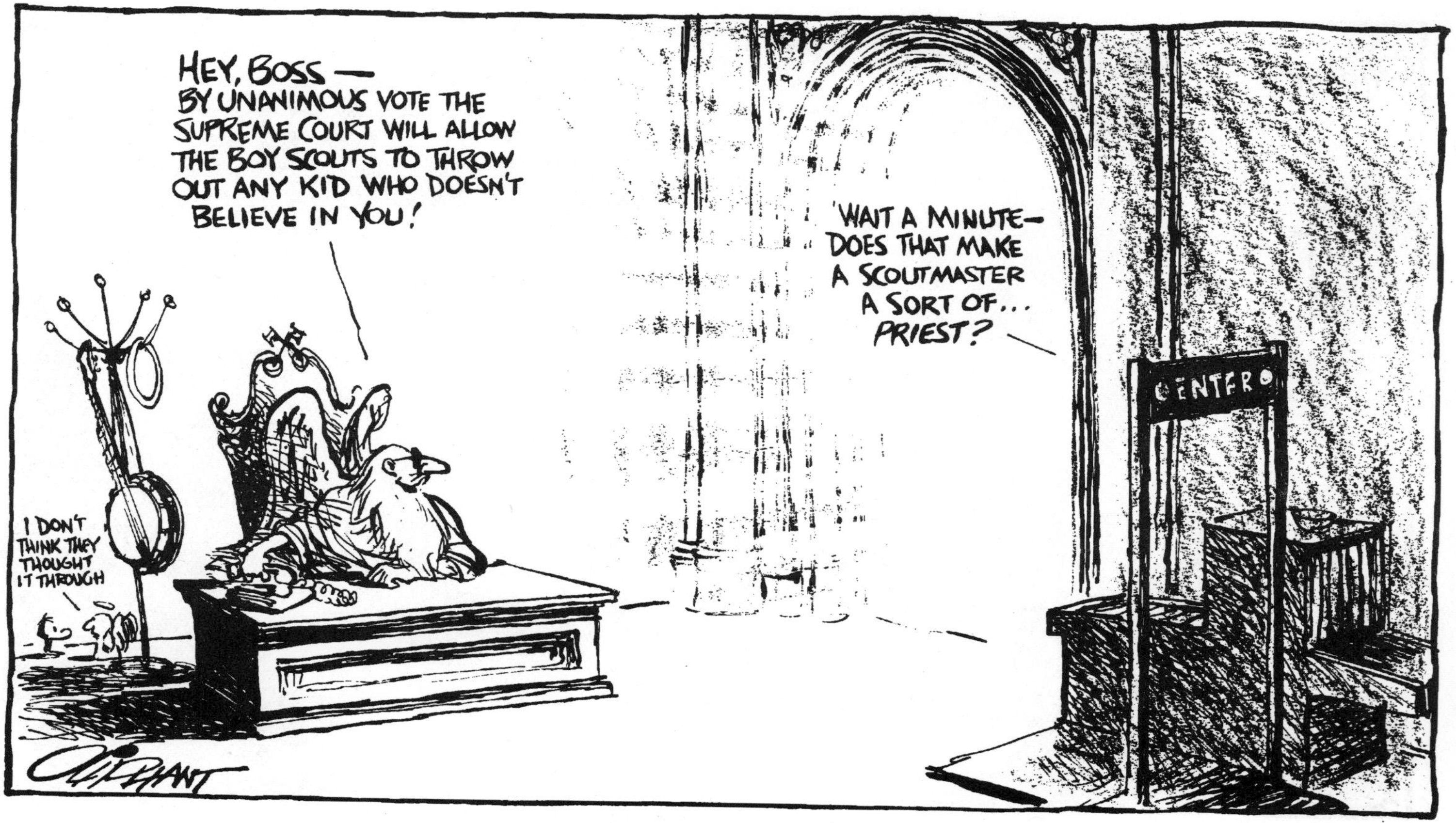
HEY, BOSS —
BY UNANIMOUS VOTE THE SUPREME COURT WILL ALLOW THE BOY SCOUTS TO THROW OUT ANY KID WHO DOESN'T BELIEVE IN YOU!
'WAIT A MINUTE— DOES THAT MAKE A SCOUTMASTER A SORT OF... PRIEST?
ENTER
I DON'T THINK THEY THOUGHT IT THROUGH
OLIPHANT

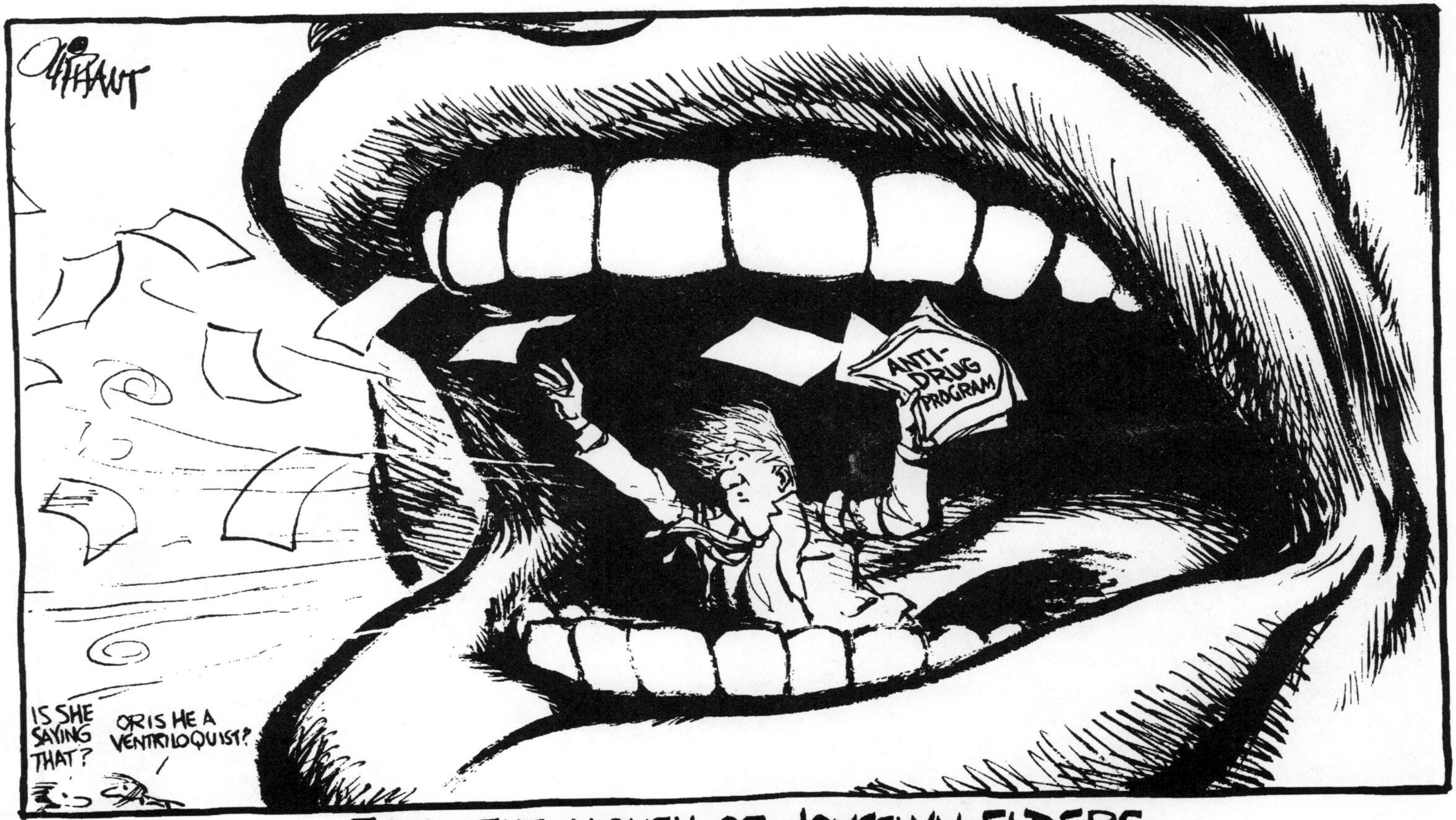
OLIPHANT
ANTI-DRUG PROGRAM
IS SHE SAYING THAT?
OR IS HE A VENTRILOQUIST?

FROM THE MOUTH OF JOYCELYN ELDERS.

December 10, 1993

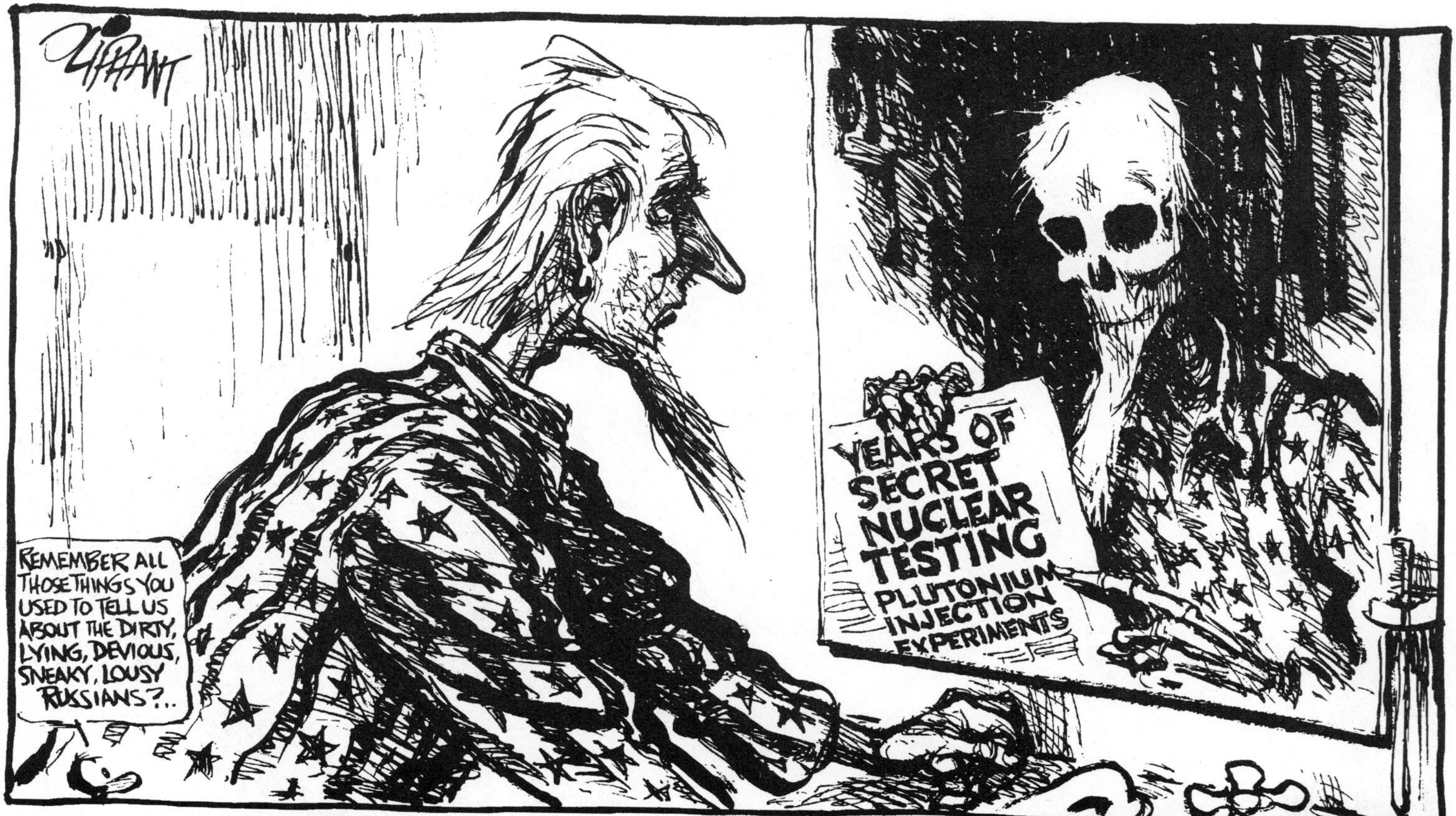
OLIPHANT
REMEMBER ALL THOSE THINGS YOU USED TO TELL US ABOUT THE DIRTY, LYING, DEVIOUS, SNEAKY, LOUSY RUSSIANS?..
YEARS OF SECRET NUCLEAR TESTING
PLUTONIUM INJECTION EXPERIMENTS

THE FACE HE HAS TO LOOK AT EVERY MORNING.

December 11, 1993

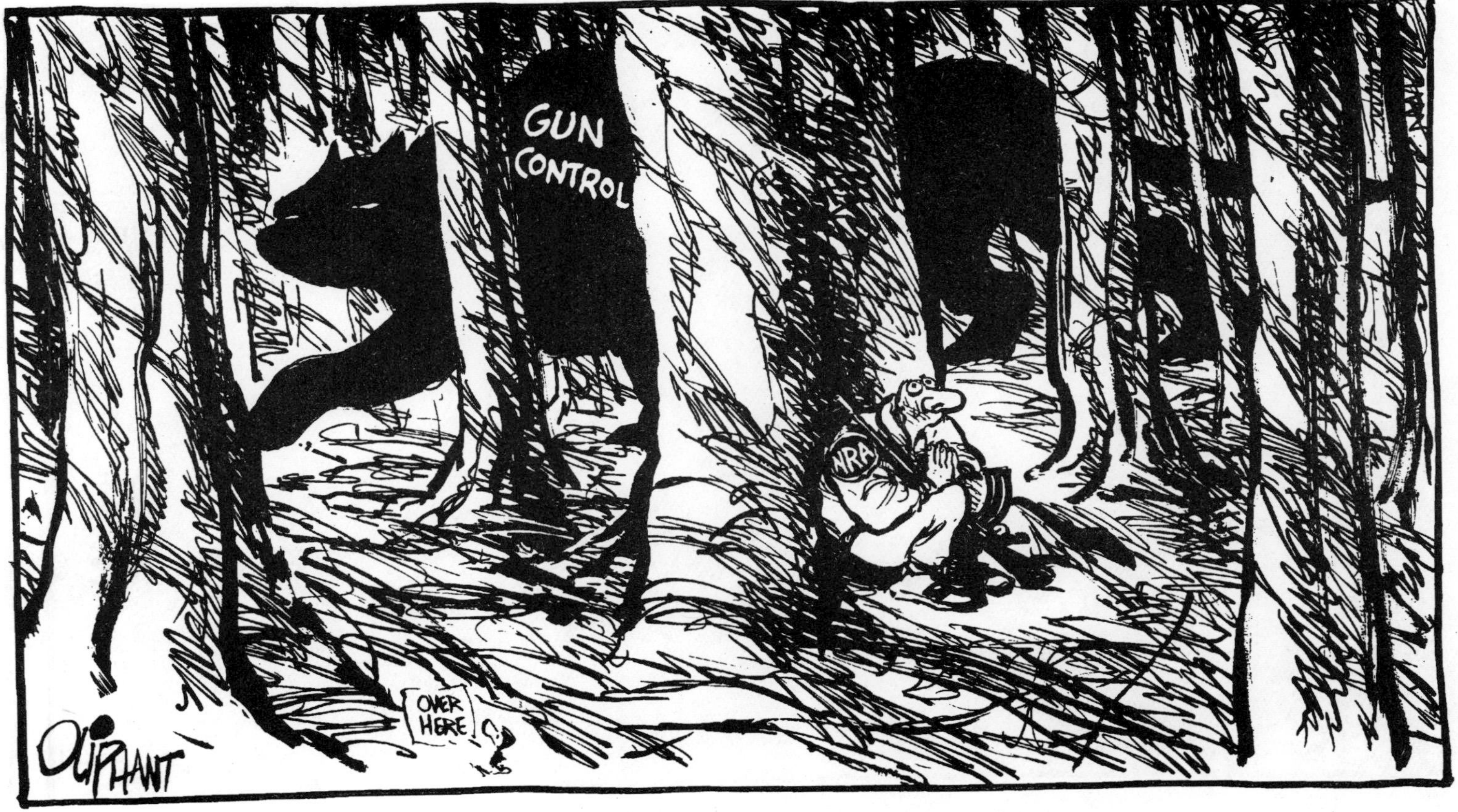
GUN CONTROL
NRA
OVER HERE
OLIPHANT

December 15, 1993

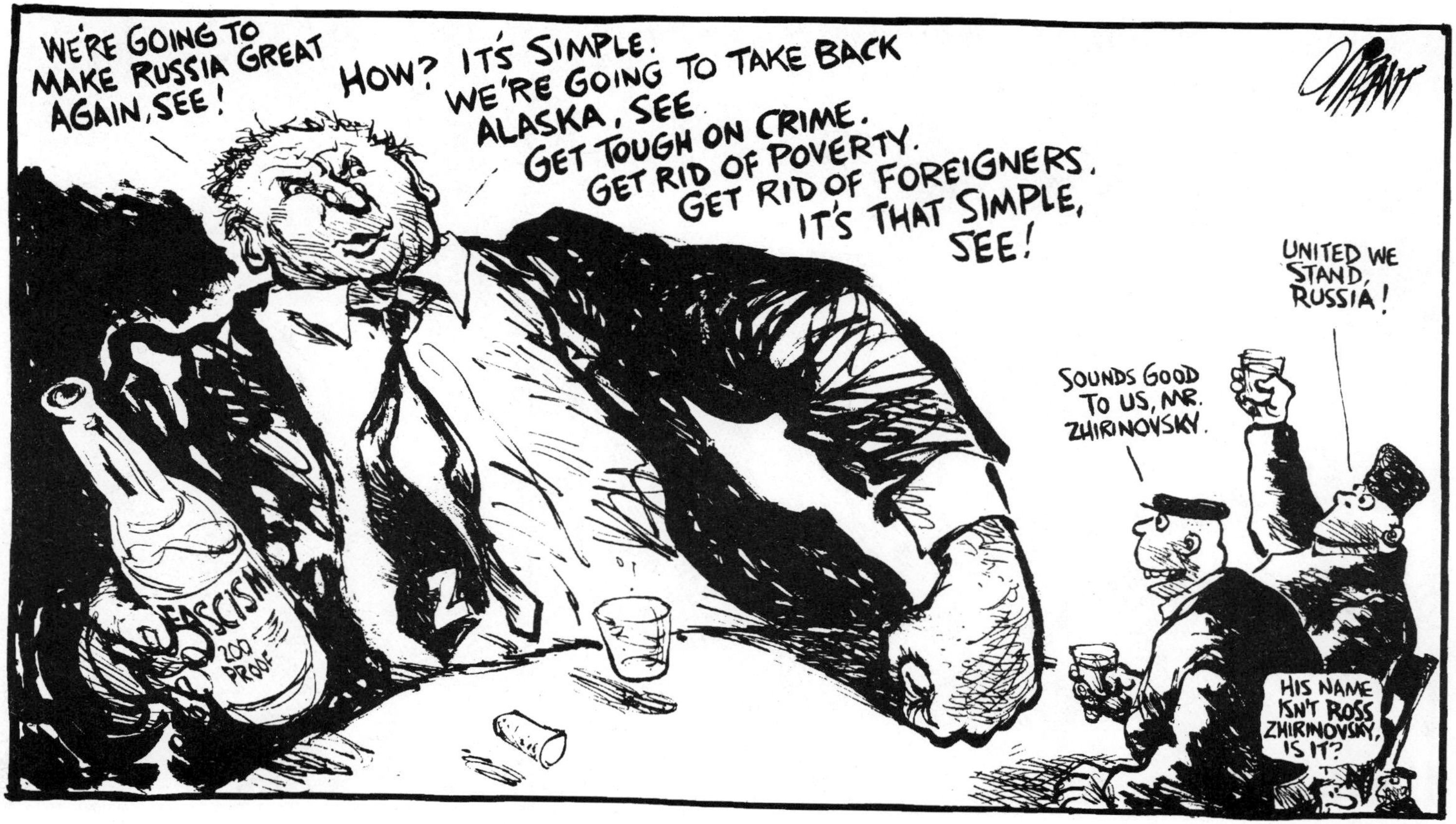
WE'RE GOING TO MAKE RUSSIA GREAT AGAIN, SEE!
HOW? IT'S SIMPLE. WE'RE GOING TO TAKE BACK ALASKA, SEE. GET TOUGH ON CRIME. GET RID OF POVERTY. GET RID OF FOREIGNERS. IT'S THAT SIMPLE, SEE!
FASCISM 200 PROOF
SOUNDS GOOD TO US, MR. ZHIRINOVSKY.
UNITED WE STAND, RUSSIA!
HIS NAME ISN'T ROSS ZHIRINOVSKY, IS IT?

December 16, 1993

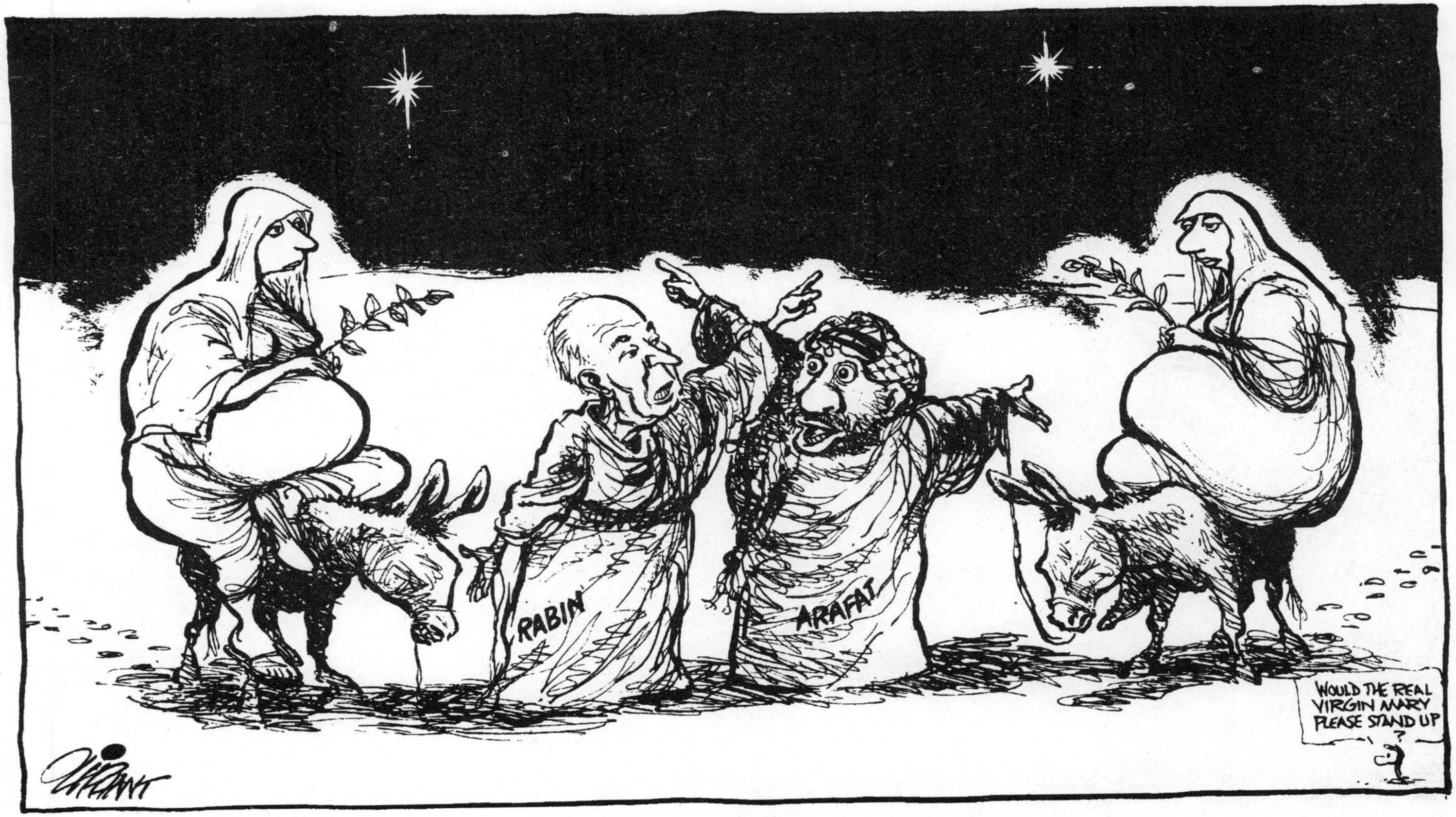
RABIN
ARAFAT
WOULD THE REAL VIRGIN MARY PLEASE STAND UP ?

December 20, 1993

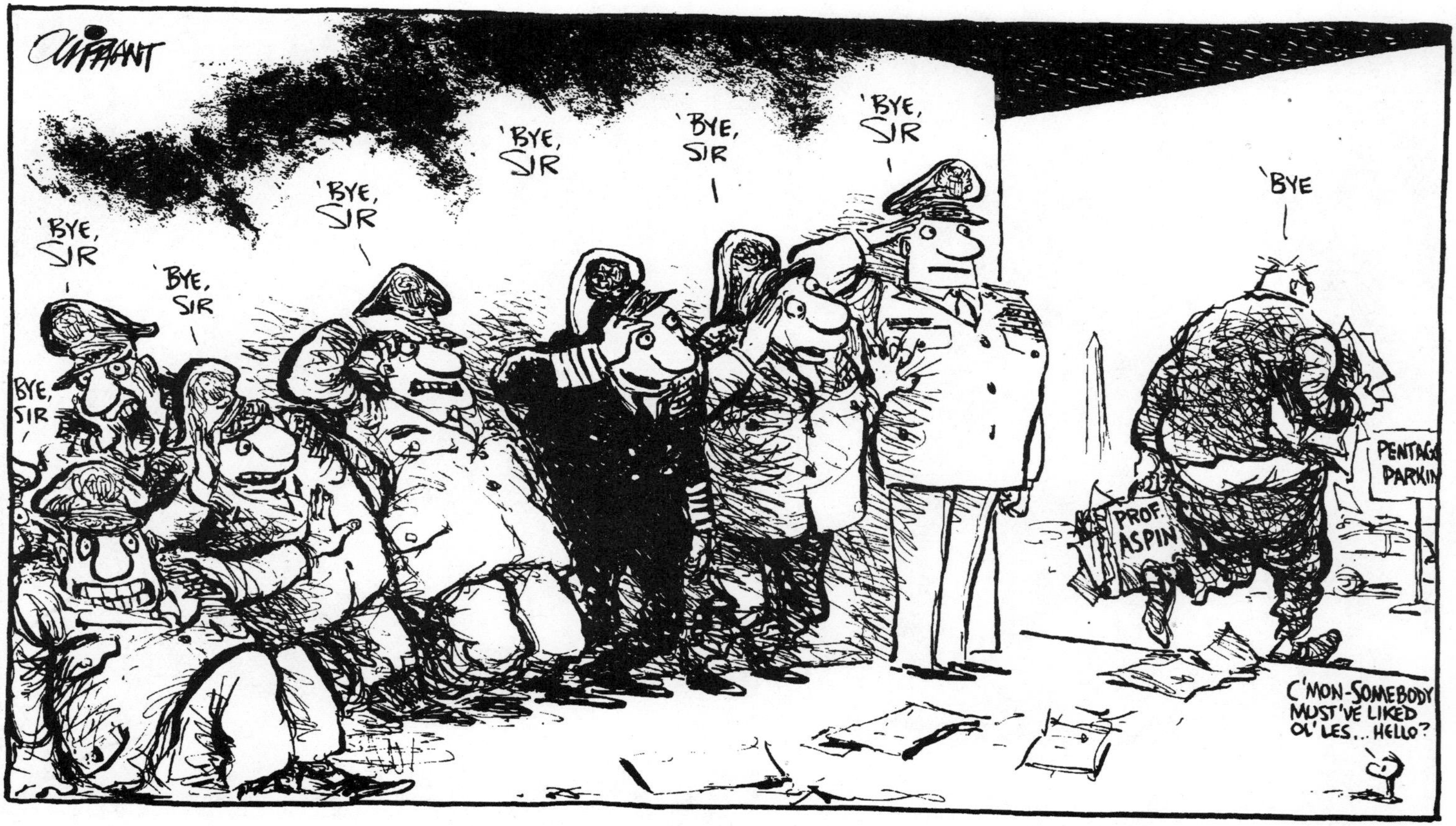

'BYE, SIR
'BYE, SIR
'BYE, SIR
'BYE, SIR
'BYE, SIR
'BYE, SIR
'BYE, SIR
'BYE
PROF. ASPIN
PENTAG
PARKIN
C'MON-SOMEBODY MUST'VE LIKED OL' LES... HELLO?

December 28, 1993

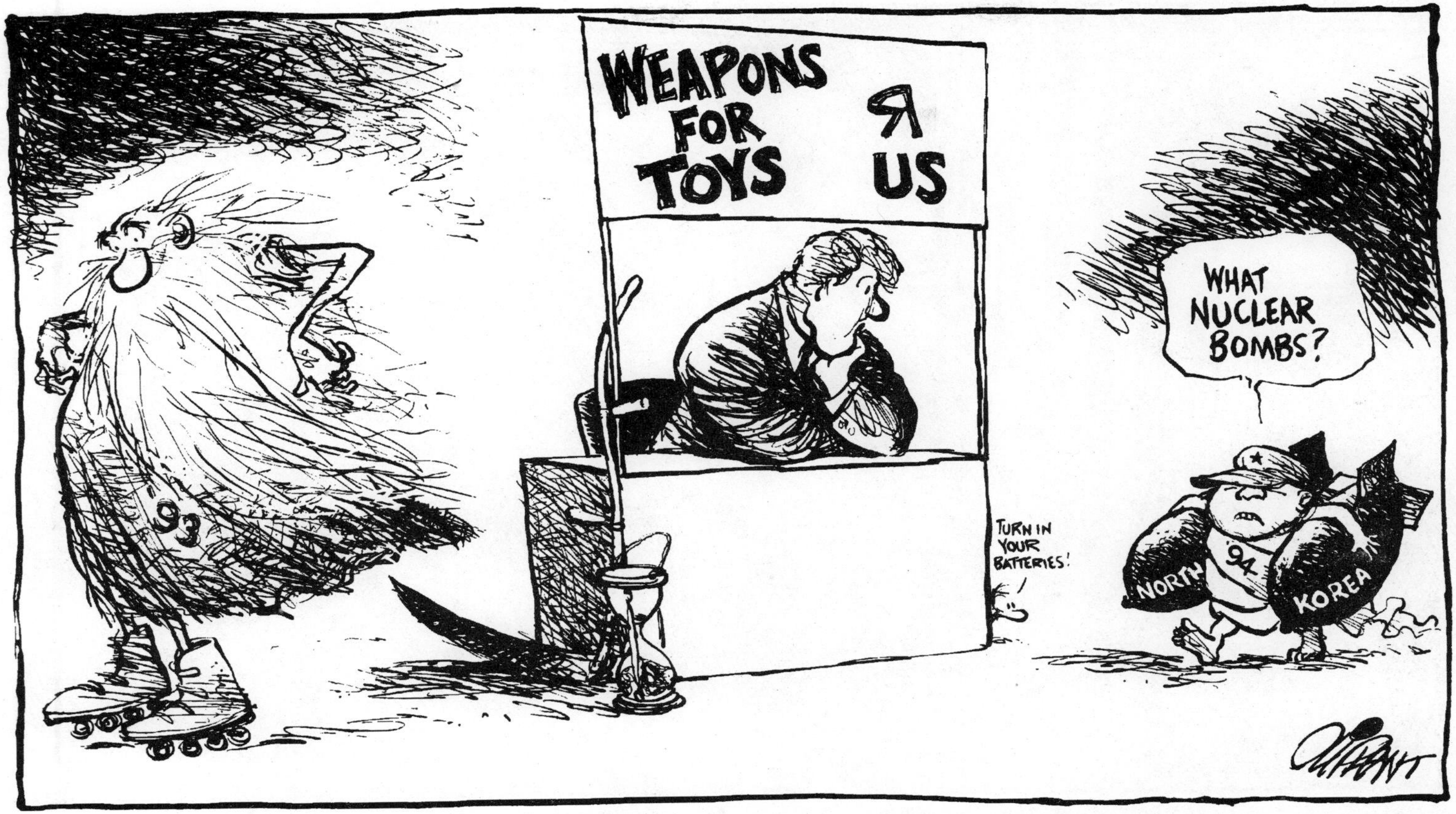
WEAPONS FOR TOYS Я US
WHAT NUCLEAR BOMBS?
TURN IN YOUR BATTERIES!
93
94
NORTH
KOREA

December 30, 1993

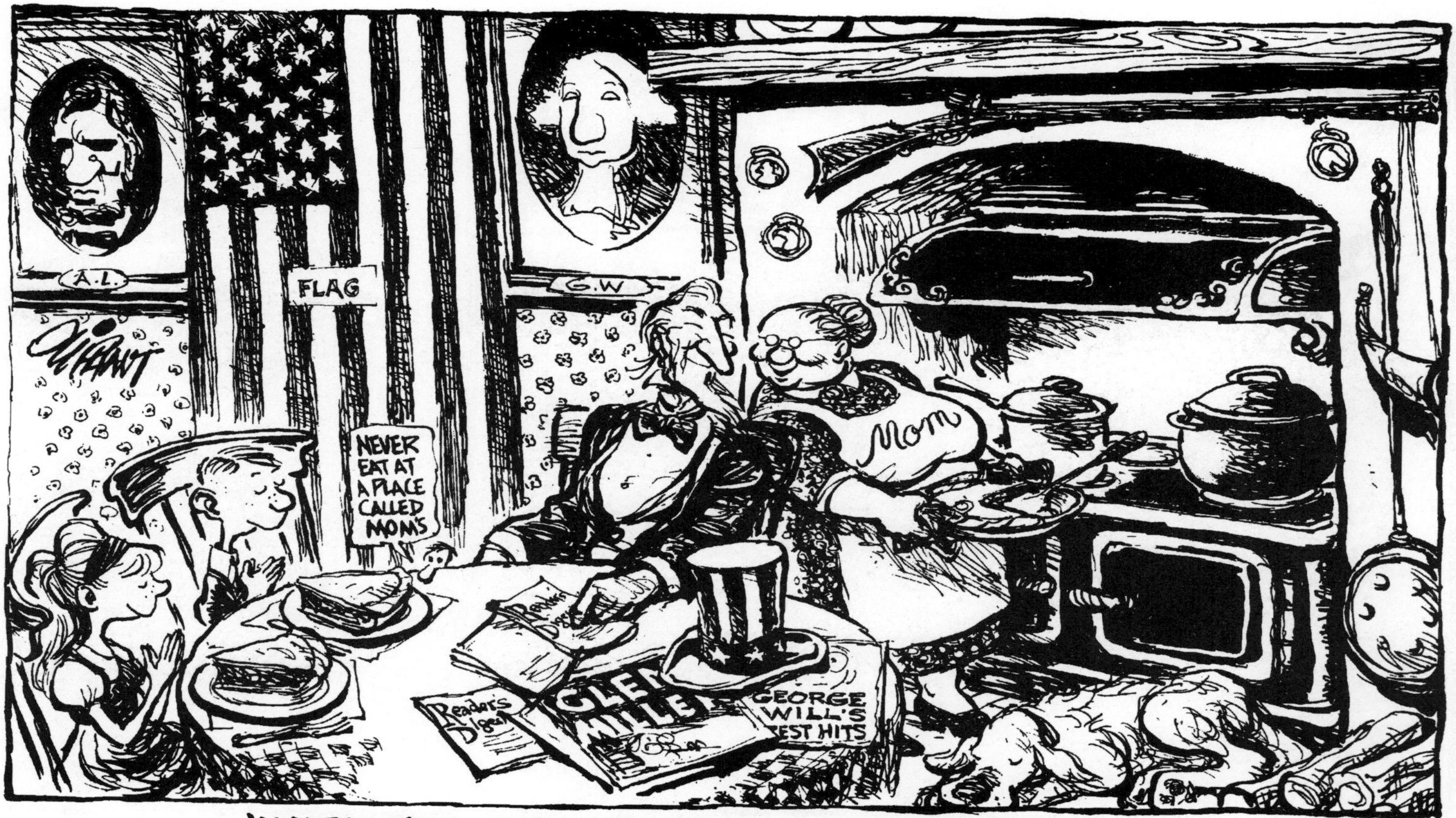
A.L.
FLAG
G.W
Mom
NEVER EAT AT A PLACE CALLED MOM'S
GEORGE WILL'S BEST HITS
Reader's Digest

'WATCH THIS—I PUT PLUTONIUM IN THE APPLE PIE.'

December 31, 1993

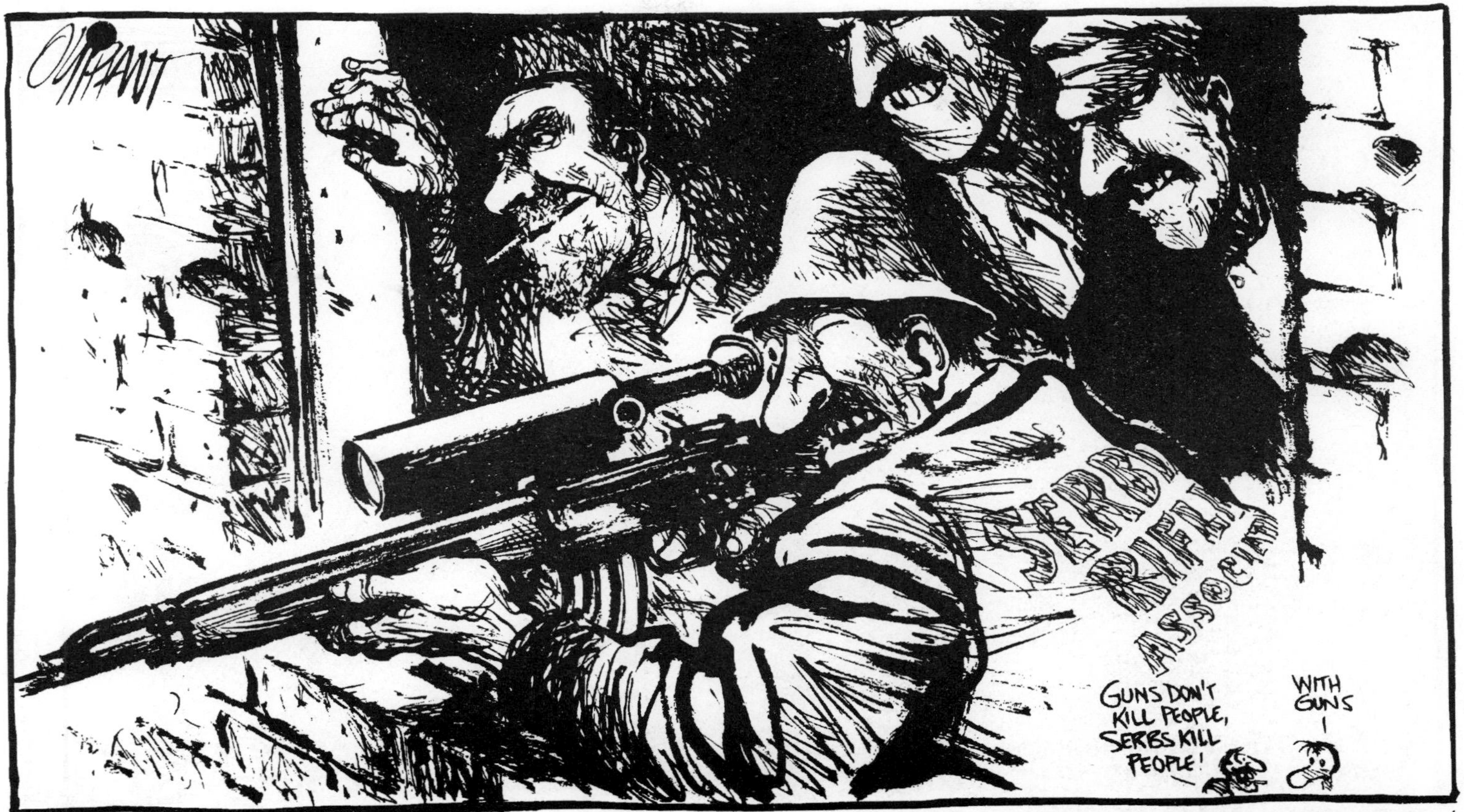
OLIPHANT
SERBIAN RIFLE ASSOCIATION
GUNS DON'T KILL PEOPLE, SERBS KILL PEOPLE!
WITH GUNS!

'HA! LOOK AT THAT CHILD DOWN THERE... THE ONE IN THE DIAPER WITH "1994" ON IT...'

January 4, 1994

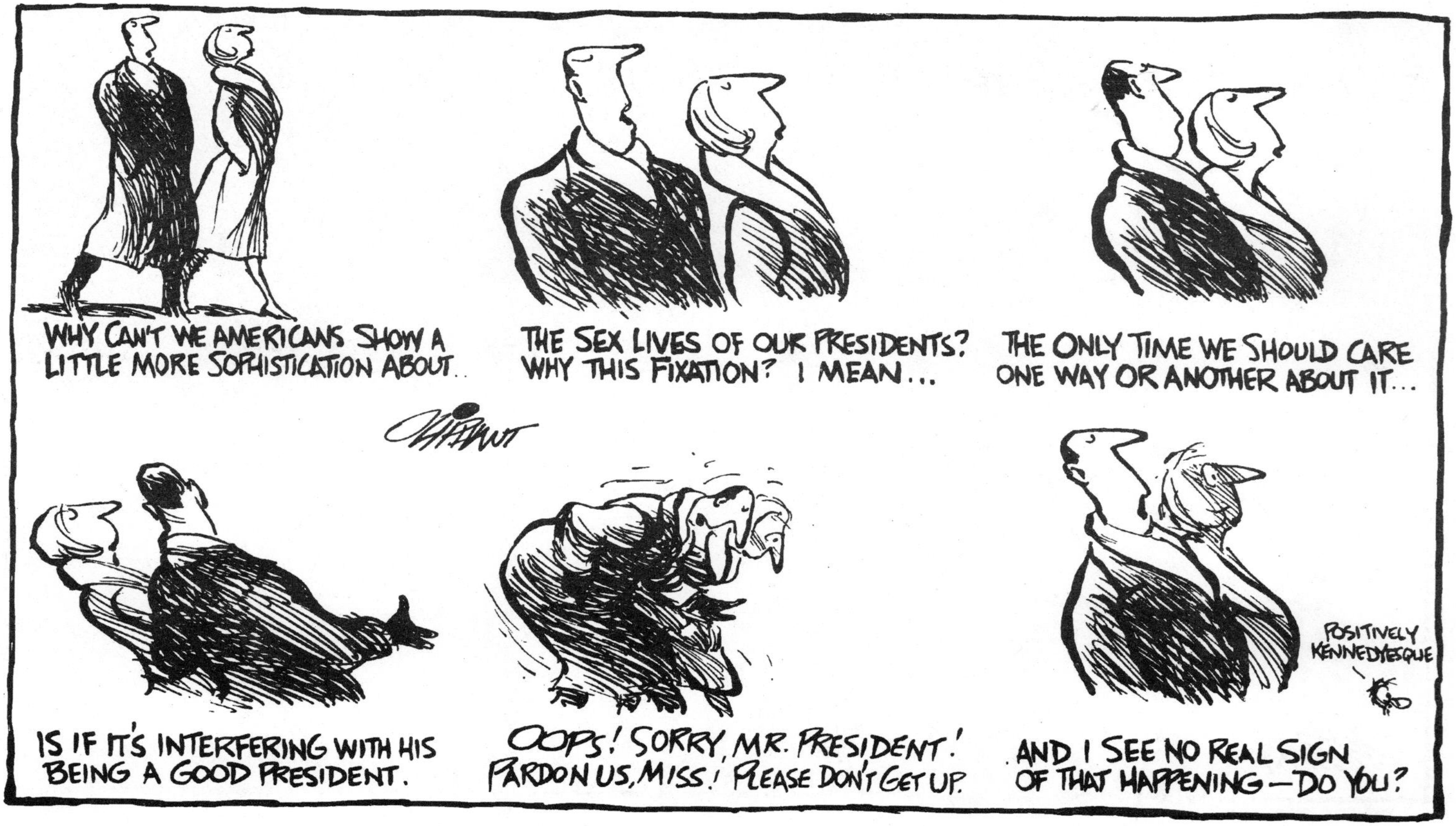
WHY CAN'T WE AMERICANS SHOW A LITTLE MORE SOPHISTICATION ABOUT...
THE SEX LIVES OF OUR PRESIDENTS? WHY THIS FIXATION? I MEAN...
THE ONLY TIME WE SHOULD CARE ONE WAY OR ANOTHER ABOUT IT...
IS IF IT'S INTERFERING WITH HIS BEING A GOOD PRESIDENT.
OOPS! SORRY, MR. PRESIDENT! PARDON US, MISS! PLEASE DON'T GET UP.
POSITIVELY KENNEDYESQUE
...AND I SEE NO REAL SIGN OF THAT HAPPENING—DO YOU?

January 4, 1994

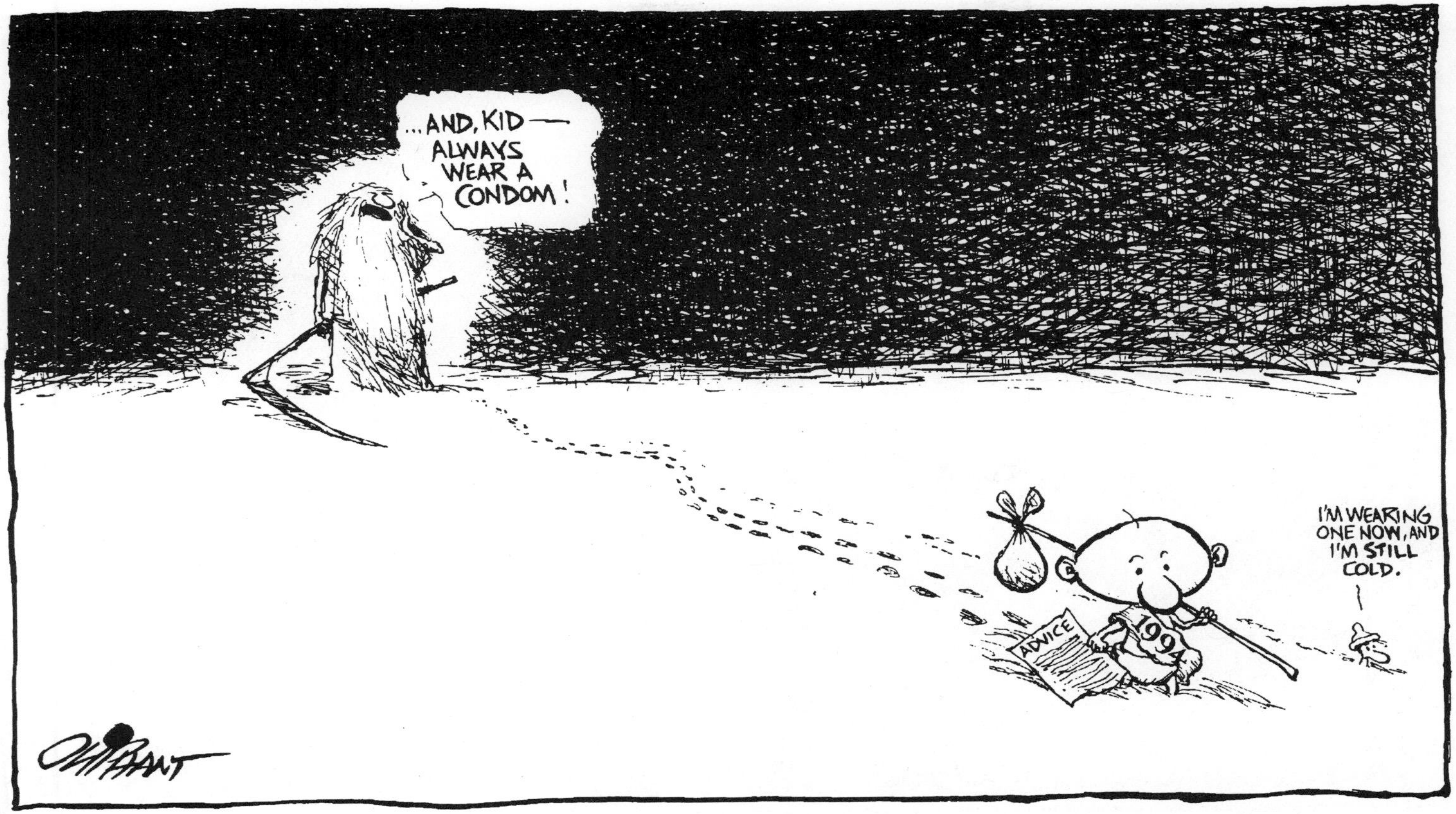
...AND, KID — ALWAYS WEAR A CONDOM!
I'M WEARING ONE NOW, AND I'M STILL COLD.
ADVICE
1994
OLIPHANT

January 5, 1994

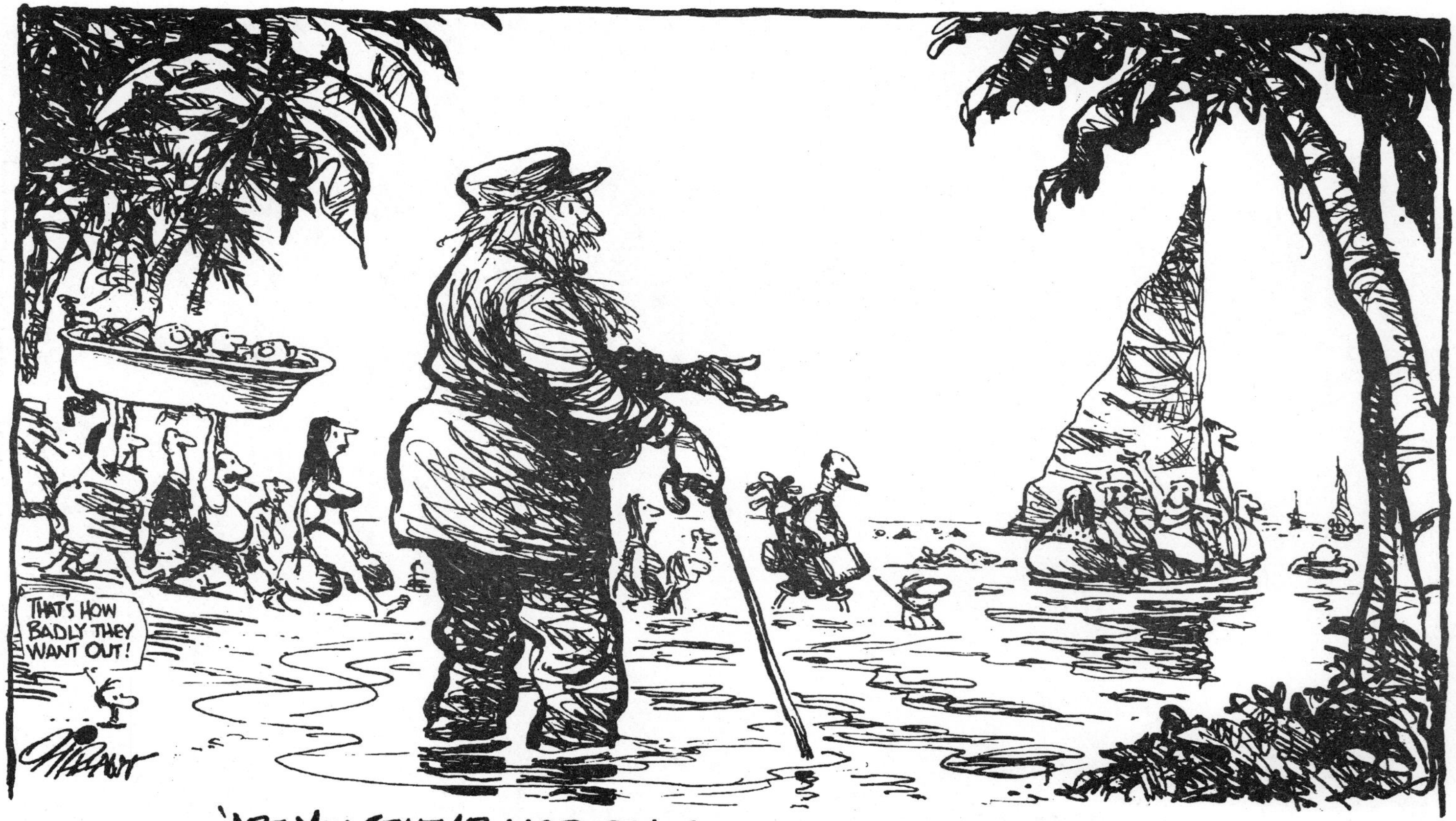
THAT'S HOW BADLY THEY WANT OUT!

'ARE YOU CRAZY? **NOBODY** GOES TO FLORIDA ANY MORE!'

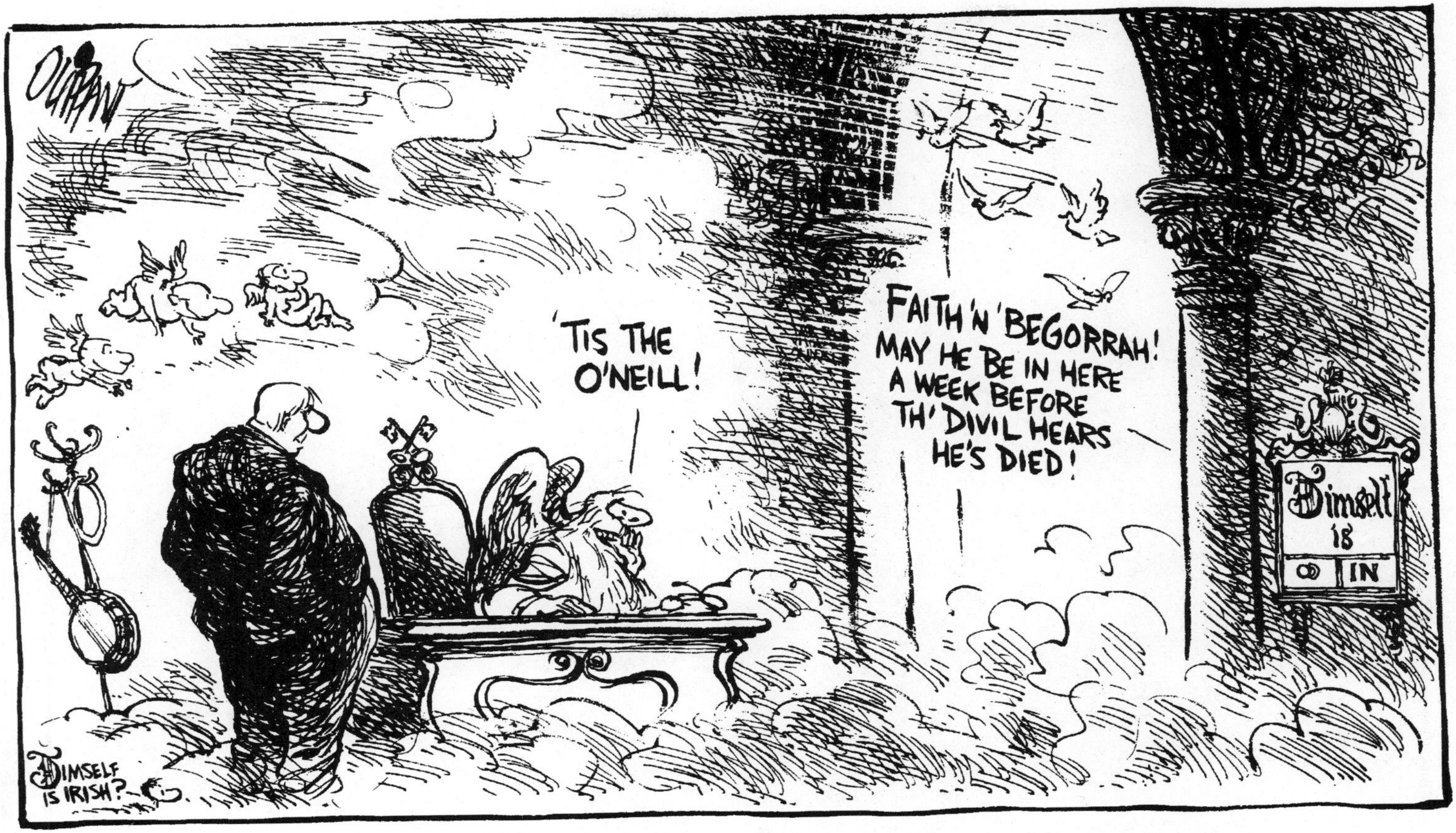
OLIPHANT
'TIS THE O'NEILL!
FAITH 'N' BEGORRAH! MAY HE BE IN HERE A WEEK BEFORE TH' DIVIL HEARS HE'S DIED!
Himself is IN
HIMSELF IS IRISH?

January 10, 1994

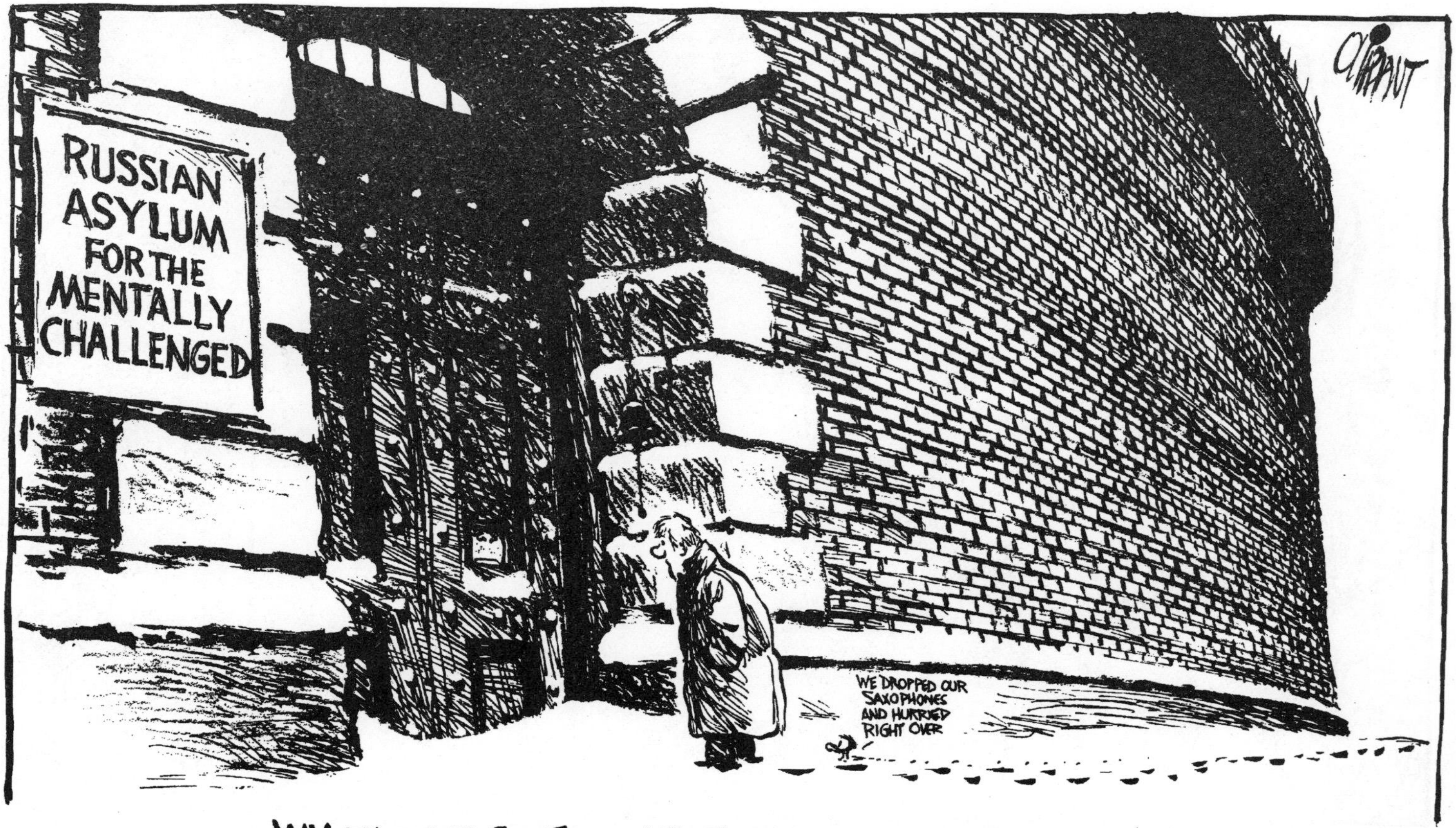
RUSSIAN ASYLUM FOR THE MENTALLY CHALLENGED
WE DROPPED OUR SAXOPHONES AND HURRIED RIGHT OVER
OLIPHANT

'MY NAME IS CLINTON... MR. ZHIRINOVSKY SENT FOR ME.'

January 12, 1994

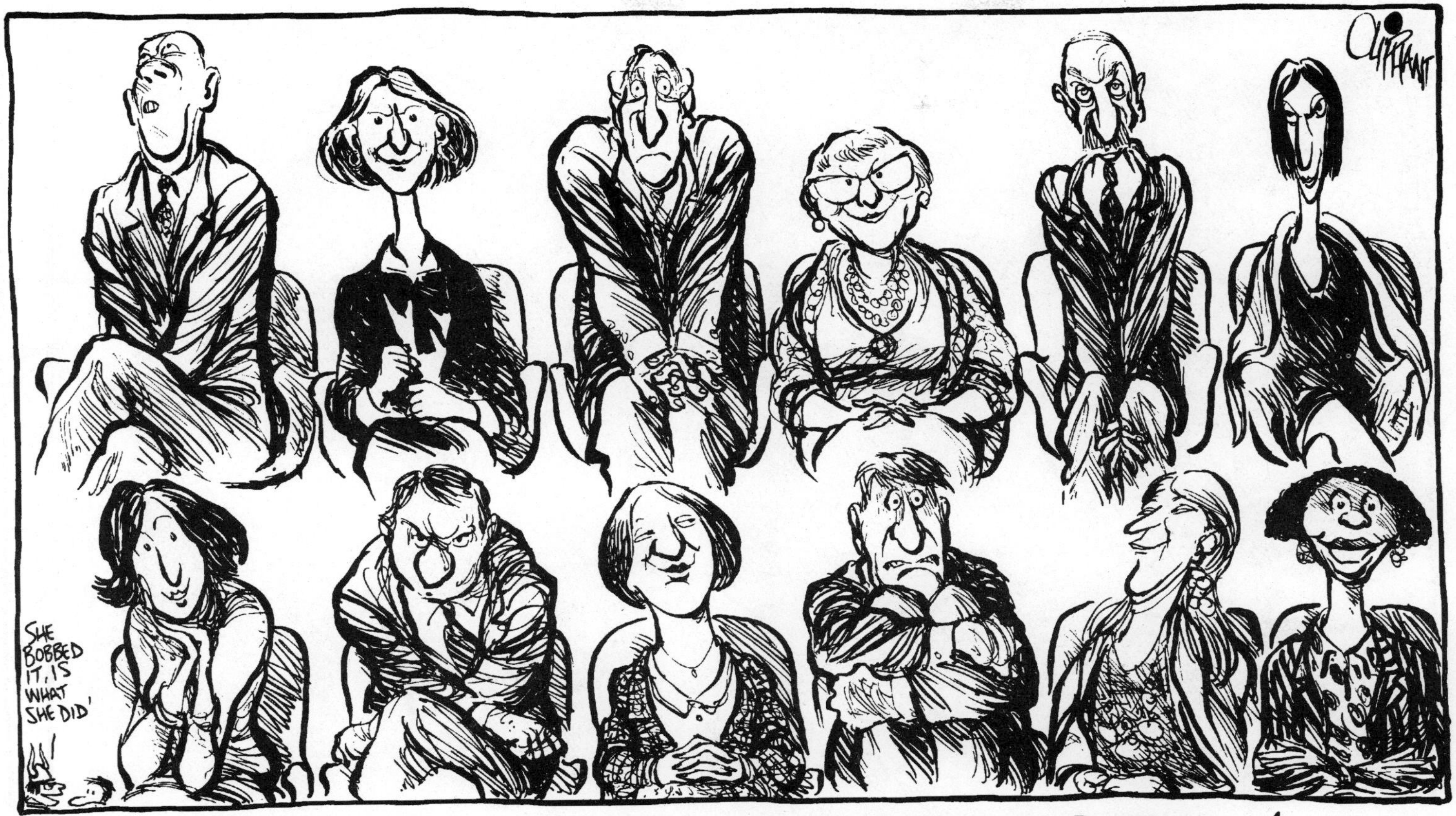
OLIPHANT
SHE BOBBED IT, IS WHAT SHE DID'

'NOW, TELL THE JURY WHAT YOU DID WITH THE KNIFE, MRS. BOBBITT...'

January 14, 1994

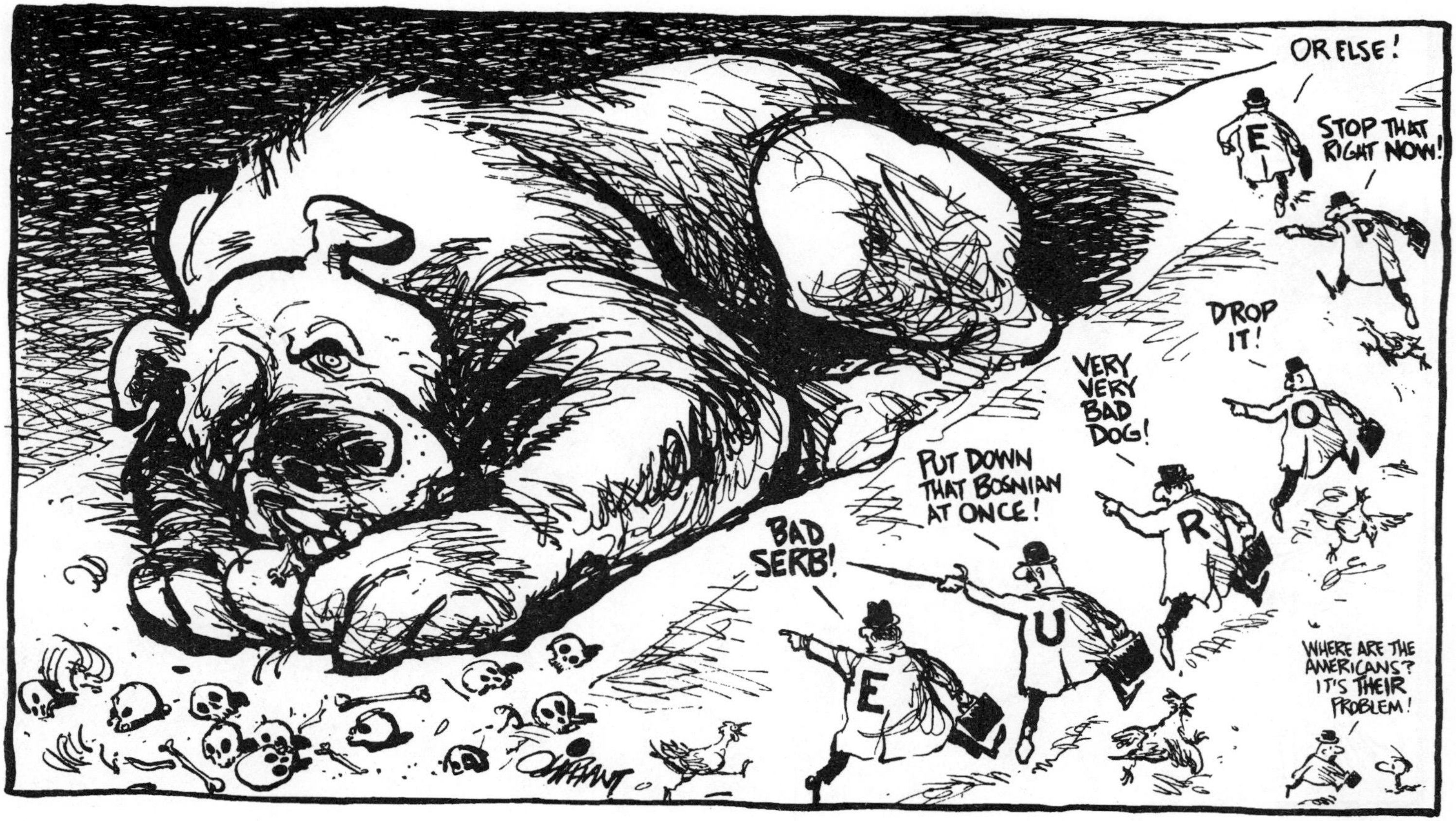

OR ELSE!
STOP THAT RIGHT NOW!
DROP IT!
VERY VERY BAD DOG!
PUT DOWN THAT BOSNIAN AT ONCE!
BAD SERB!
WHERE ARE THE AMERICANS? IT'S THEIR PROBLEM!
E
P
O
R
U
E

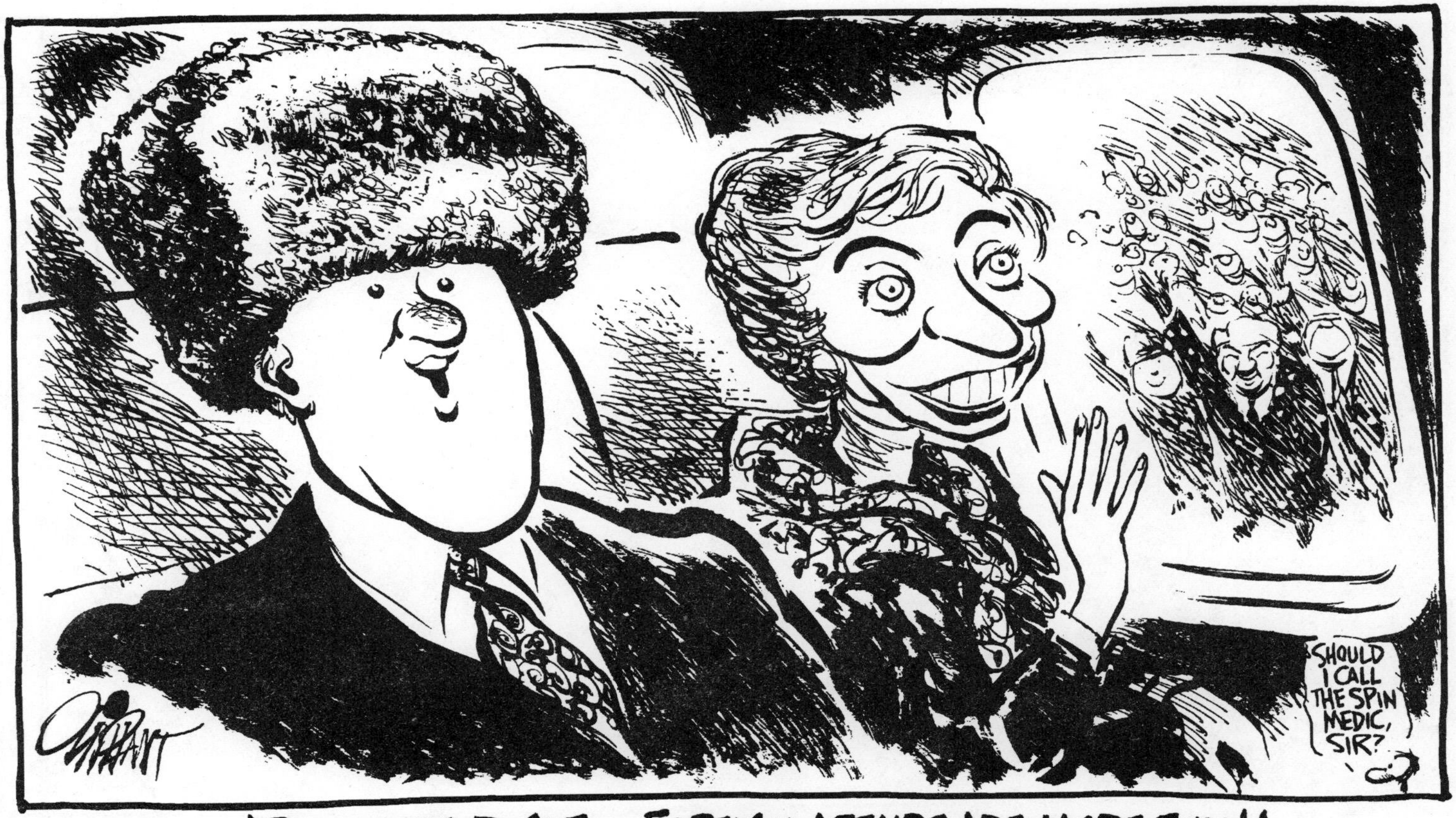
SHOULD I CALL THE SPIN MEDIC, SIR?

'BUSH WAS RIGHT—FOREIGN AFFAIRS ARE MORE FUN!'

January 19, 1994

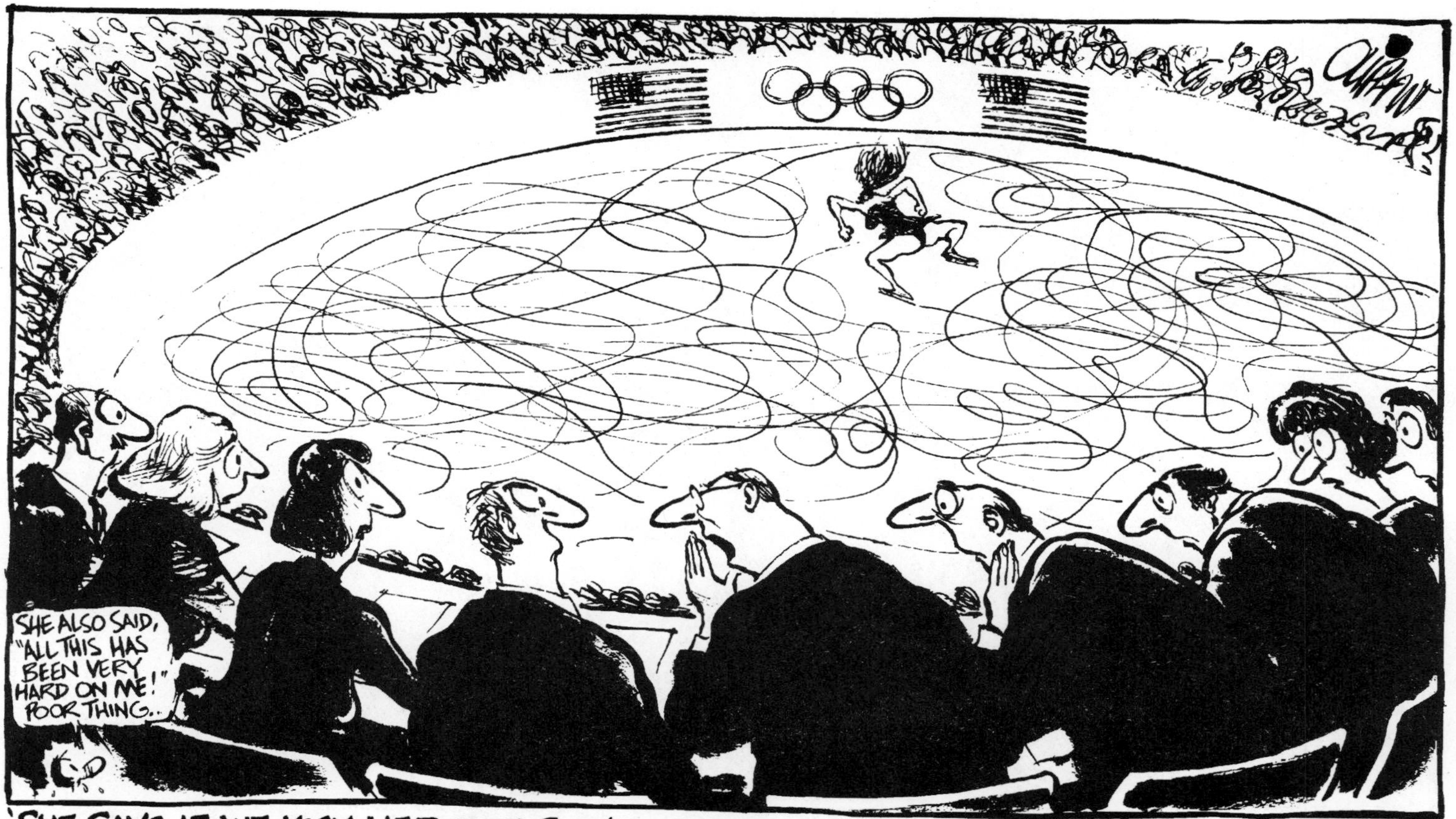
SHE ALSO SAID, "ALL THIS HAS BEEN VERY HARD ON ME!" POOR THING..

'SHE SAYS IF WE KICK HER OUT, SHE'LL BREAK OUR GODDAM KNEES – PASS IT ON...'

January 19, 1994

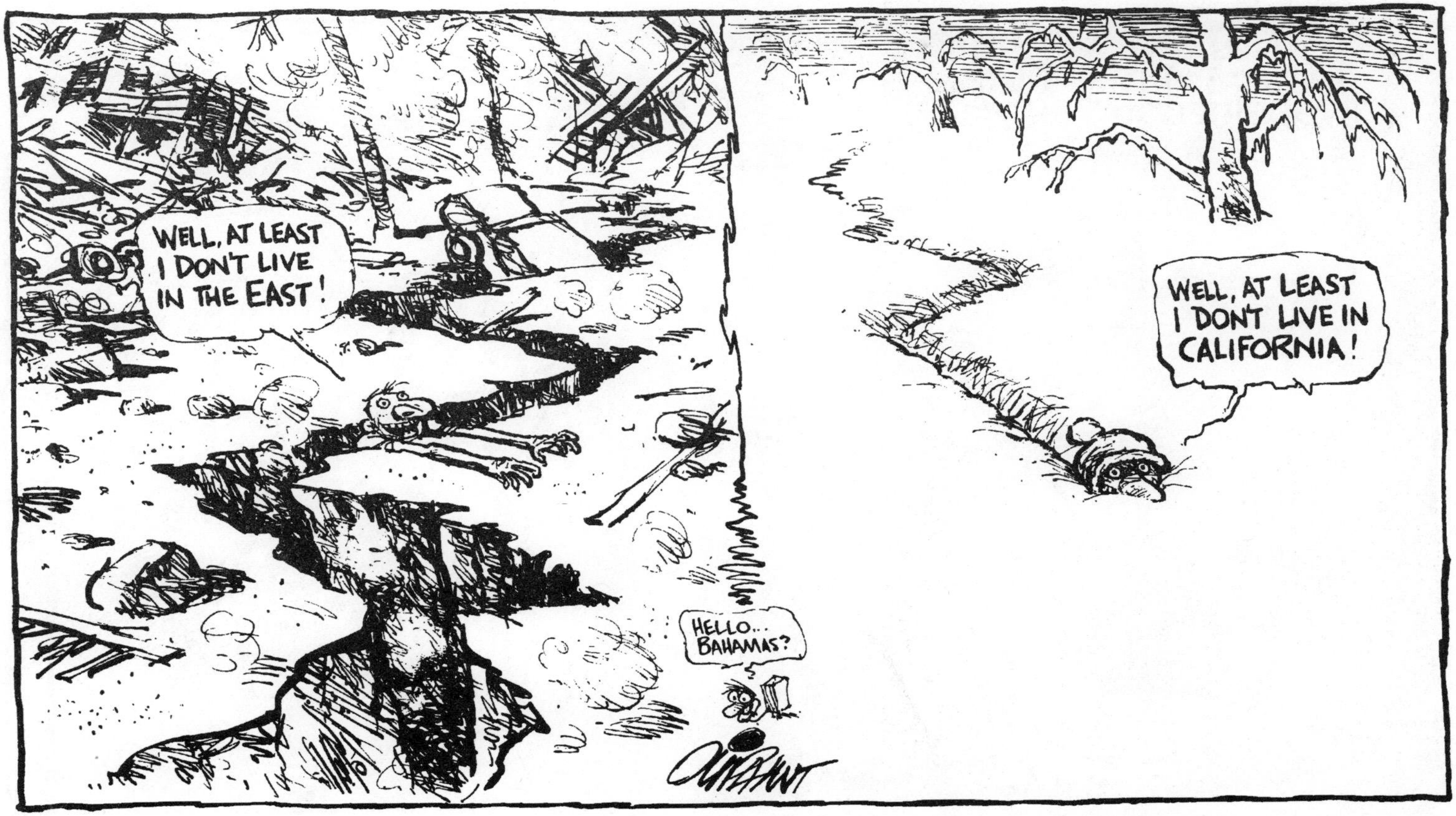
WELL, AT LEAST I DON'T LIVE IN THE EAST!
HELLO... BAHAMAS?
WELL, AT LEAST I DON'T LIVE IN CALIFORNIA!

January 20, 1994

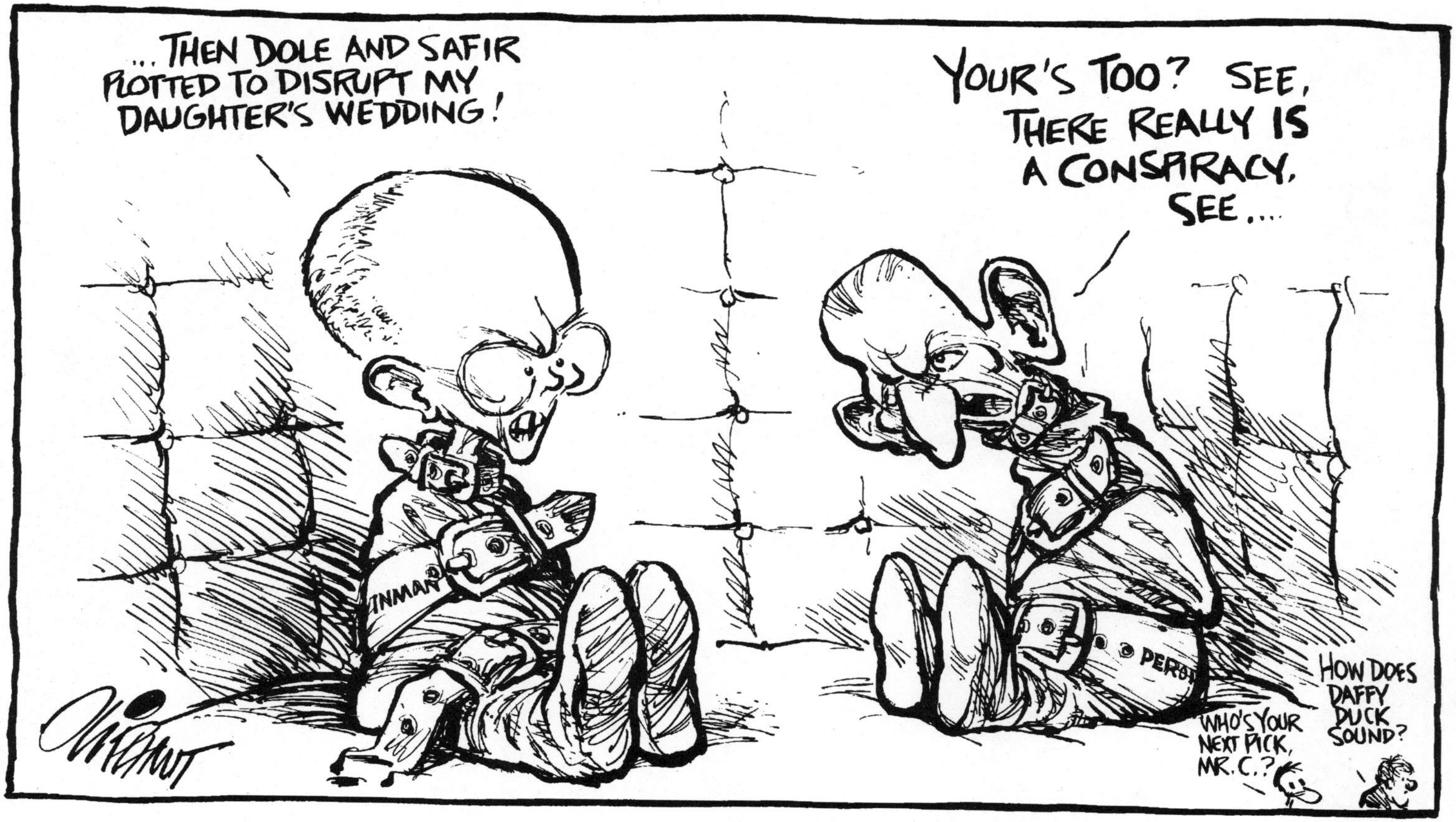
...THEN DOLE AND SAFIR PLOTTED TO DISRUPT MY DAUGHTER'S WEDDING!
YOUR'S TOO? SEE, THERE REALLY IS A CONSPIRACY, SEE...
INMAN
PEROT
WHO'S YOUR NEXT PICK, MR. C.?
HOW DOES DAFFY DUCK SOUND?

January 21, 1994

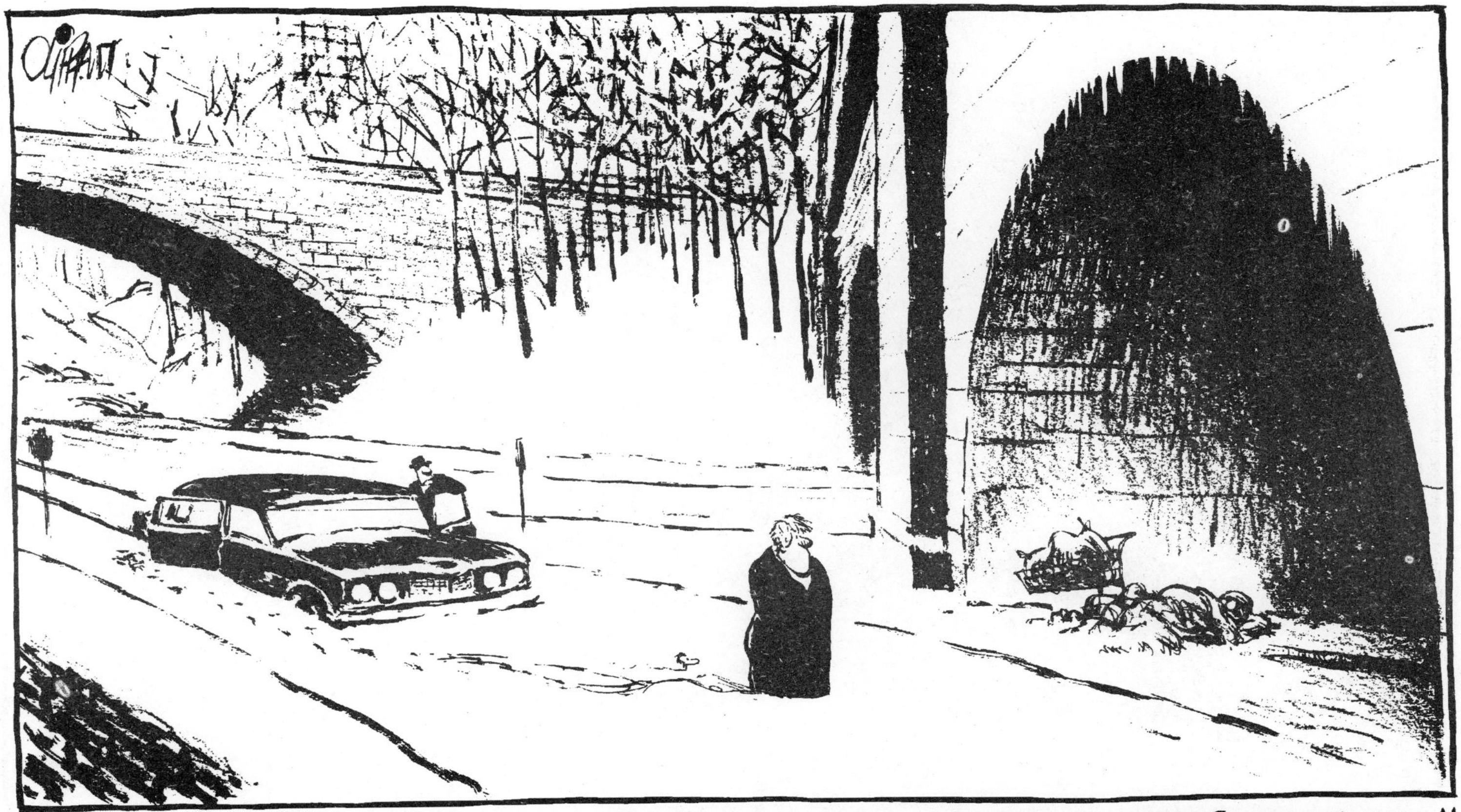

'NO, I DON'T WANT TO BE SECRETARY OF DEFENSE — THAT JOB HAS A LOUSY COMFORT LEVEL!'

January 26, 1994

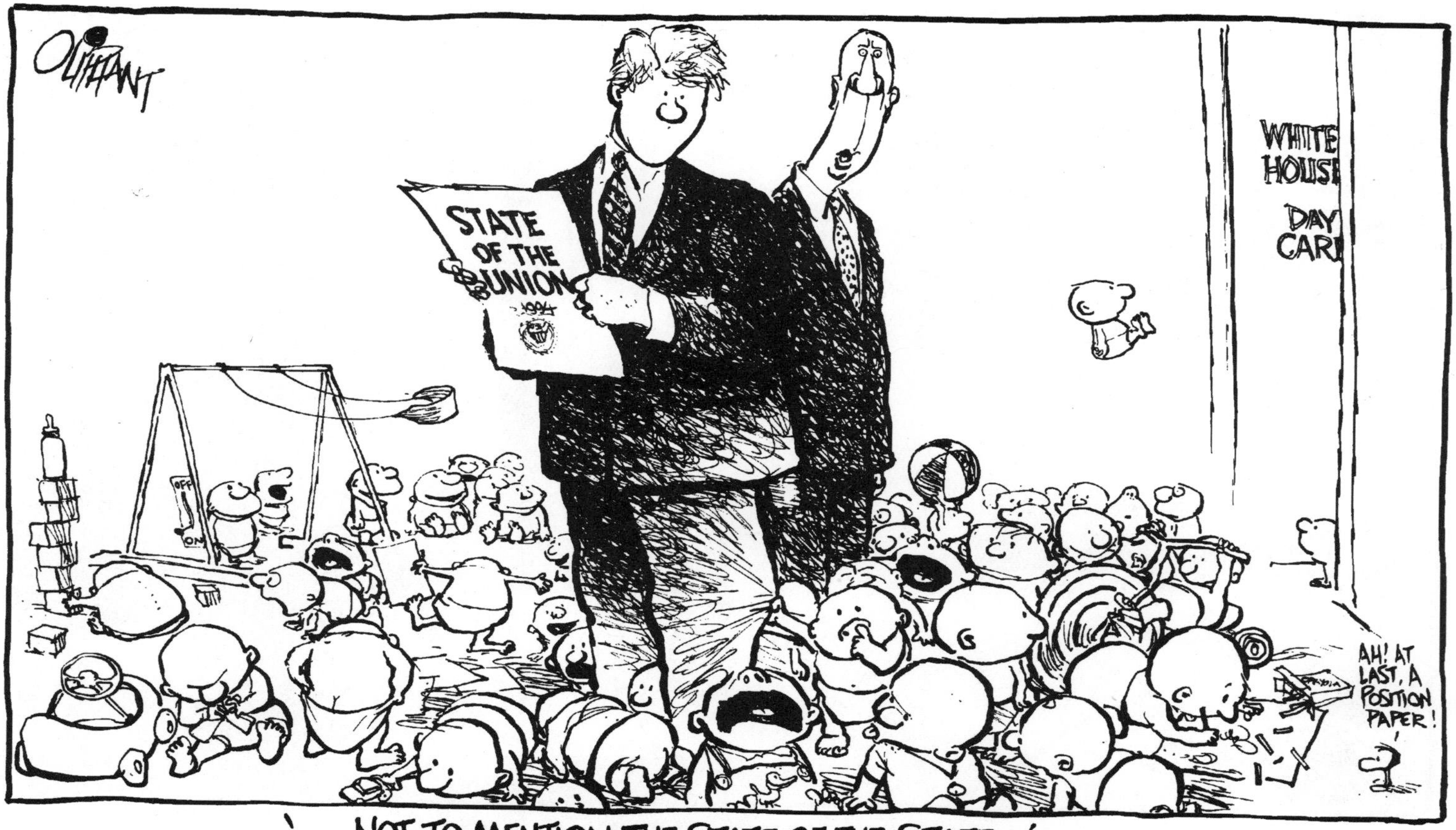
OLIPHANT
STATE OF THE UNION
1994
WHITE HOUSE
DAY CARE
AH! AT LAST, A POSITION PAPER!

'... NOT TO MENTION THE STATE OF THE STAFF.'

January 27, 1994

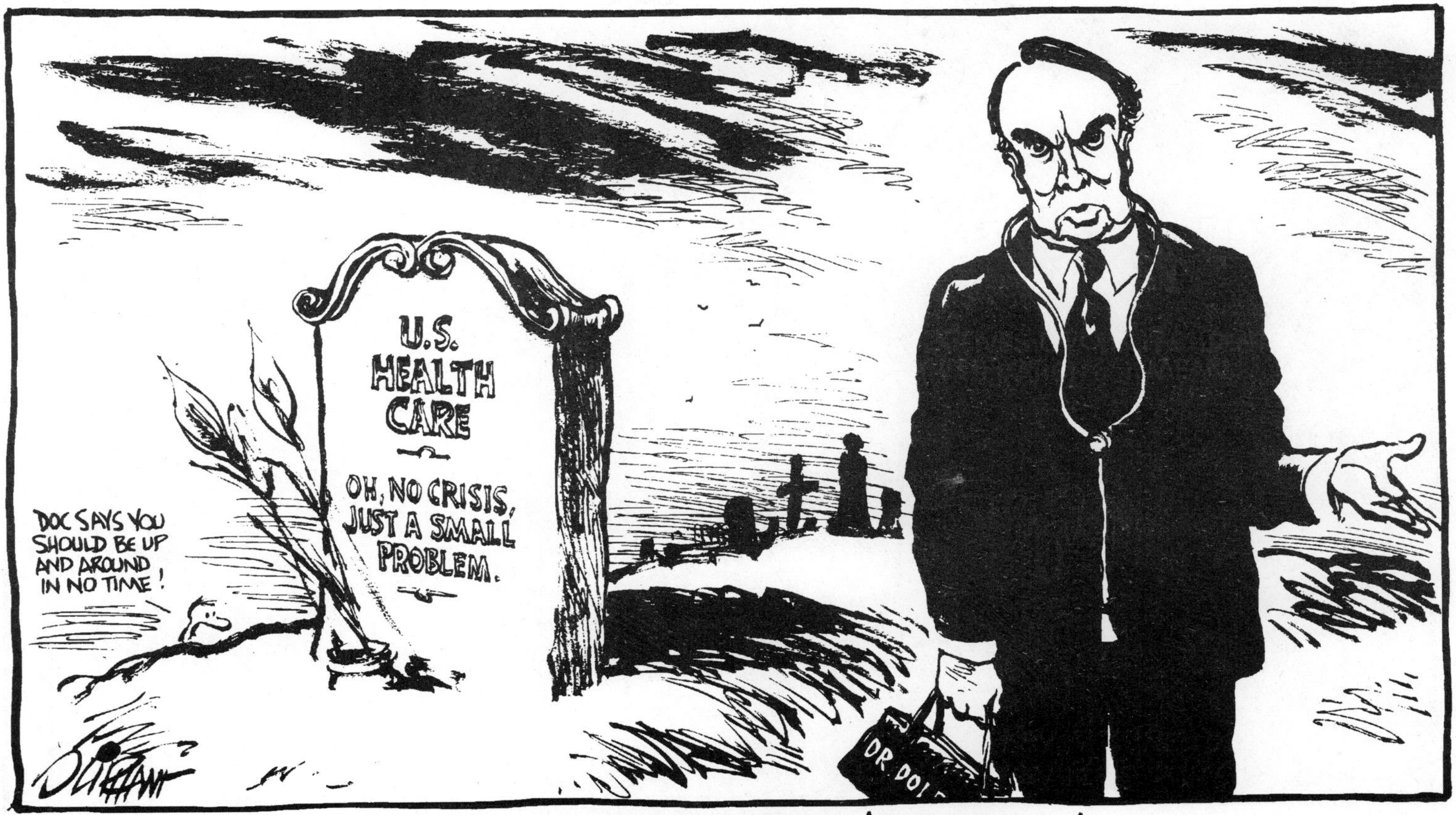
U.S. HEALTH CARE
OH, NO CRISIS, JUST A SMALL PROBLEM.
DOC SAYS YOU SHOULD BE UP AND AROUND IN NO TIME!
DR DOLE

'SO, THE ASPIRIN DIDN'T WORK...'

January 28, 1994

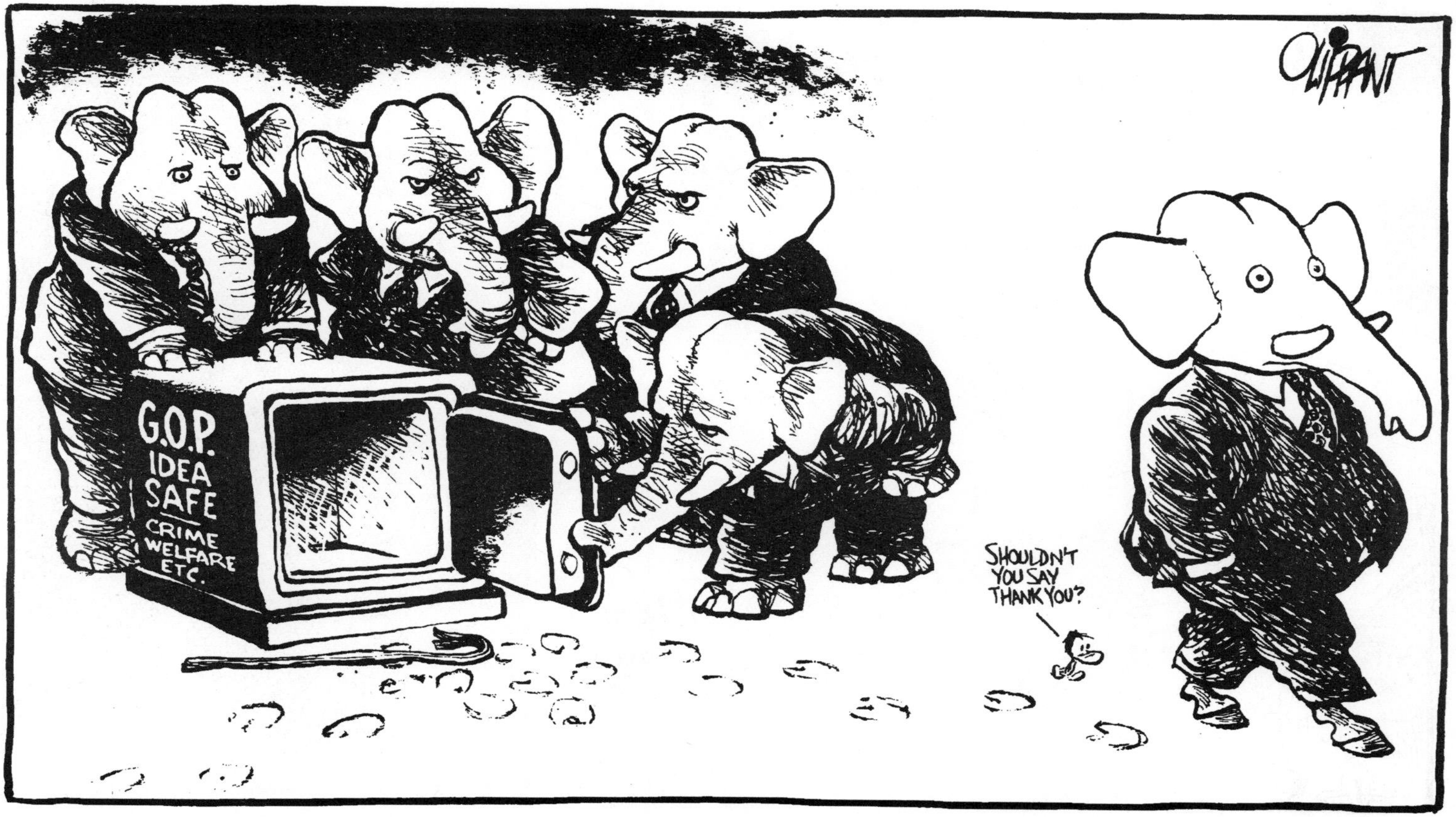
OLIPHANT
G.O.P.
IDEA
SAFE
CRIME
WELFARE
ETC.
SHOULDN'T YOU SAY THANK YOU?

January 29, 1994

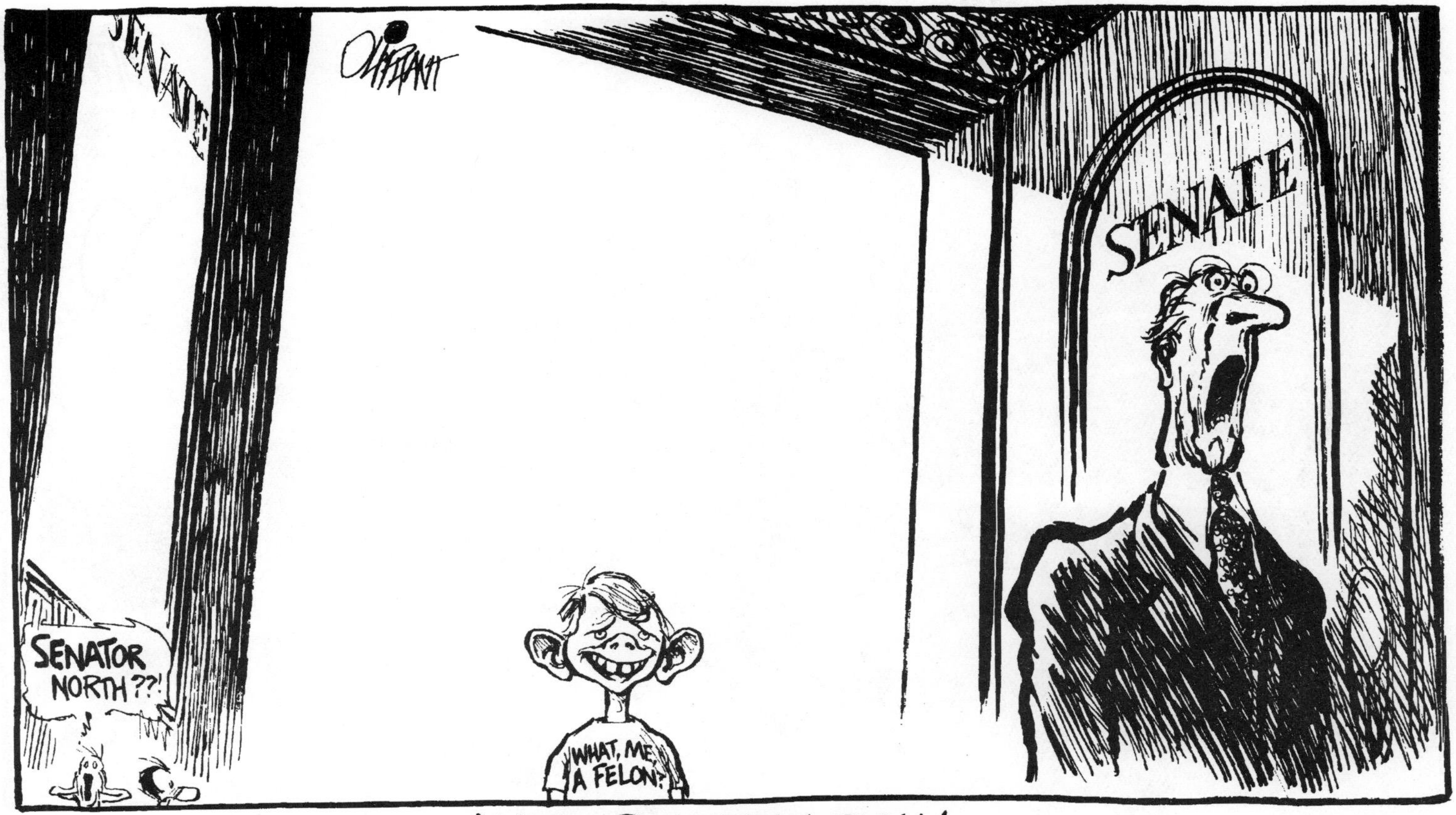
SENATE
OLIPHANT
SENATE
SENATOR NORTH??!
WHAT, ME, A FELON?

'HE'S BAAAAAACK!!'

February 2, 1994

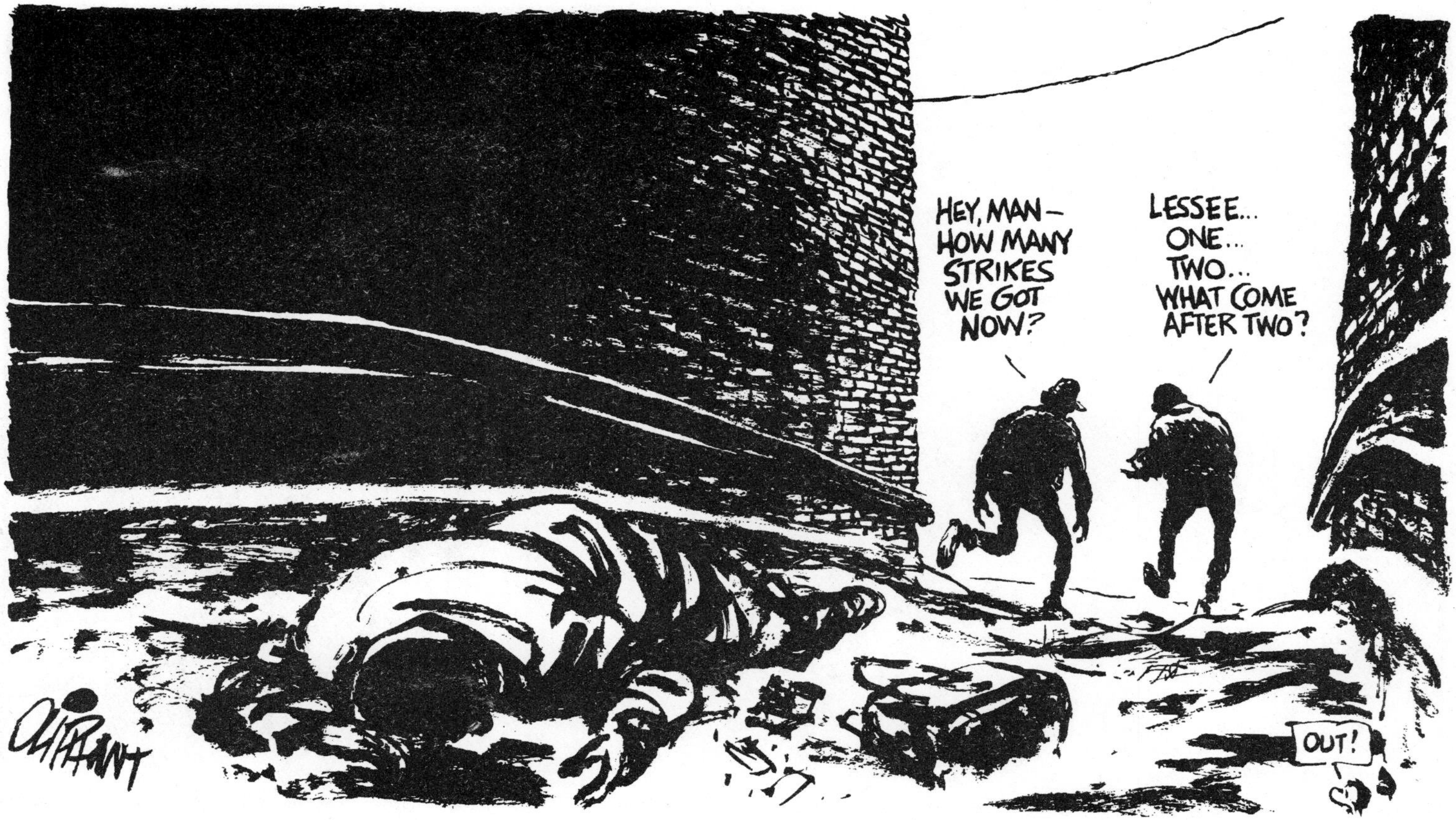
HEY, MAN-
HOW MANY
STRIKES
WE GOT
NOW?
LESSEE...
ONE...
TWO...
WHAT COME
AFTER TWO?
OUT!
OLIPHANT

February 3, 1994

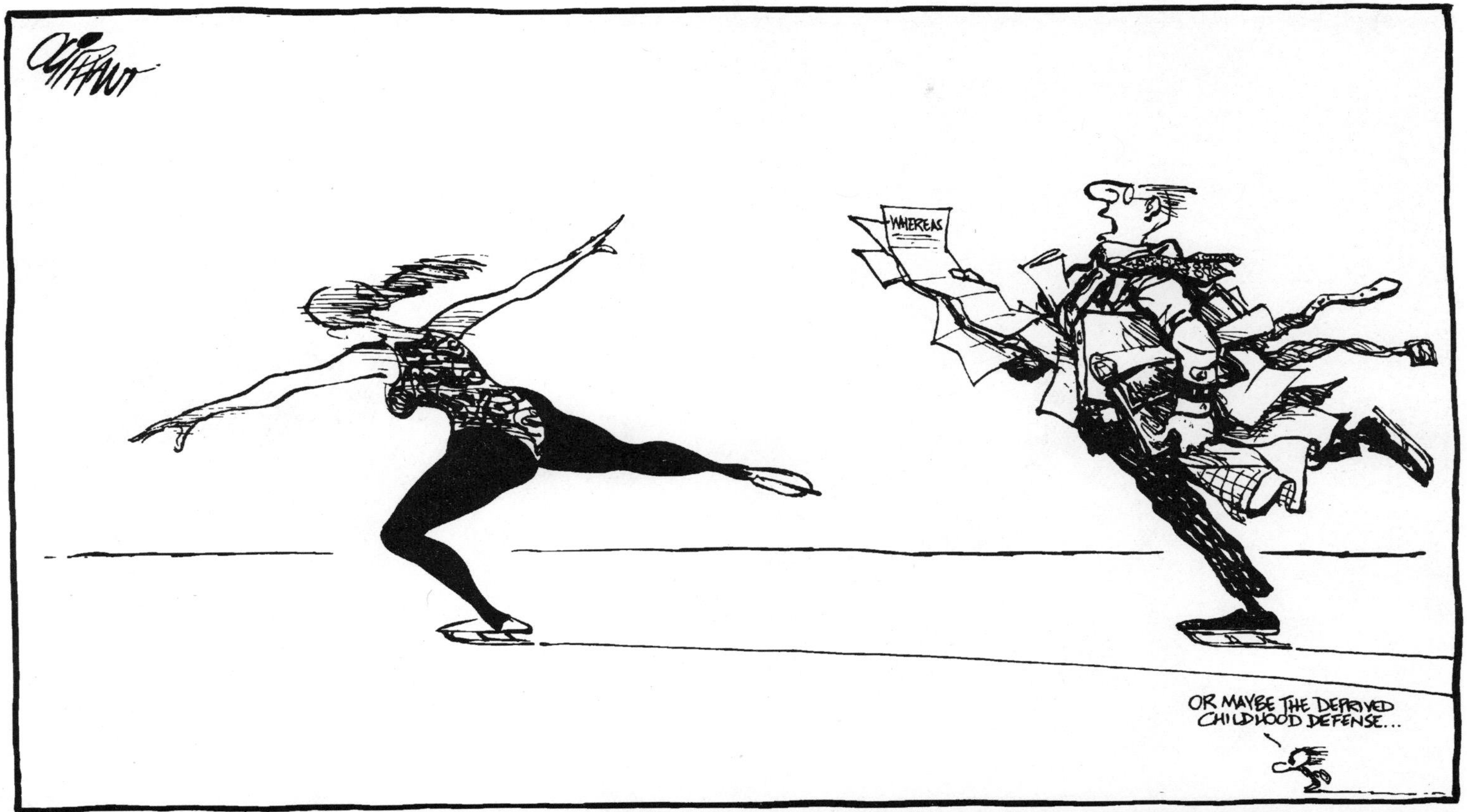
WHEREAS
OR MAYBE THE DEPRIVED CHILDHOOD DEFENSE...

'...THEN THERE'S "NOT GUILTY BY REASON OF INSANITY"— THAT'S BEEN WORKING QUITE WELL LATELY.'

February 4, 1994

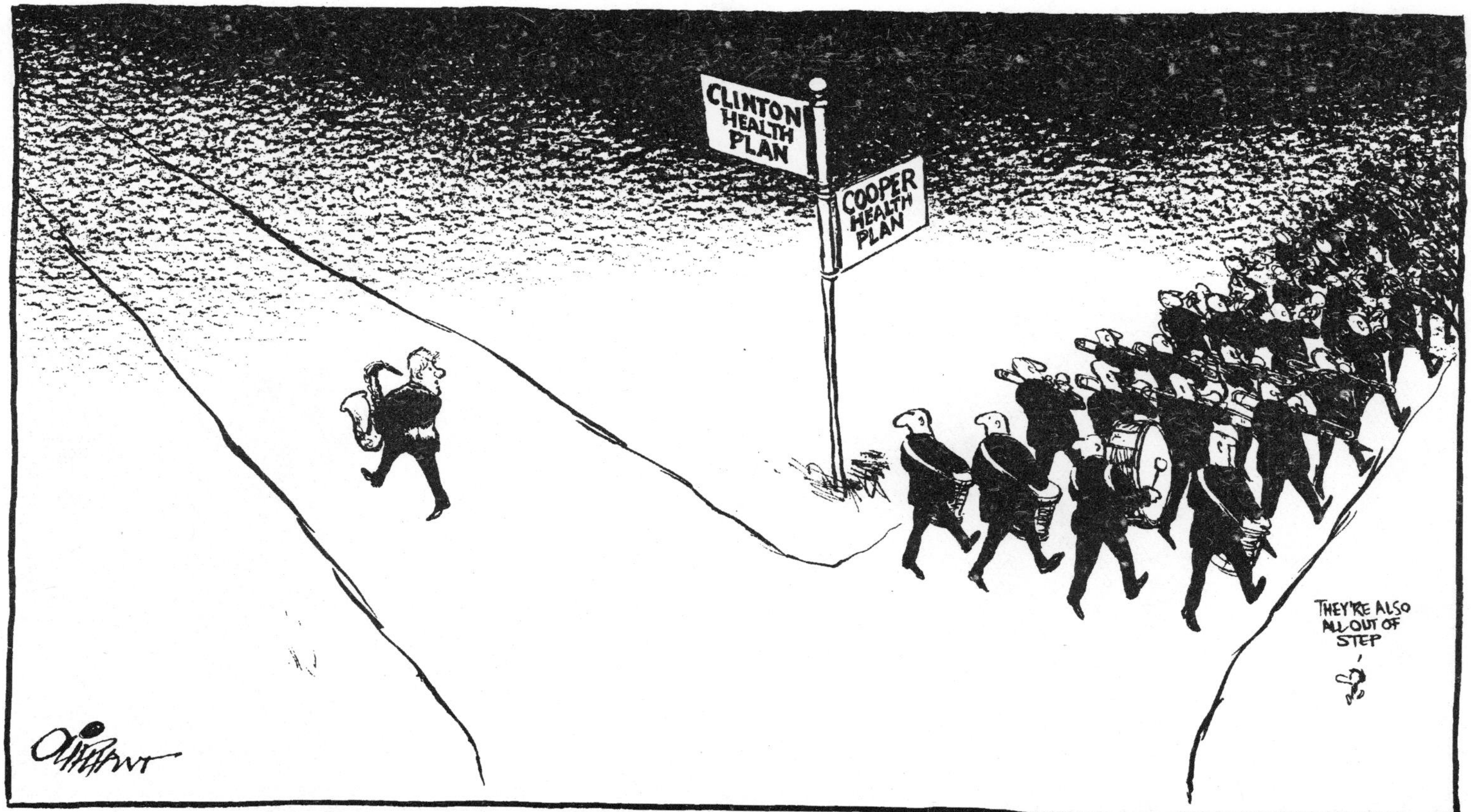
CLINTON HEALTH PLAN
COOPER HEALTH PLAN
THEY'RE ALSO ALL OUT OF STEP

'Y'ALL MUST HEAR A DIFFERENT DRUMMER.'

February 7, 1994

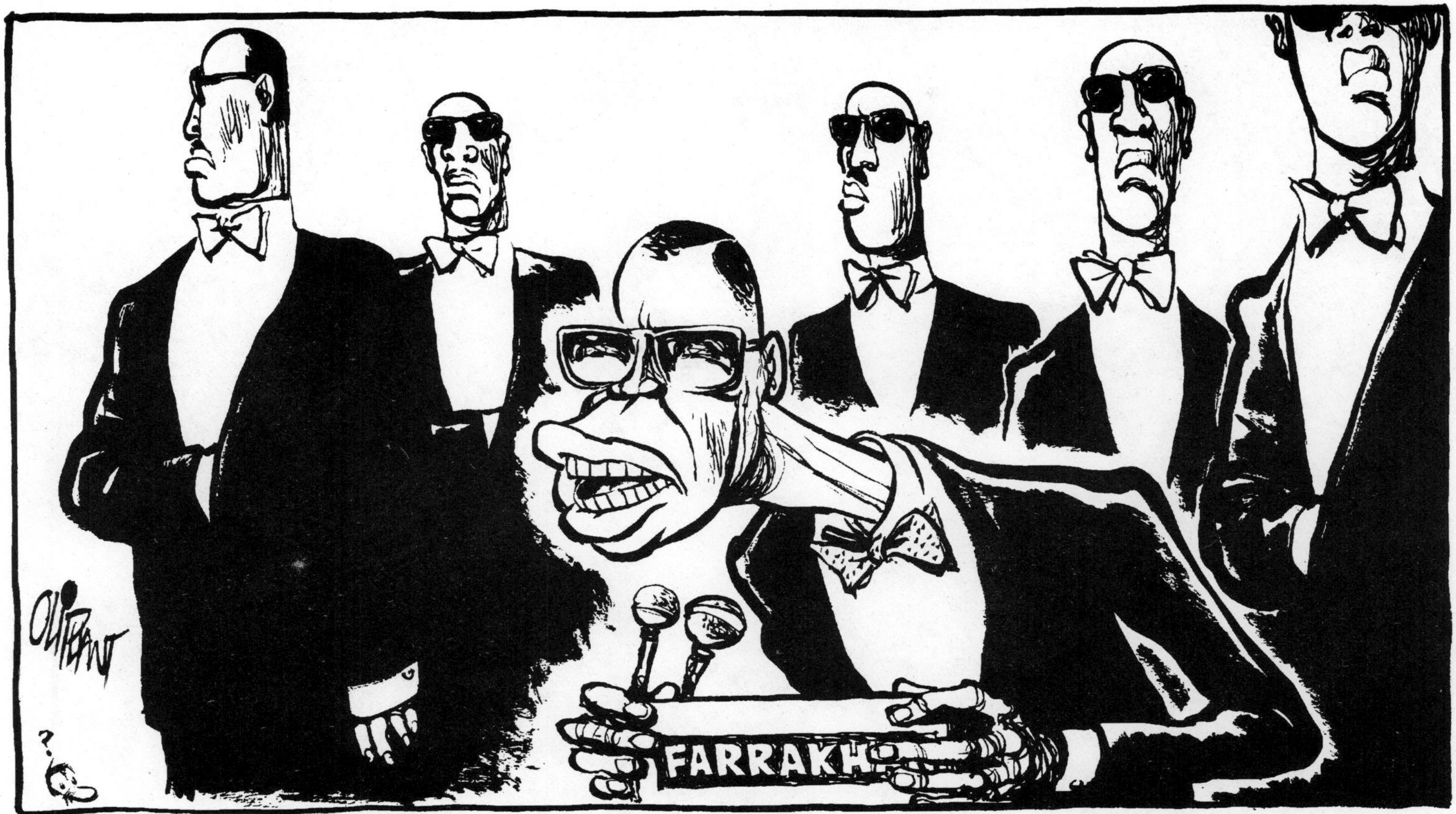
OLIPHANT
FARRAKH

'I PUBLICLY REPUDIATE BROTHER KHALID'S MEAN, VILE, VICIOUS, MALICIOUS SPEECH ABOUT THE MEAN, VILE, VICIOUS, MALICIOUS YOU-KNOW-WHOS.'

February 9, 1994

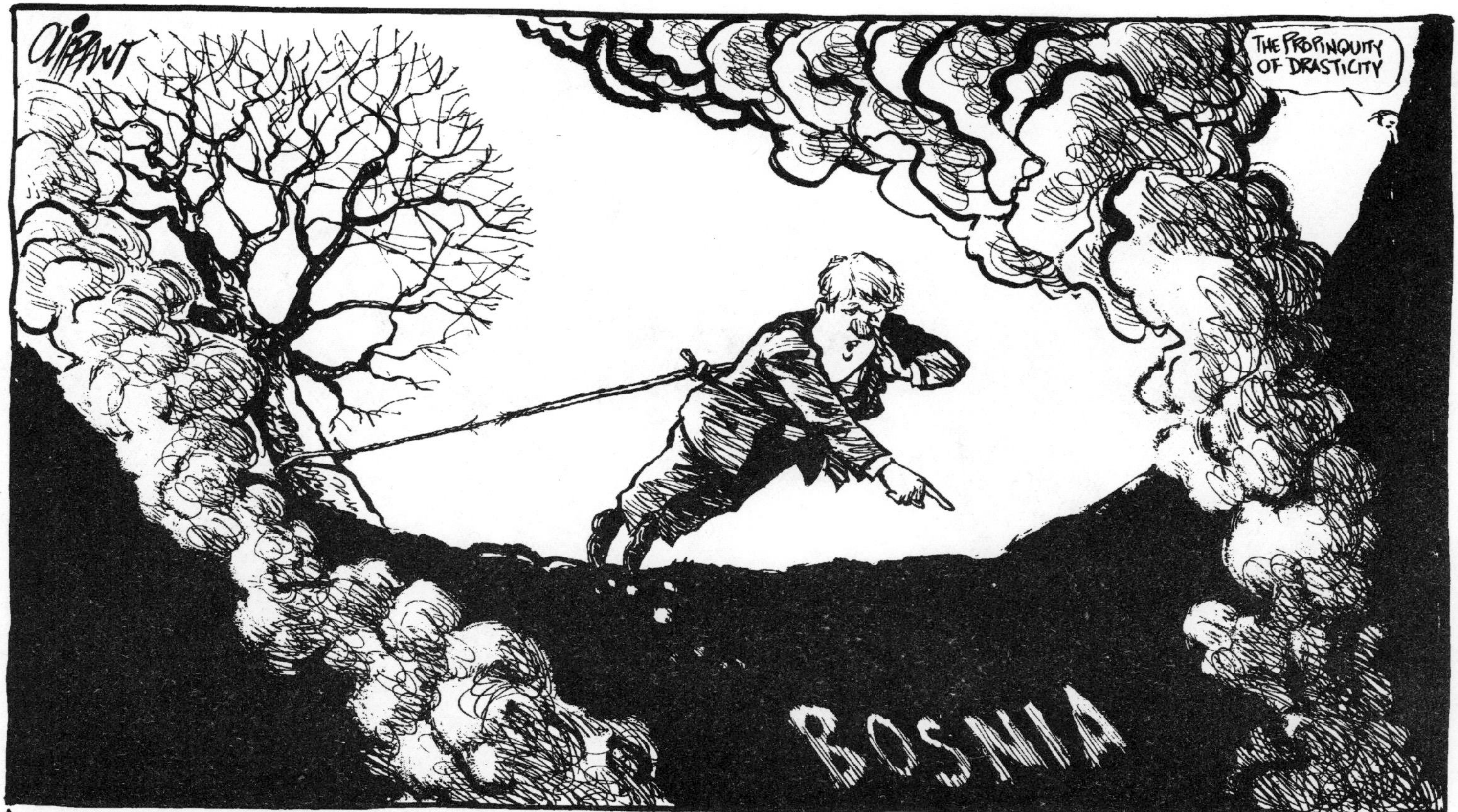
OLIPHANT
THE PROPINQUITY OF DRASTICITY
BOSNIA

'NOW, KNOCK THAT OFF, DOWN THERE, OR I'M GOING TO HAVE TO DO SOMETHING DRASTIC!'

February 10, 1994

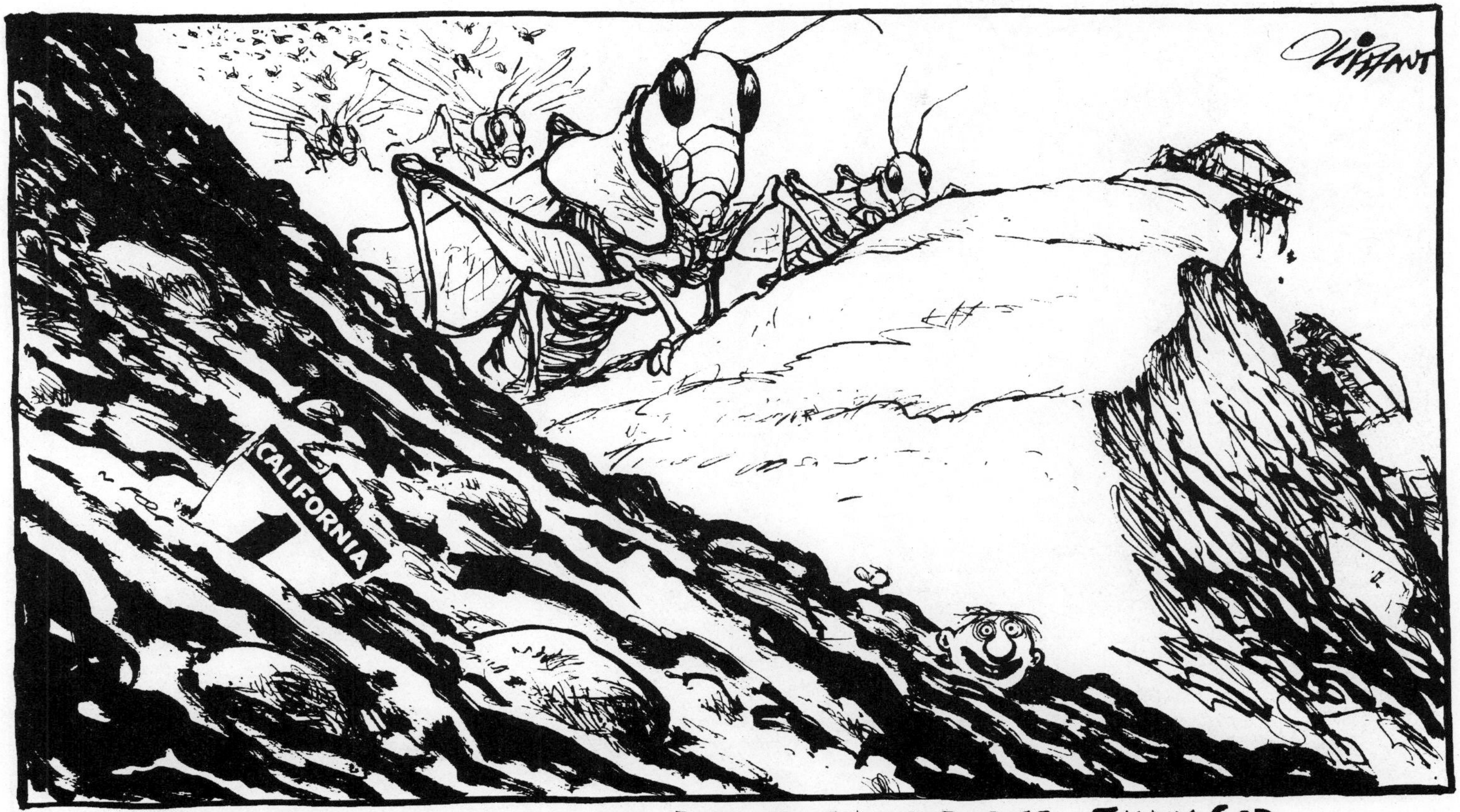
OLIPHANT
CALIFORNIA
1

'RIOTS, FIRES, EARTHQUAKES, DROUGHT, MUDSLIDES ... THANK GOD NOTHING ELSE CAN HAPPEN TO US!'

February 11, 1994

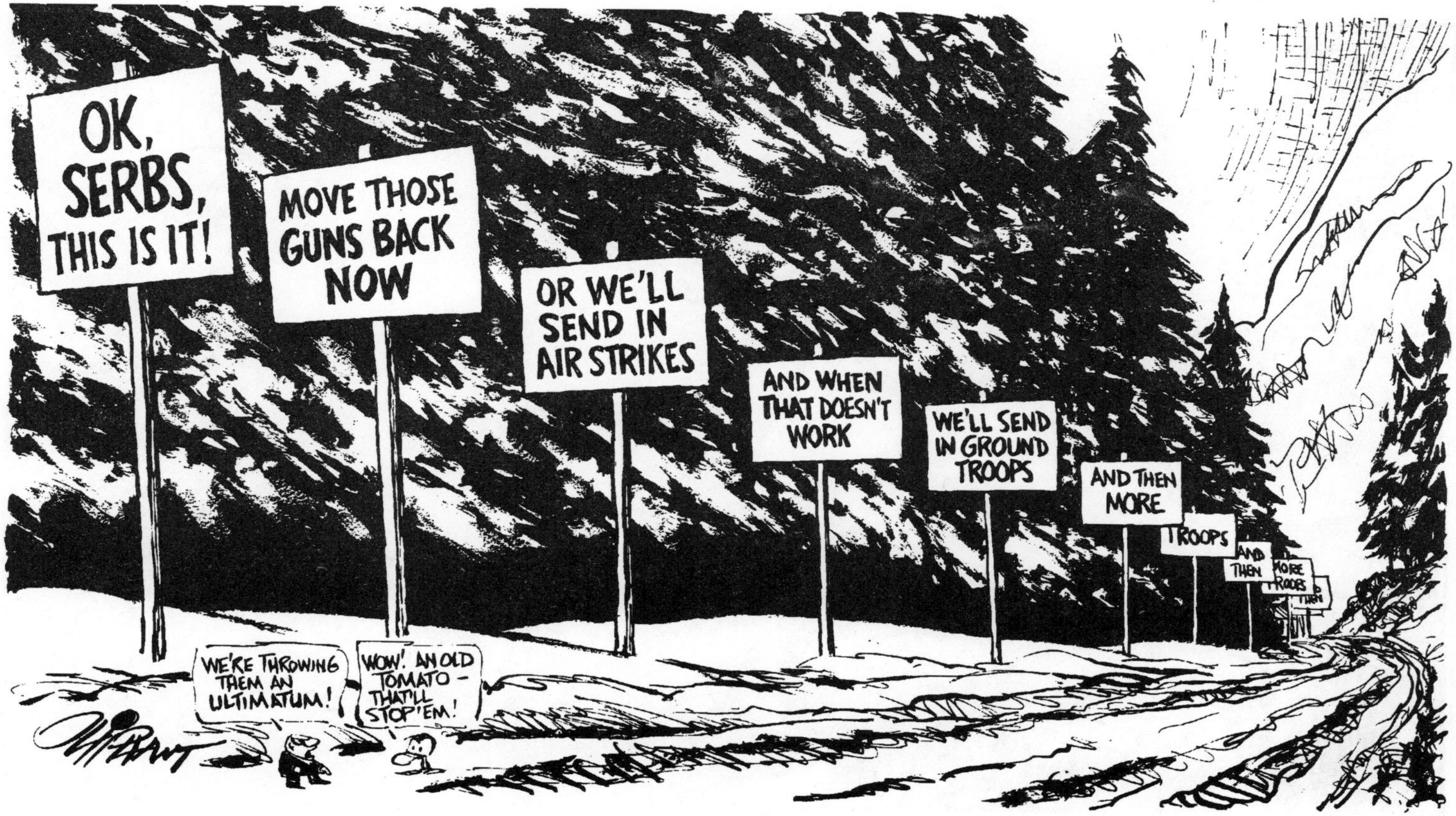
OK, SERBS, THIS IS IT!
MOVE THOSE GUNS BACK NOW
OR WE'LL SEND IN AIR STRIKES
AND WHEN THAT DOESN'T WORK
WE'LL SEND IN GROUND TROOPS
AND THEN MORE
TROOPS
AND THEN
MORE TROOPS
WE'RE THROWING THEM AN ULTIMATUM!
WOW! AN OLD TOMATO - THAT'LL STOP 'EM!

February 12, 1994

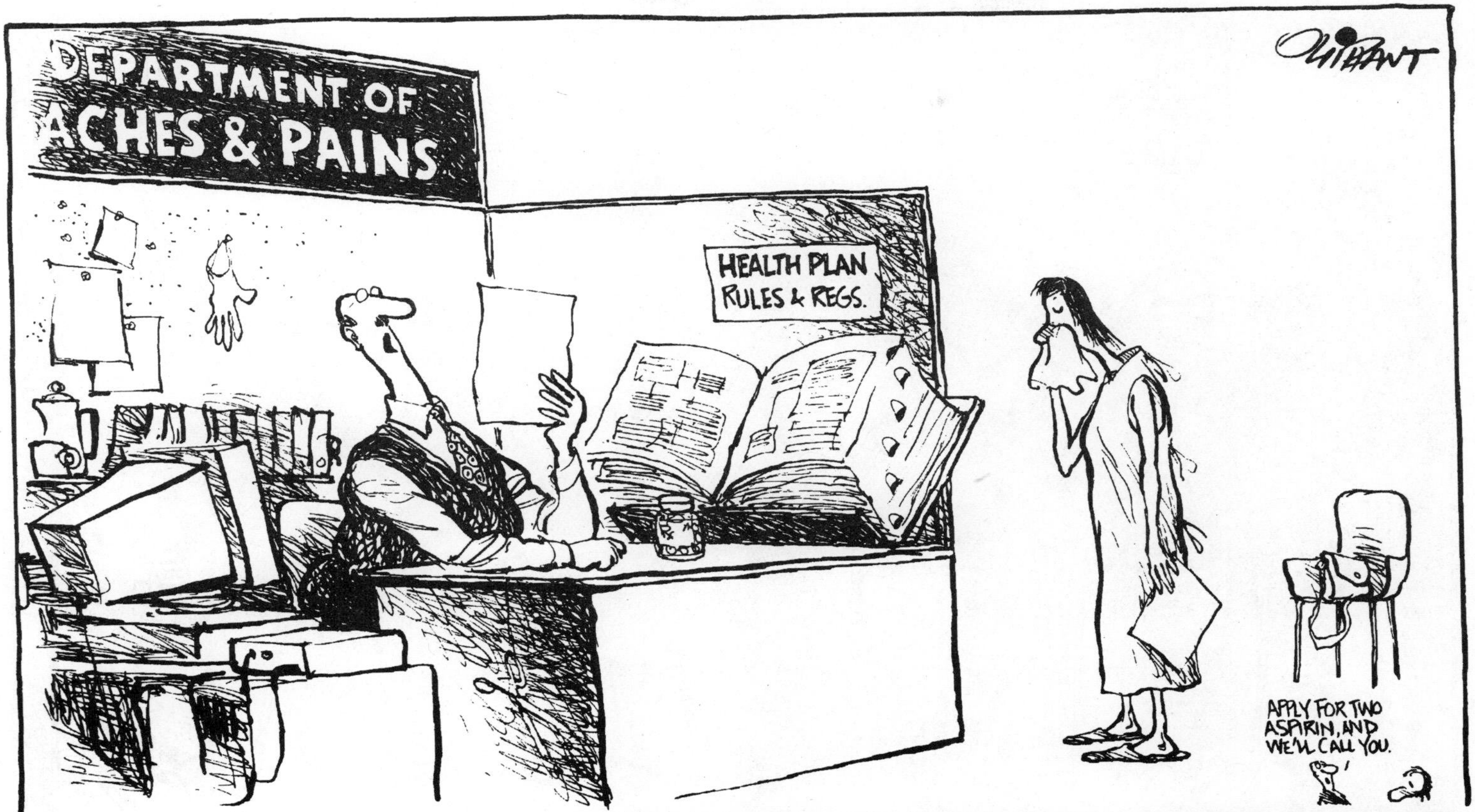
DEPARTMENT OF
ACHES & PAINS
HEALTH PLAN
RULES & REGS.
OLIPHANT
APPLY FOR TWO ASPIRIN, AND WE'LL CALL YOU.

'NORMALLY, MADAM, YOU SHOULD GO TO THE DEPARTMENT OF COUGHS AND COLDS FOR TREATMENT. HOWEVER, YOUR PROSTATE EXAMINATION WAS FAVORABLE, SO WE CAN TREAT YOU UNDER PART B, SUBSECTION IV...'

February 16, 1994

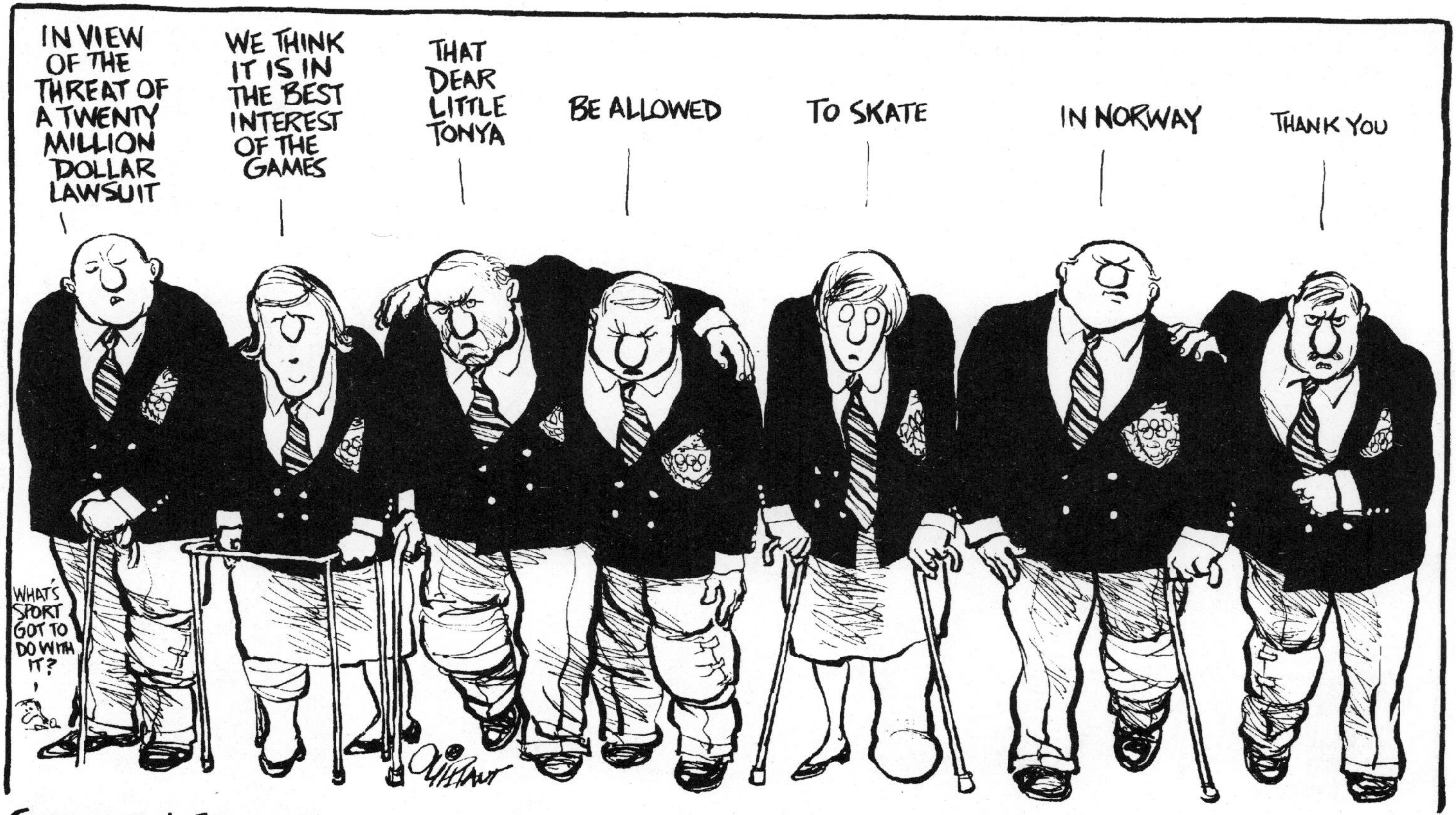
IN VIEW OF THE THREAT OF A TWENTY MILLION DOLLAR LAWSUIT
WE THINK IT IS IN THE BEST INTEREST OF THE GAMES
THAT DEAR LITTLE TONYA
BE ALLOWED
TO SKATE
IN NORWAY
THANK YOU
WHAT'S SPORT GOT TO DO WITH IT?

SUDDENLY, SOME THUG RUSHED IN, AND KNEECAPPED THE ENTIRE U.S. OLYMPIC COMMITTEE.

February 17, 1994

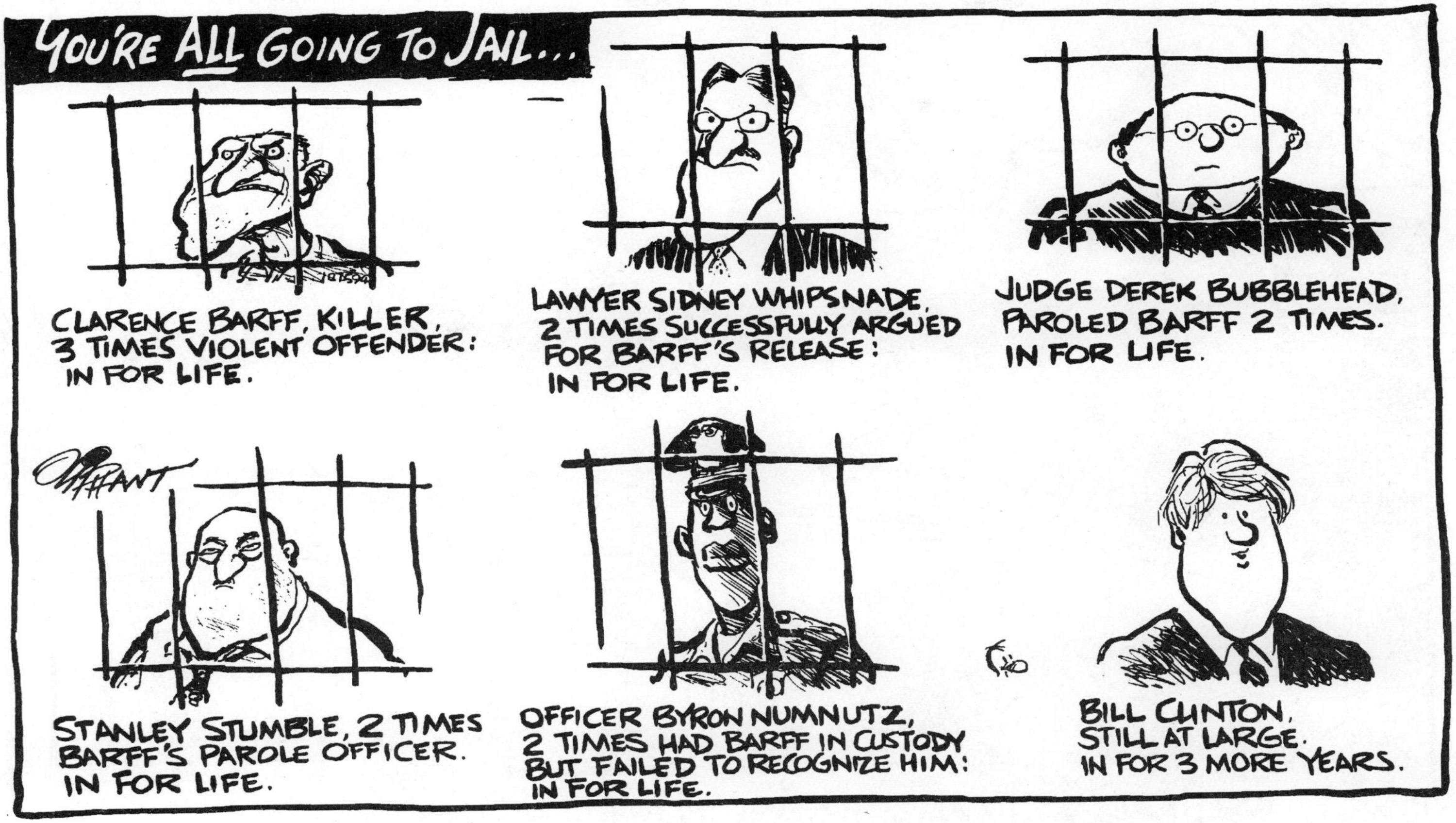

YOU'RE ALL GOING TO JAIL...
CLARENCE BARFF, KILLER, 3 TIMES VIOLENT OFFENDER: IN FOR LIFE.
LAWYER SIDNEY WHIPSNADE, 2 TIMES SUCCESSFULLY ARGUED FOR BARFF'S RELEASE: IN FOR LIFE.
JUDGE DEREK BUBBLEHEAD, PAROLED BARFF 2 TIMES. IN FOR LIFE.
STANLEY STUMBLE, 2 TIMES BARFF'S PAROLE OFFICER. IN FOR LIFE.
OFFICER BYRON NUMNUTZ, 2 TIMES HAD BARFF IN CUSTODY BUT FAILED TO RECOGNIZE HIM: IN FOR LIFE.
BILL CLINTON, STILL AT LARGE. IN FOR 3 MORE YEARS.
OLIPHANT

February 18, 1994

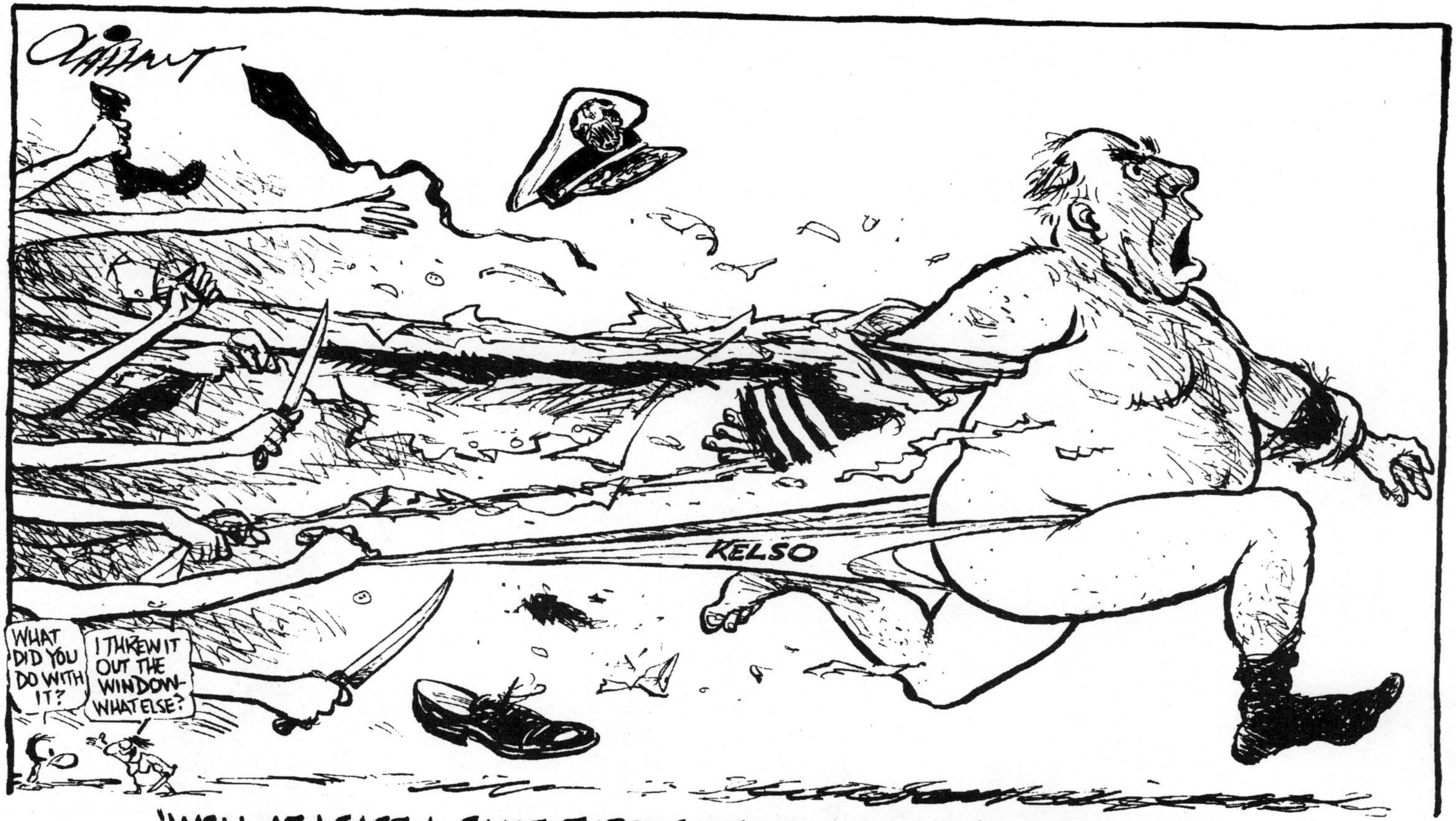
KELSO
WHAT DID YOU DO WITH IT?
I THREW IT OUT THE WINDOW- WHAT ELSE?

'WELL, AT LEAST I CAME THROUGH THAT WITH MY HONOR INTACT!'

February 23, 1994

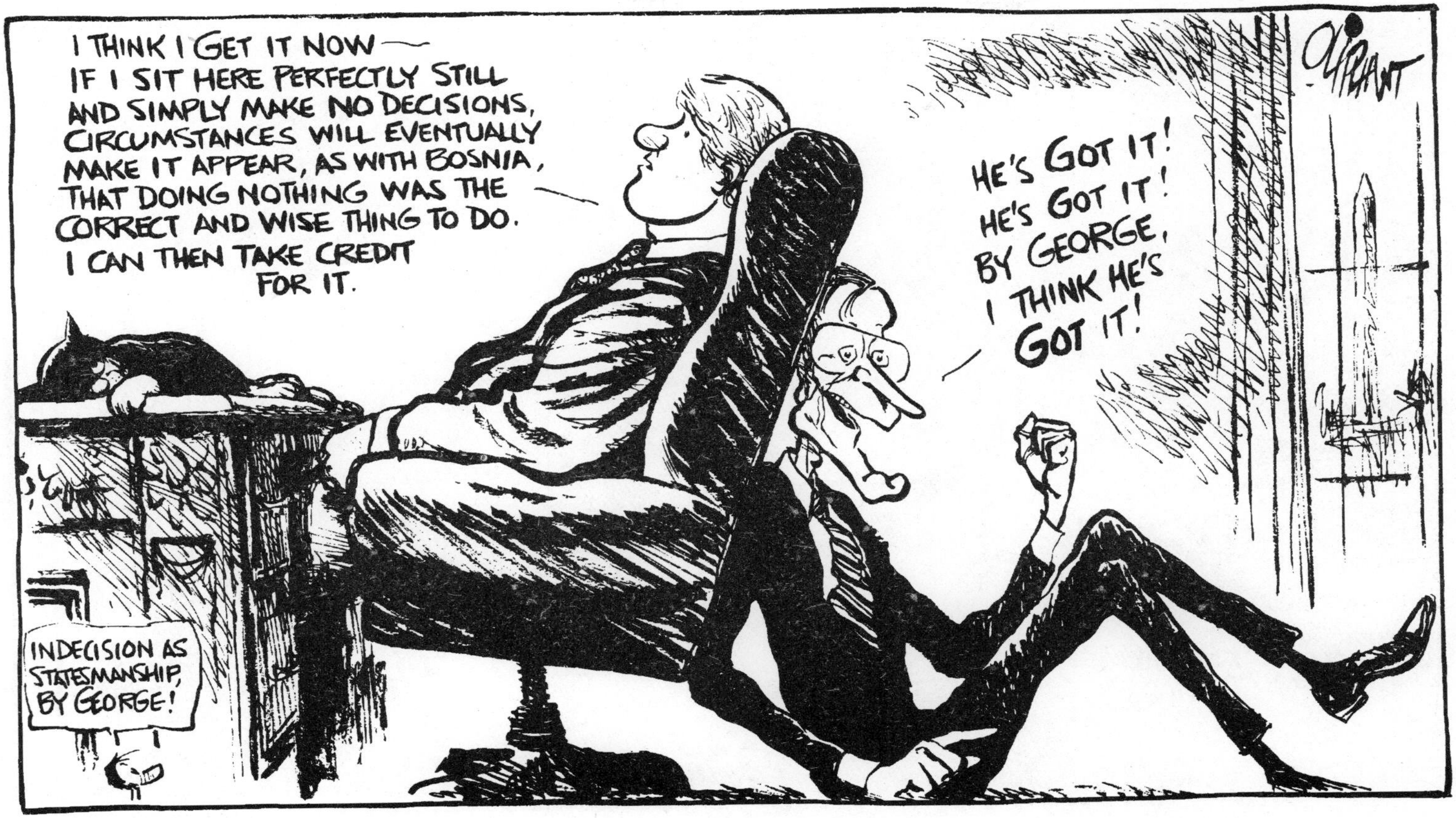
I THINK I GET IT NOW— IF I SIT HERE PERFECTLY STILL AND SIMPLY MAKE NO DECISIONS, CIRCUMSTANCES WILL EVENTUALLY MAKE IT APPEAR, AS WITH BOSNIA, THAT DOING NOTHING WAS THE CORRECT AND WISE THING TO DO. I CAN THEN TAKE CREDIT FOR IT.
HE'S GOT IT! HE'S GOT IT! BY GEORGE, I THINK HE'S GOT IT!
INDECISION AS STATESMANSHIP, BY GEORGE!
OLIPHANT

February 24, 1994

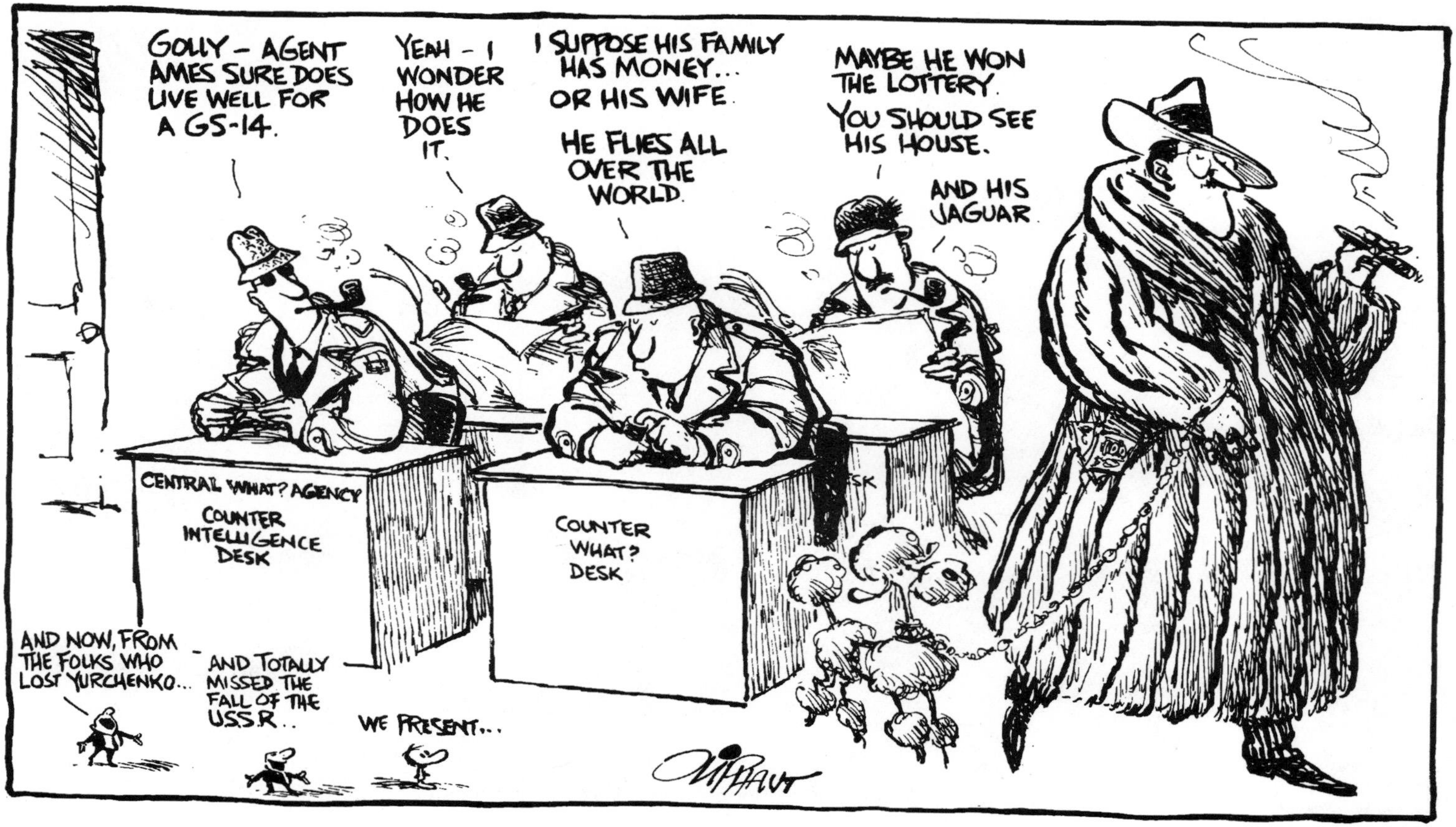
GOLLY - AGENT AMES SURE DOES LIVE WELL FOR A GS-14.
YEAH - I WONDER HOW HE DOES IT.
I SUPPOSE HIS FAMILY HAS MONEY... OR HIS WIFE.
HE FLIES ALL OVER THE WORLD.
MAYBE HE WON THE LOTTERY.
YOU SHOULD SEE HIS HOUSE.
AND HIS JAGUAR.
CENTRAL WHAT? AGENCY
COUNTER INTELLIGENCE DESK
COUNTER WHAT? DESK
AND NOW, FROM THE FOLKS WHO LOST YURCHENKO...
AND TOTALLY MISSED THE FALL OF THE USSR..
WE PRESENT...
OLIPHANT

February 24, 1994

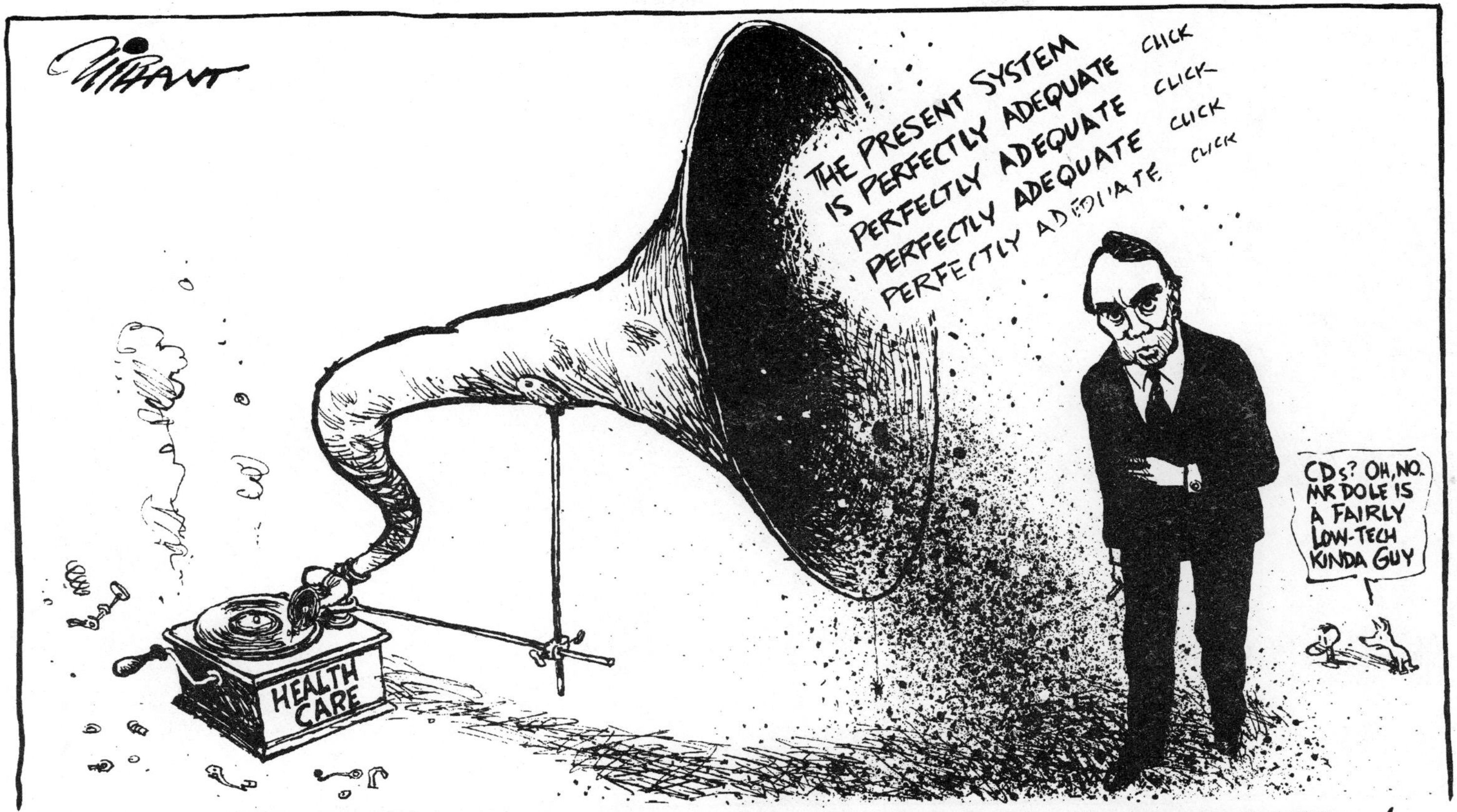
THE PRESENT SYSTEM
IS PERFECTLY ADEQUATE
CLICK
PERFECTLY ADEQUATE
CLICK
PERFECTLY ADEQUATE
CLICK
PERFECTLY ADEQUATE
CLICK
HEALTH CARE
CDs? OH, NO. MR DOLE IS A FAIRLY LOW-TECH KINDA GUY

'SEE, IT DOESN'T NEED REPLACEMENT, JUST A FEW MINOR ADJUSTMENTS...'

February 25, 1994

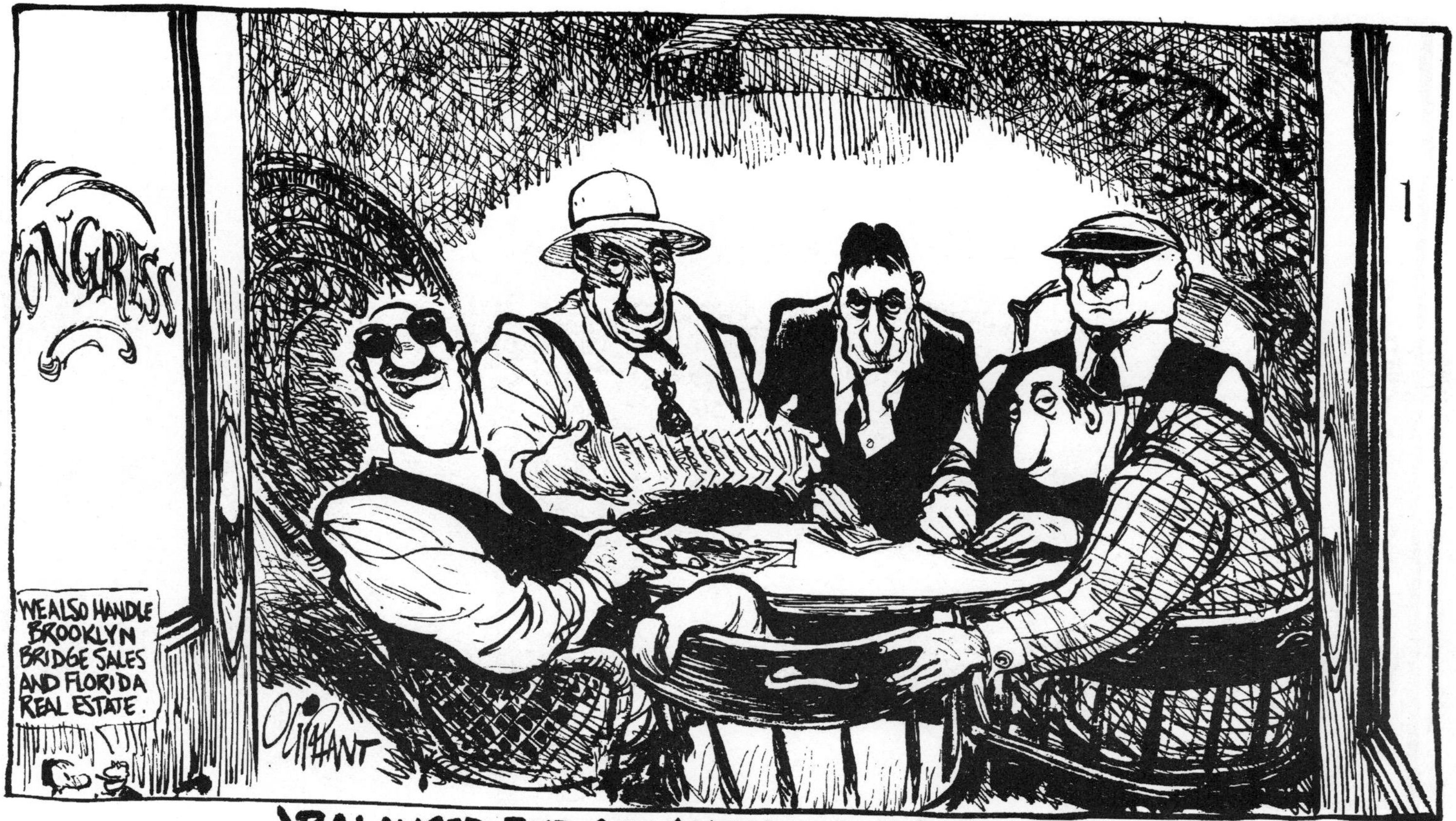
CONGRESS
WE ALSO HANDLE BROOKLYN BRIDGE SALES AND FLORIDA REAL ESTATE.
OLIPHANT

'BALANCED BUDGET AMENDMENT, ANYONE?'

March 2, 1994

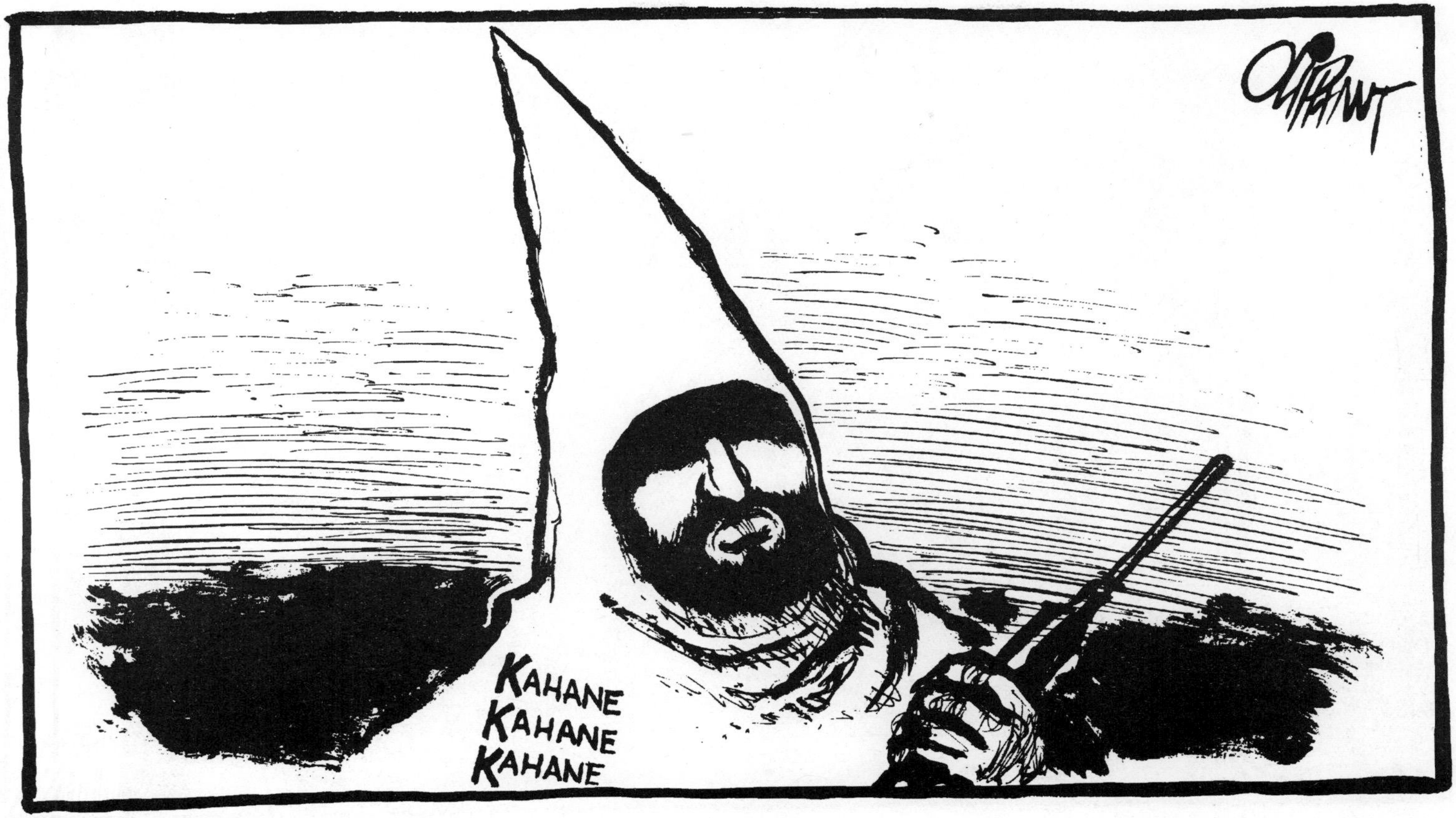
KAHANE
KAHANE
KAHANE

March 3, 1994

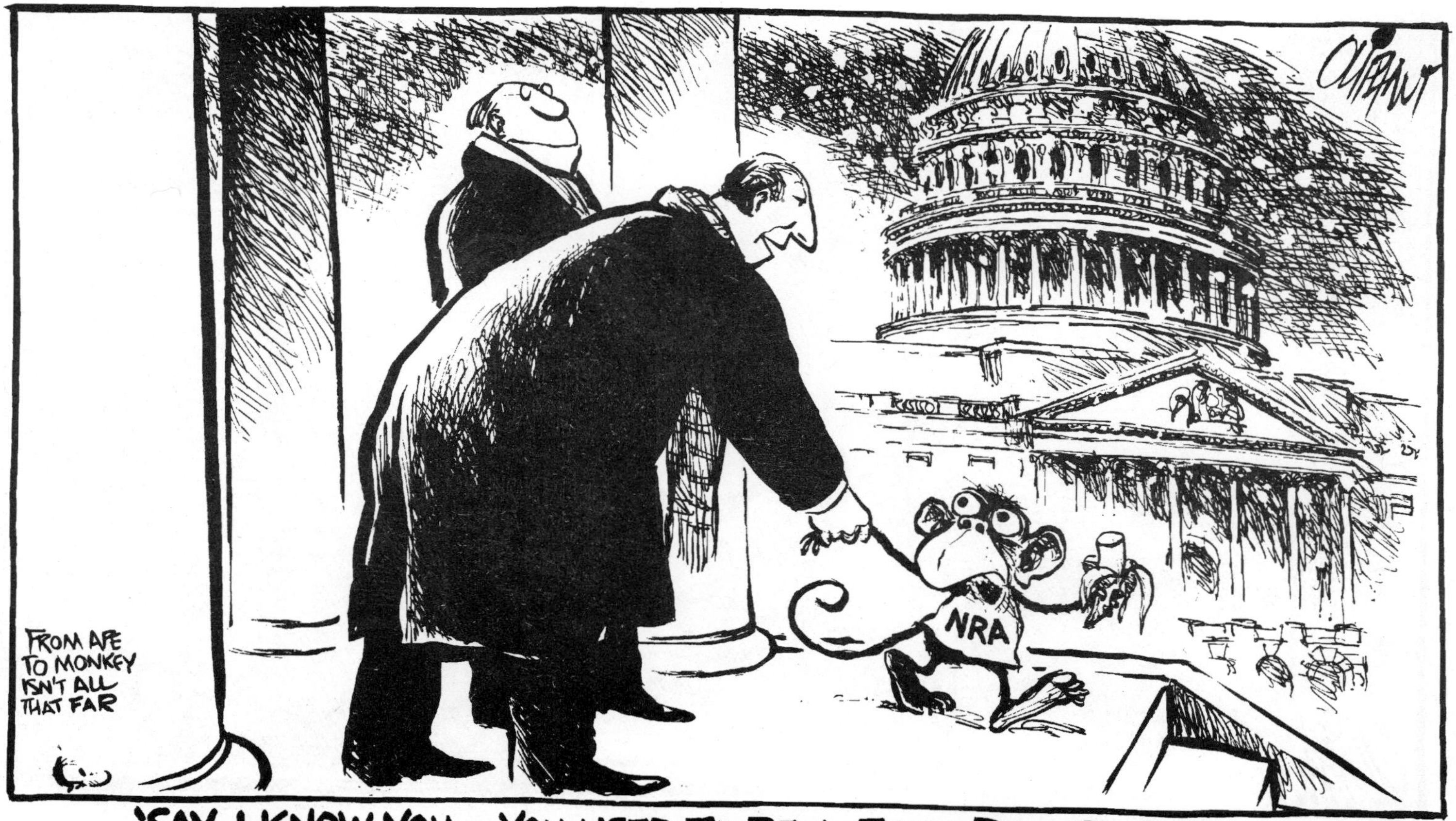
OLIPHANT
FROM APE TO MONKEY ISN'T ALL THAT FAR
NRA

'SAY, I KNOW YOU—YOU USED TO BE A 500-POUND GORILLA!'

March 4, 1994

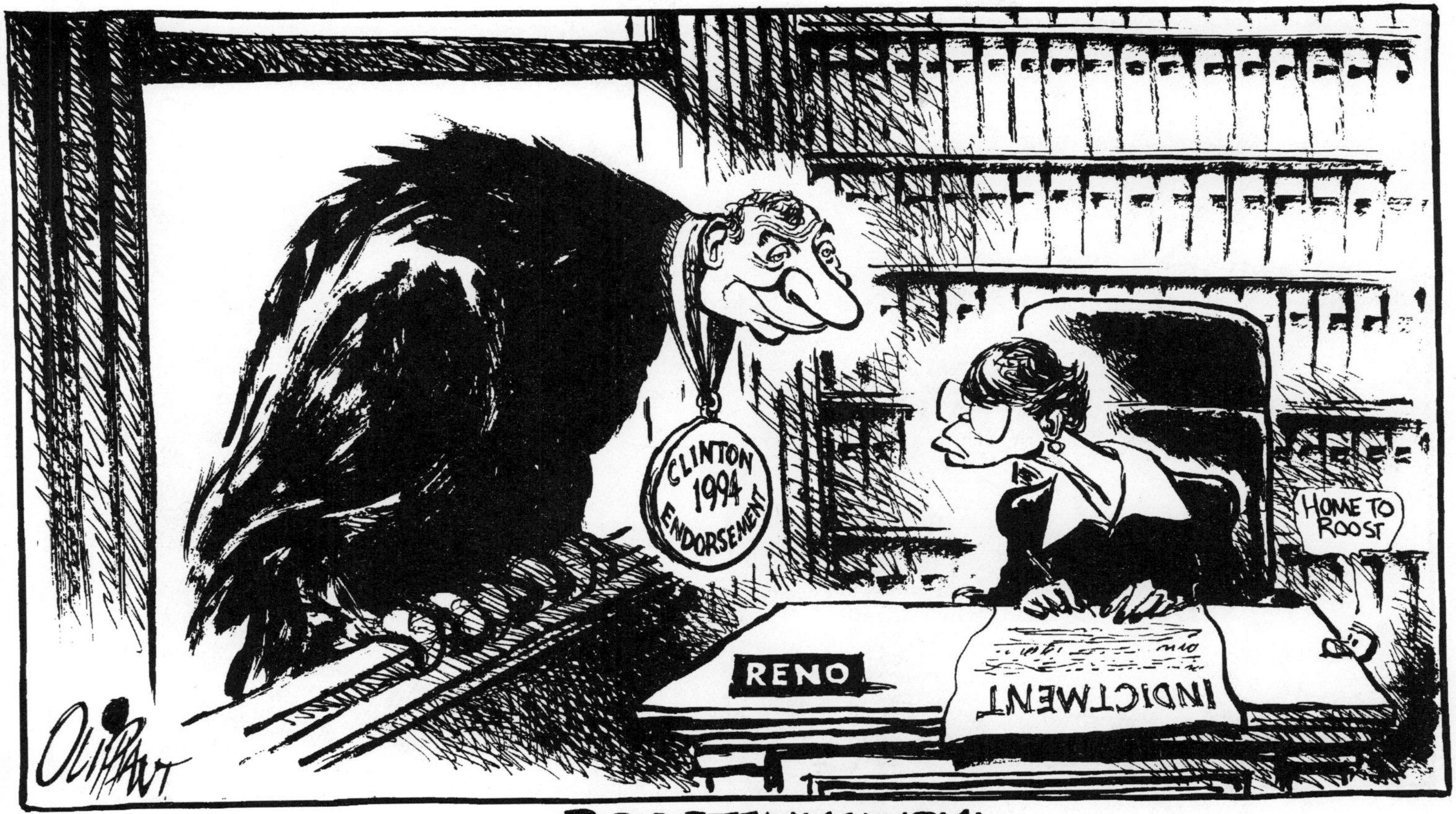
CLINTON
1994
ENDORSEMENT
HOME TO
ROOST
RENO
INDICTMENT
OLIPHANT

ROOSTENKOWSKI.

March 5, 1994

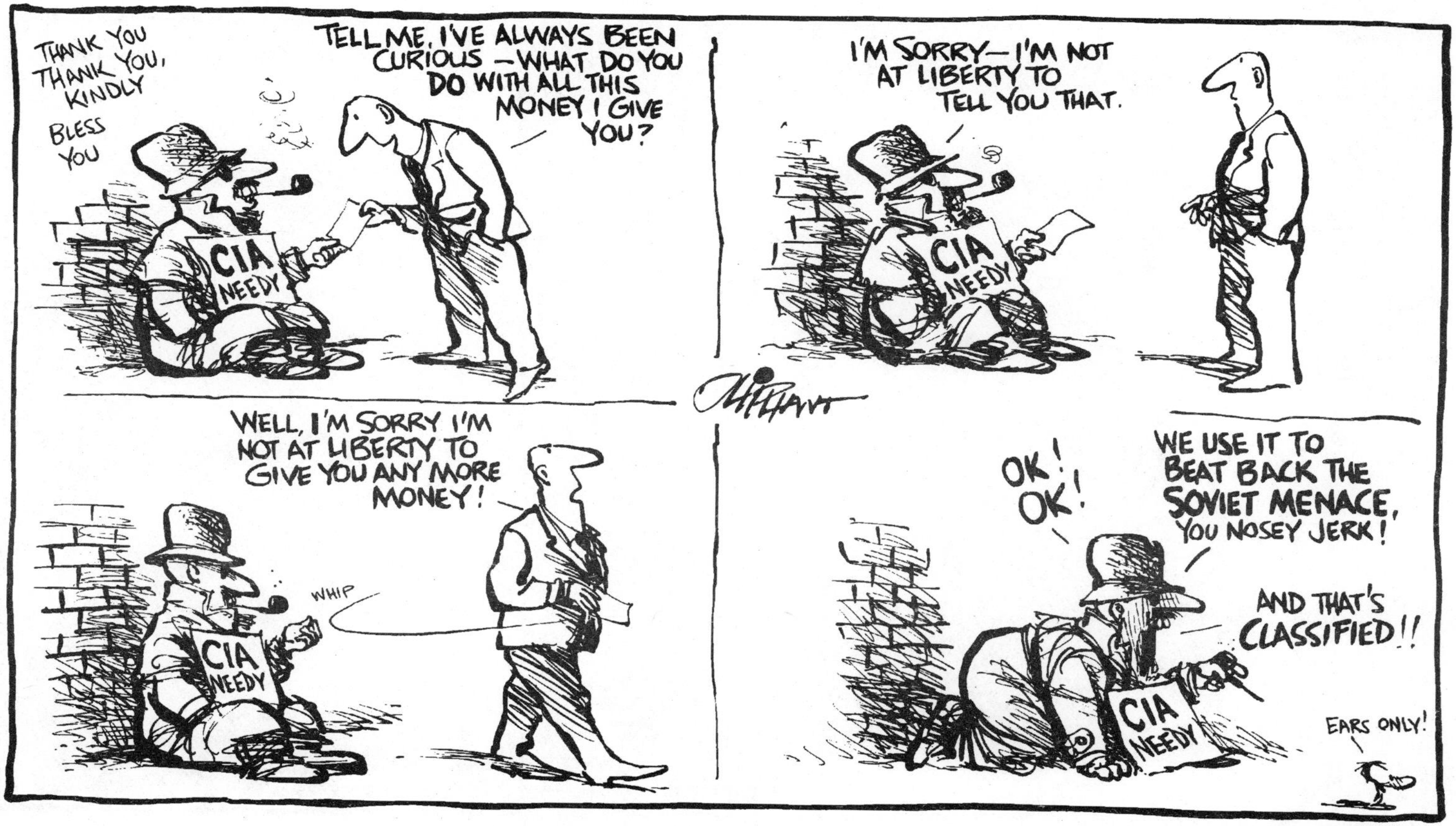

THANK YOU THANK YOU, KINDLY
BLESS YOU
TELL ME, I'VE ALWAYS BEEN CURIOUS — WHAT DO YOU DO WITH ALL THIS MONEY I GIVE YOU?
CIA NEEDY
I'M SORRY— I'M NOT AT LIBERTY TO TELL YOU THAT.
CIA NEEDY
WELL, I'M SORRY I'M NOT AT LIBERTY TO GIVE YOU ANY MORE MONEY!
WHIP
CIA NEEDY
OK! OK!
WE USE IT TO BEAT BACK THE SOVIET MENACE, YOU NOSEY JERK!
AND THAT'S CLASSIFIED!!
CIA NEEDY
EARS ONLY!

March 9, 1994

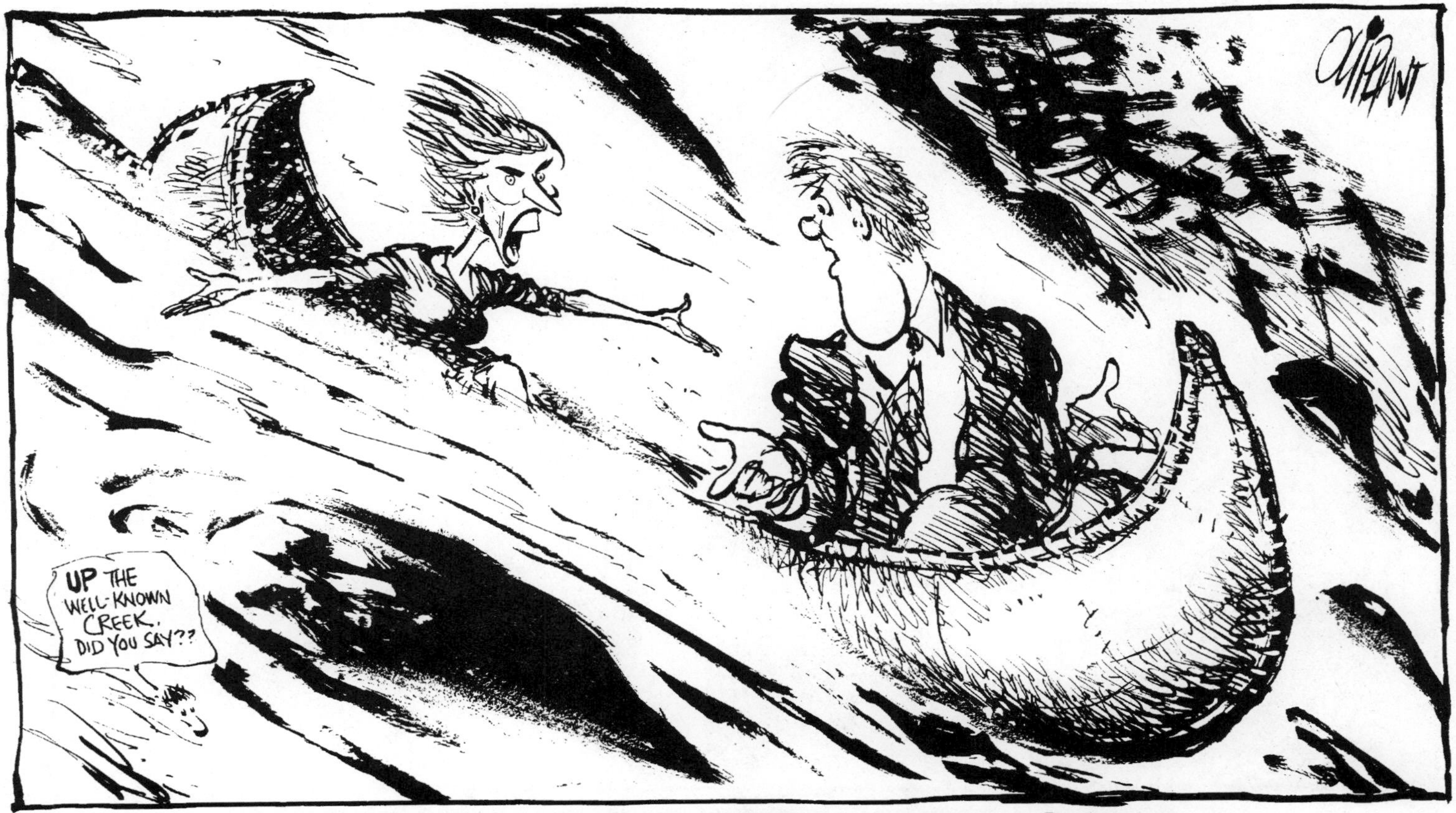

OLIPHANT
UP THE WELL-KNOWN CREEK, DID YOU SAY??

UP THE WELL-KNOWN WHITEWATER CREEK, WITHOUT A PADDLE...

March 10, 1994

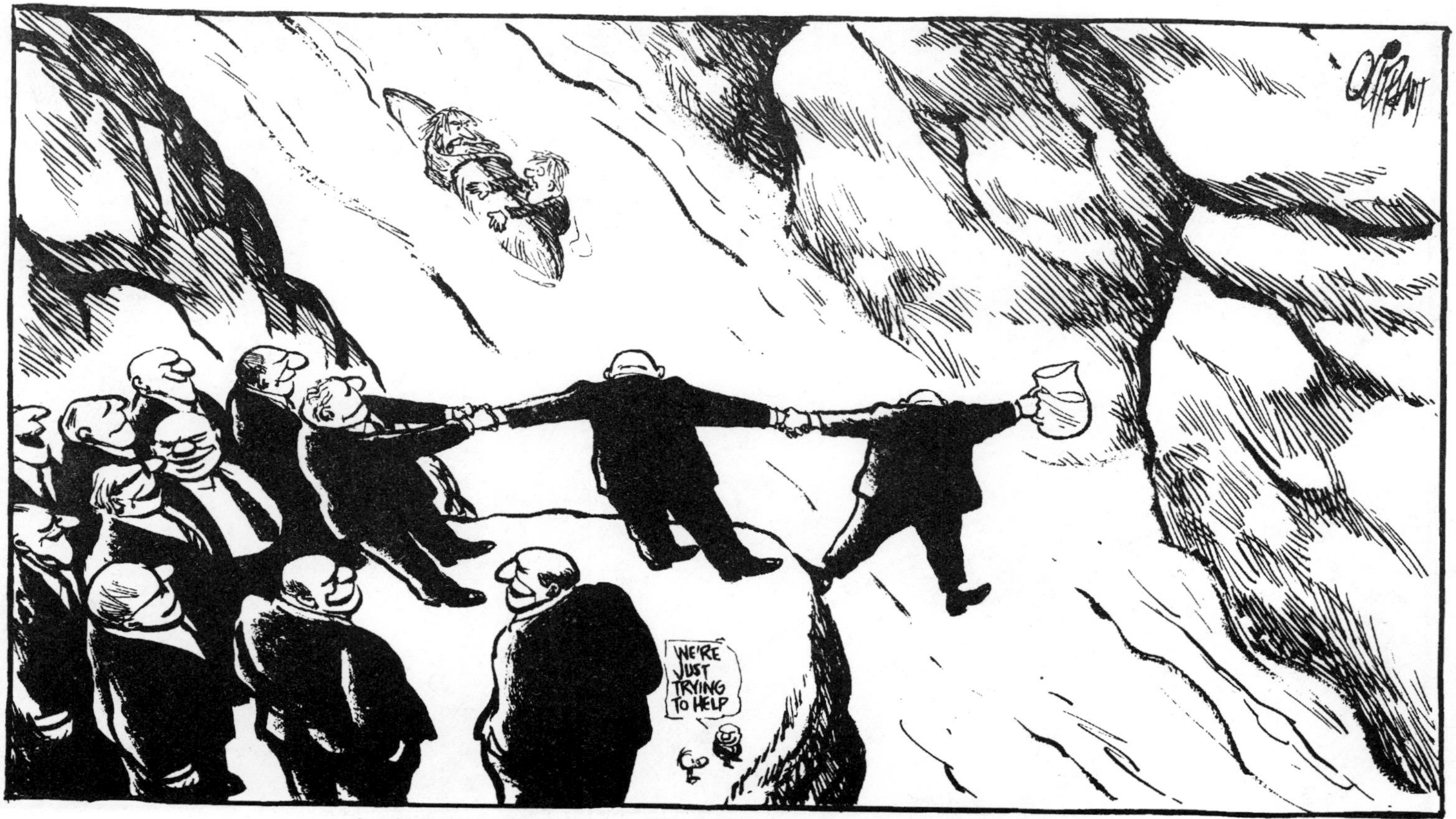
WE'RE JUST TRYING TO HELP

WHITEWATER II — THE REPUBLICAN PERSPECTIVE.

March 11,1994

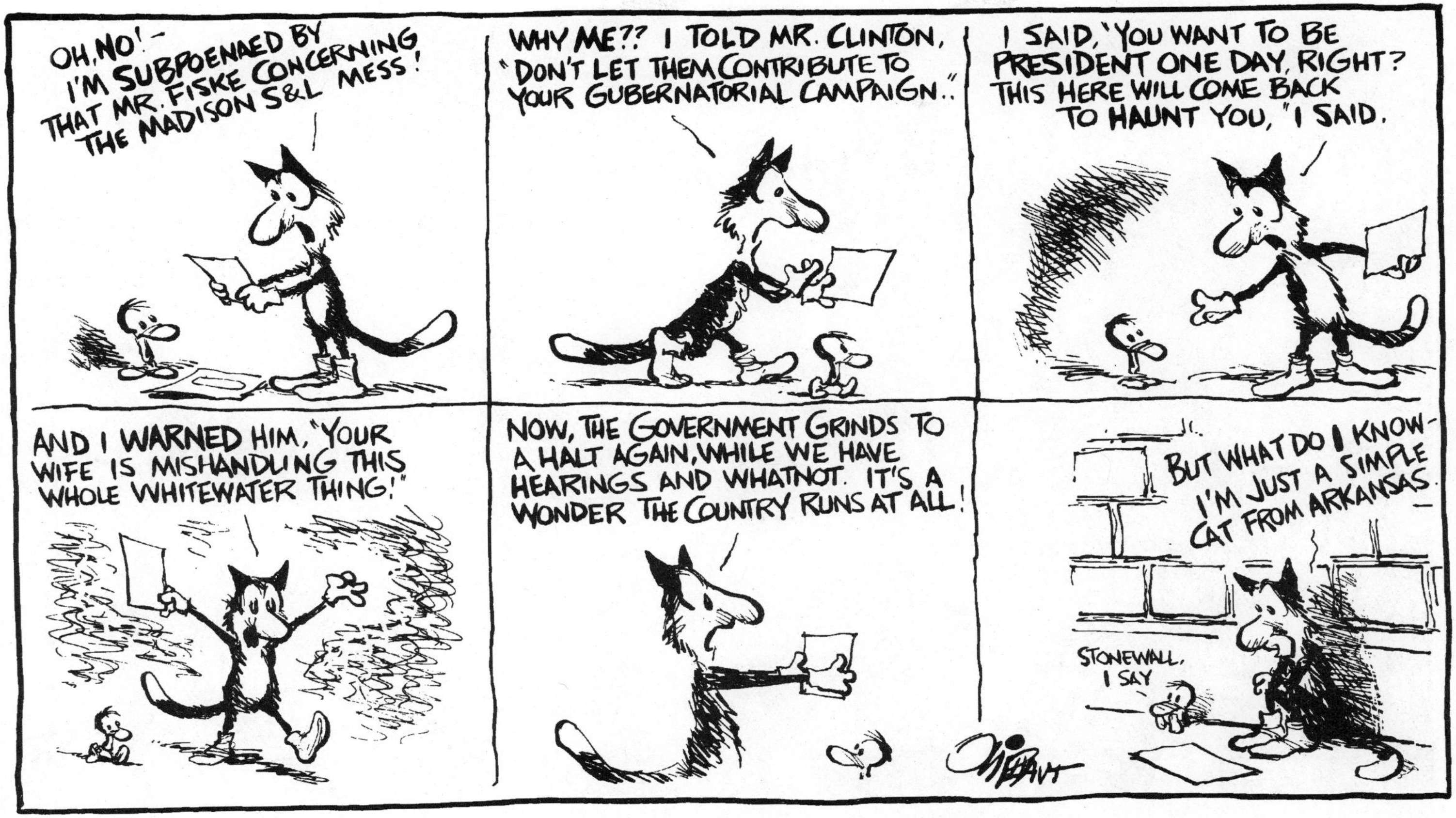

OH, NO! - I'M SUBPOENAED BY THAT MR. FISKE CONCERNING THE MADISON S&L MESS!
WHY ME?? I TOLD MR. CLINTON, "DON'T LET THEM CONTRIBUTE TO YOUR GUBERNATORIAL CAMPAIGN."
I SAID, "YOU WANT TO BE PRESIDENT ONE DAY, RIGHT? THIS HERE WILL COME BACK TO HAUNT YOU," I SAID.
AND I WARNED HIM, "YOUR WIFE IS MISHANDLING THIS WHOLE WHITEWATER THING!"
NOW, THE GOVERNMENT GRINDS TO A HALT AGAIN, WHILE WE HAVE HEARINGS AND WHATNOT. IT'S A WONDER THE COUNTRY RUNS AT ALL!
BUT WHAT DO I KNOW - I'M JUST A SIMPLE CAT FROM ARKANSAS -
STONEWALL, I SAY

March 12,1994

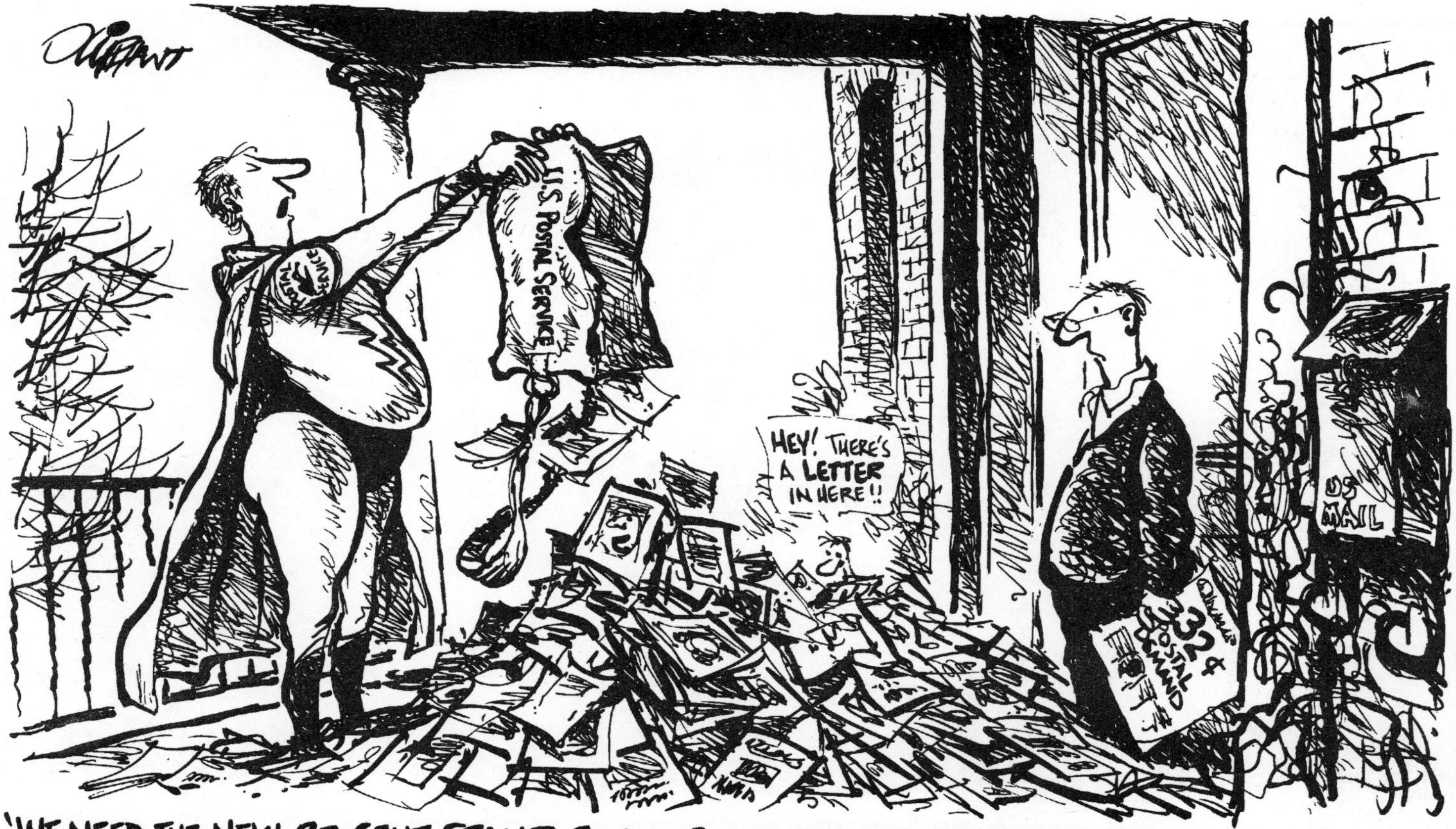
OLIPHANT
U.S. POSTAL SERVICE
HEY! THERE'S A LETTER IN HERE!!
US MAIL

'WE NEED THE NEW 32-CENT STAMP SO WE CAN AFFORD TO BRING YOU ALL THESE CATALOGS AND NUISANCE DIRECT-MAIL JUNK THAT YOU NEVER ASKED FOR IN THE FIRST PLACE!'

March 16, 1994

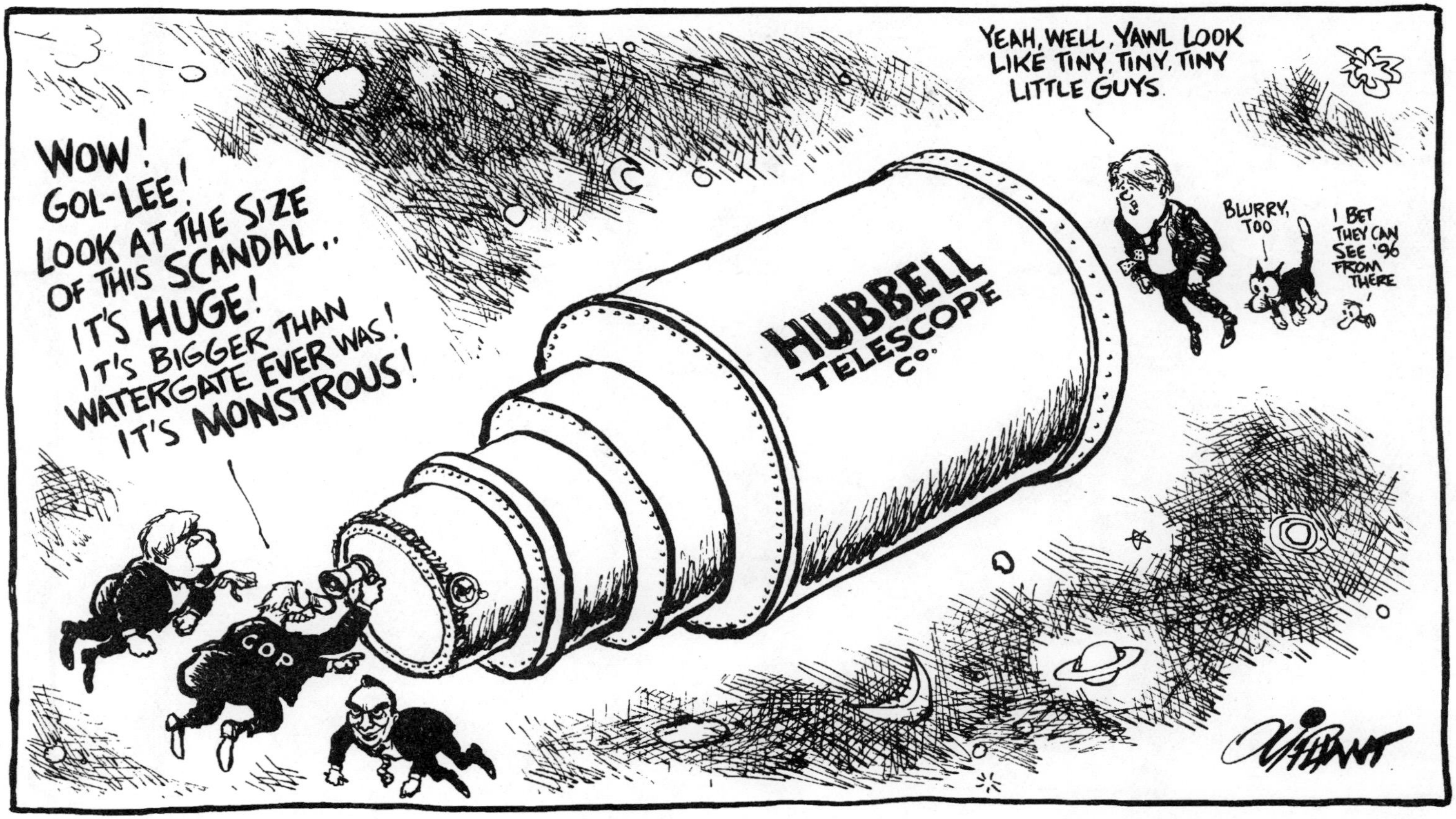
WOW! GOL-LEE! LOOK AT THE SIZE OF THIS SCANDAL.. IT'S HUGE! IT'S BIGGER THAN WATERGATE EVER WAS! IT'S MONSTROUS!
YEAH, WELL, YAWL LOOK LIKE TINY, TINY, TINY LITTLE GUYS.
BLURRY, TOO
I BET THEY CAN SEE '96 FROM THERE
HUBBELL TELESCOPE Co.
GOP
OLIPHANT

March 19, 1994

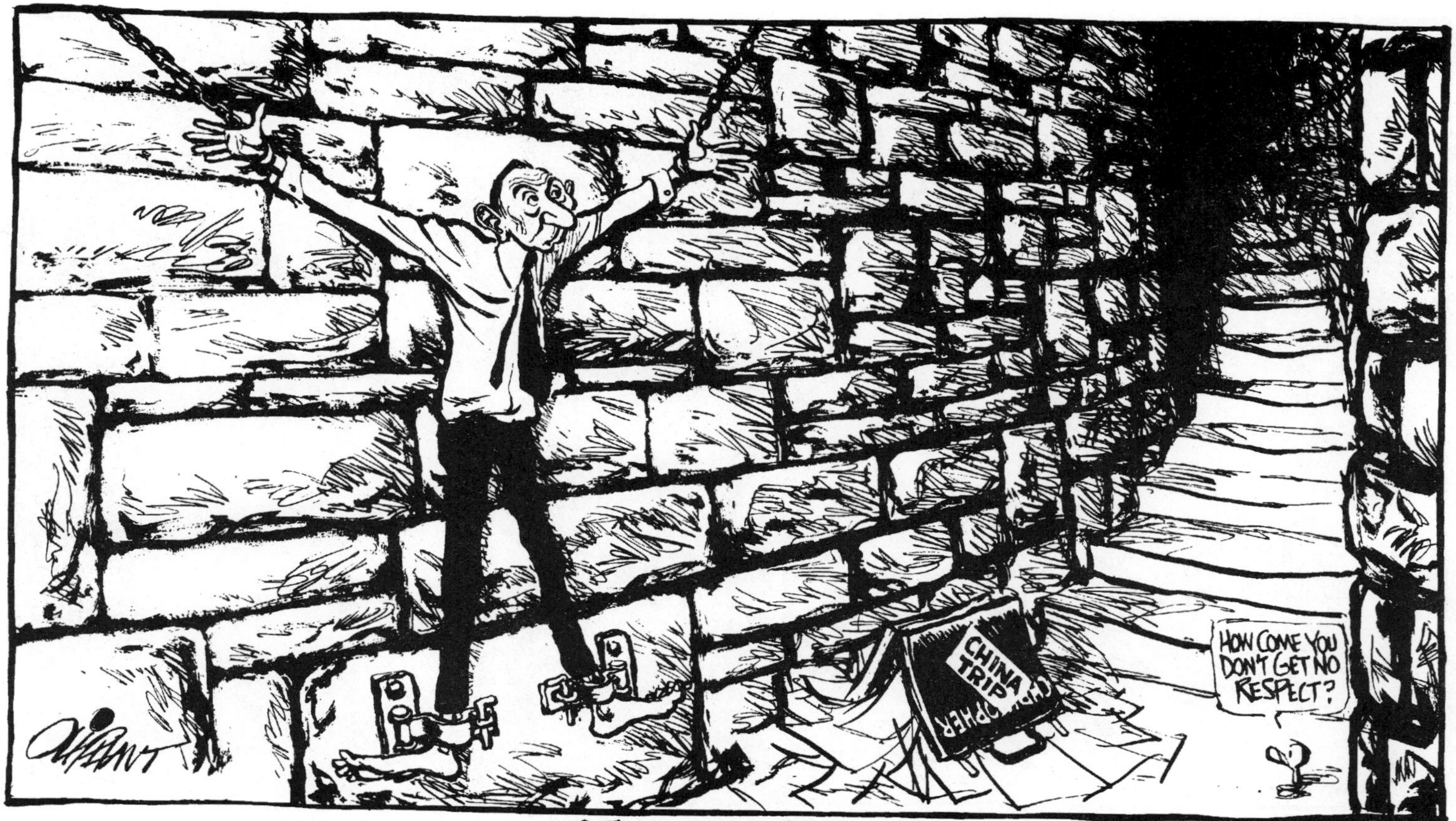
CHINA TRIP
HOW COME YOU DON'T GET NO RESPECT?

OF HUMAN RIGHTS.

March 23, 1994

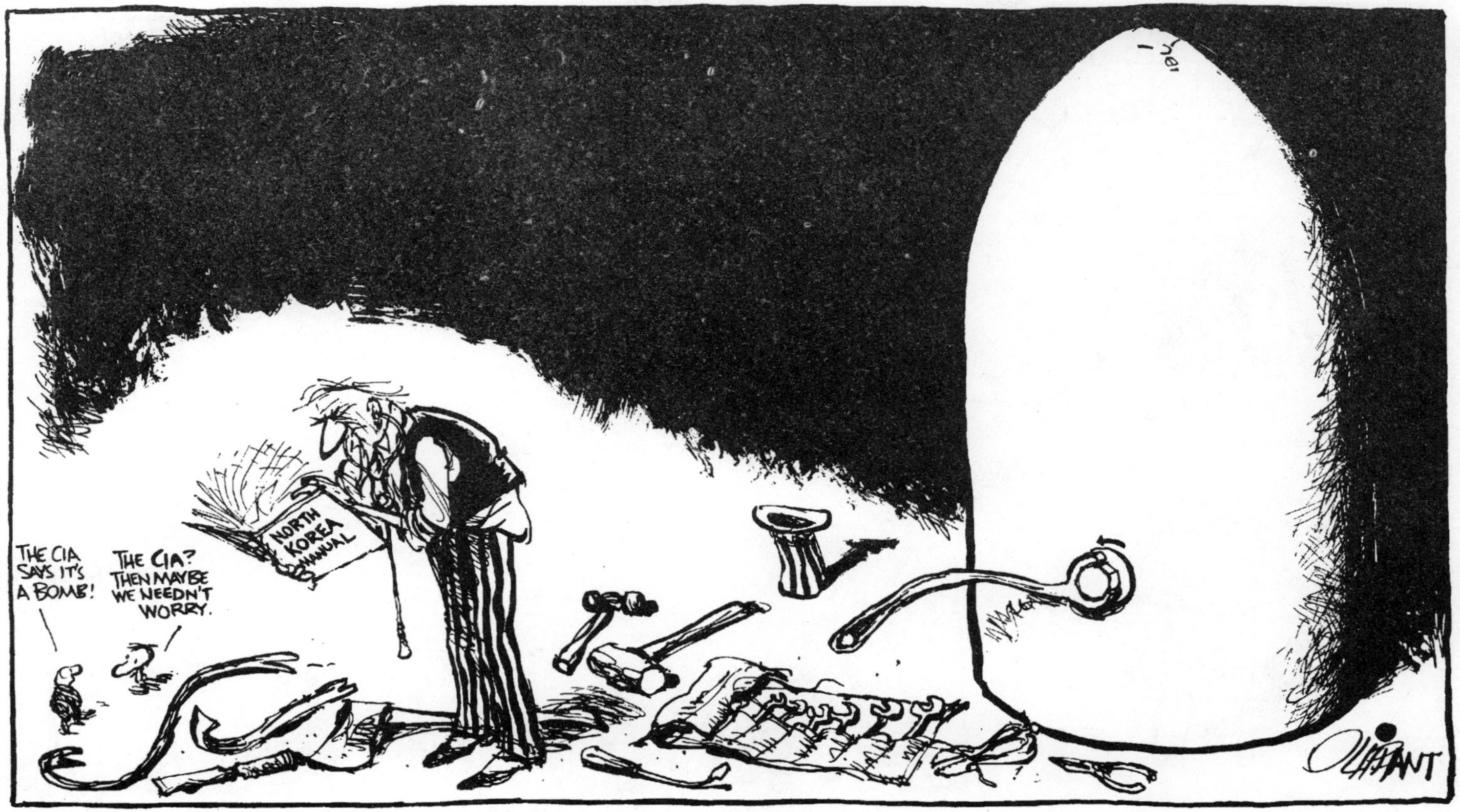
NORTH KOREA MANUAL
THE CIA SAYS IT'S A BOMB!
THE CIA? THEN MAYBE WE NEEDN'T WORRY.
OLIPHANT

March 25, 1994

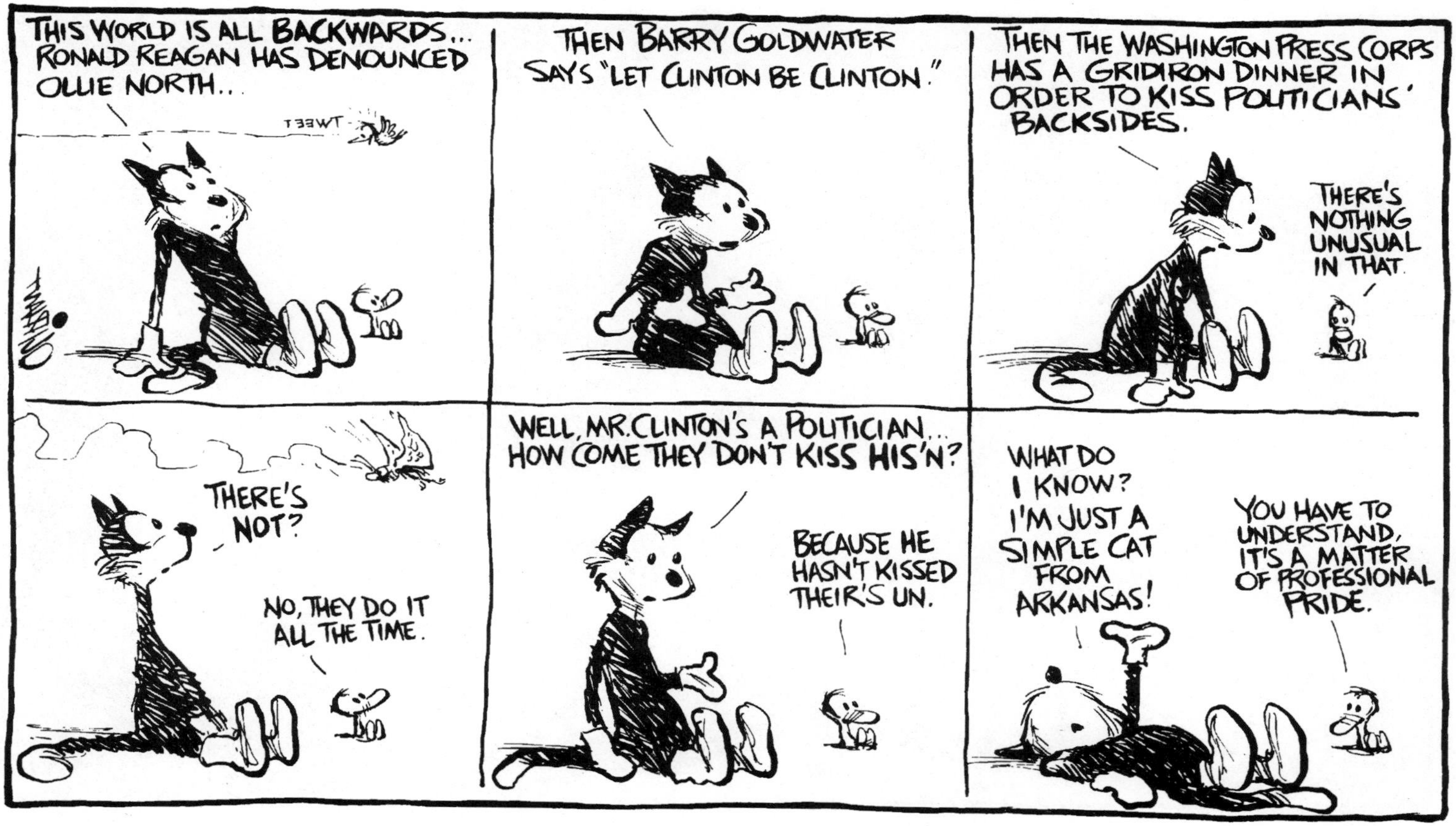
THIS WORLD IS ALL BACKWARDS... RONALD REAGAN HAS DENOUNCED OLLIE NORTH...
TWEET
THEN BARRY GOLDWATER SAYS "LET CLINTON BE CLINTON."
THEN THE WASHINGTON PRESS CORPS HAS A GRIDIRON DINNER IN ORDER TO KISS POLITICIANS' BACKSIDES.
THERE'S NOTHING UNUSUAL IN THAT.
THERE'S NOT?
NO, THEY DO IT ALL THE TIME.
WELL, MR. CLINTON'S A POLITICIAN... HOW COME THEY DON'T KISS HIS'N?
BECAUSE HE HASN'T KISSED THEIR'S UN.
WHAT DO I KNOW? I'M JUST A SIMPLE CAT FROM ARKANSAS!
YOU HAVE TO UNDERSTAND, IT'S A MATTER OF PROFESSIONAL PRIDE.

March 25, 1994

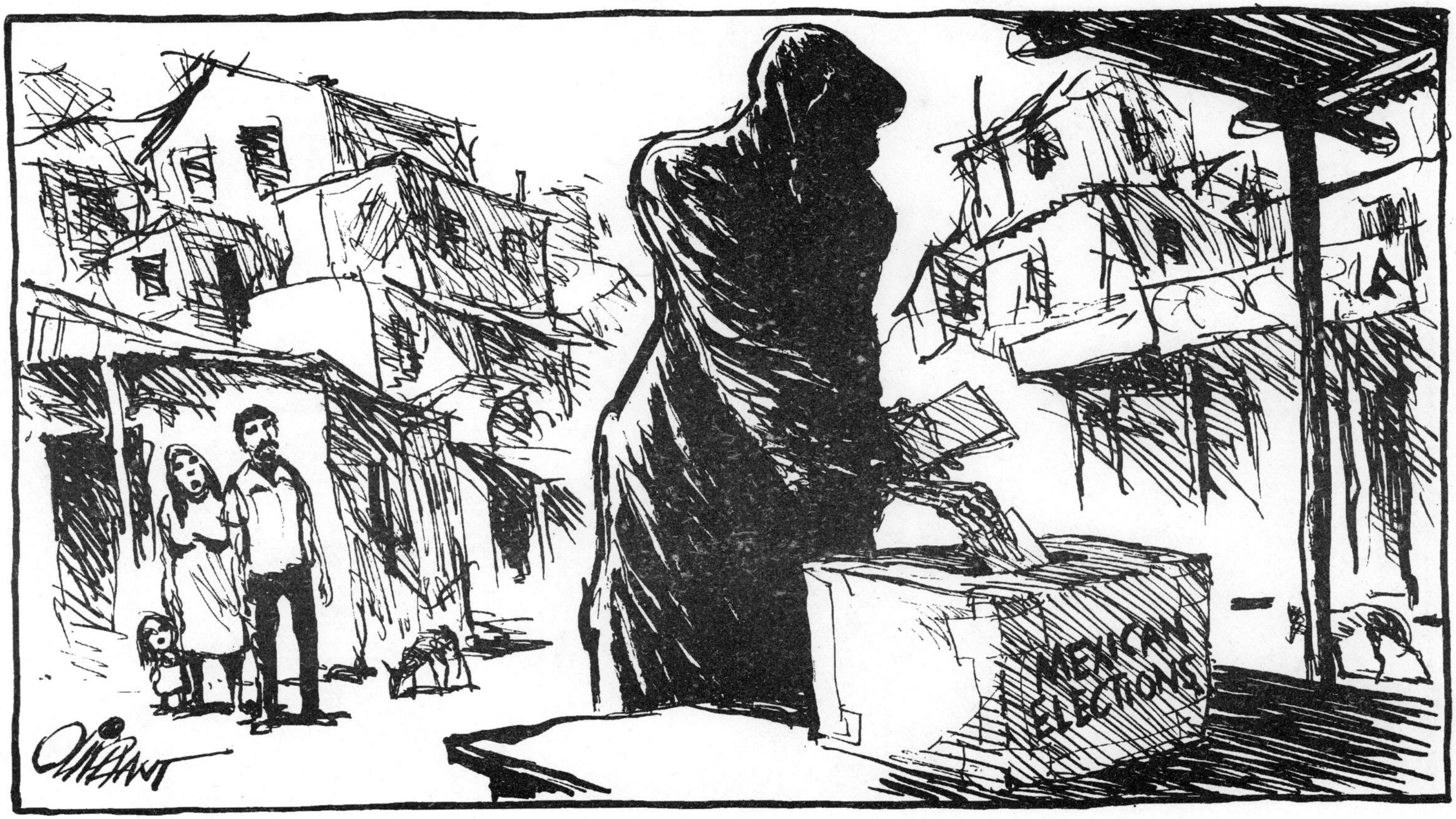
MEXICAN ELECTIONS
OLIPHANT

March 31, 1994

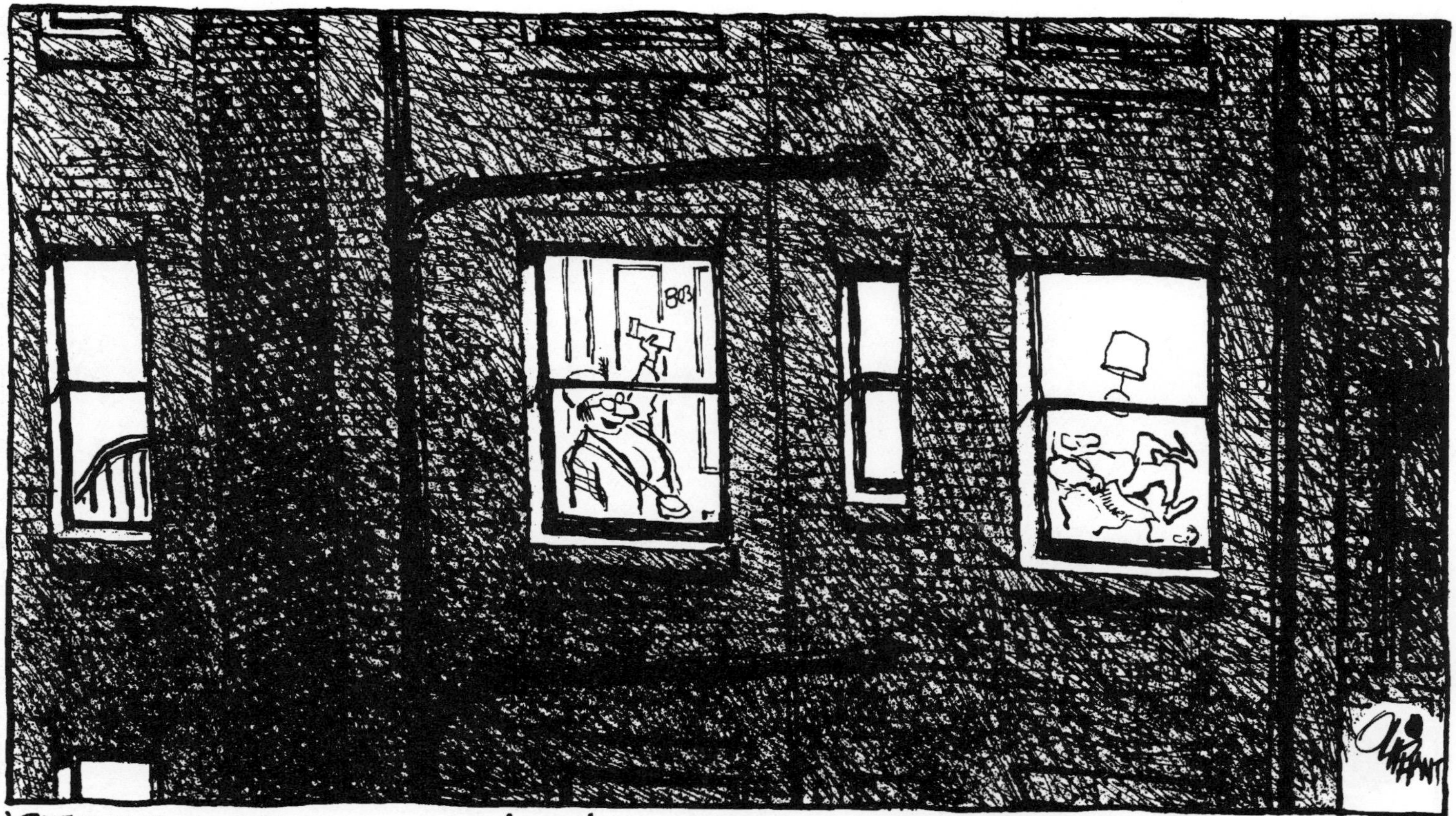

'CATTLE FUTURES IS WHERE IT'S AT! I JUST PUT ALL OUR SAVINGS IN CATTLE FUTURES!'

April 1, 1994

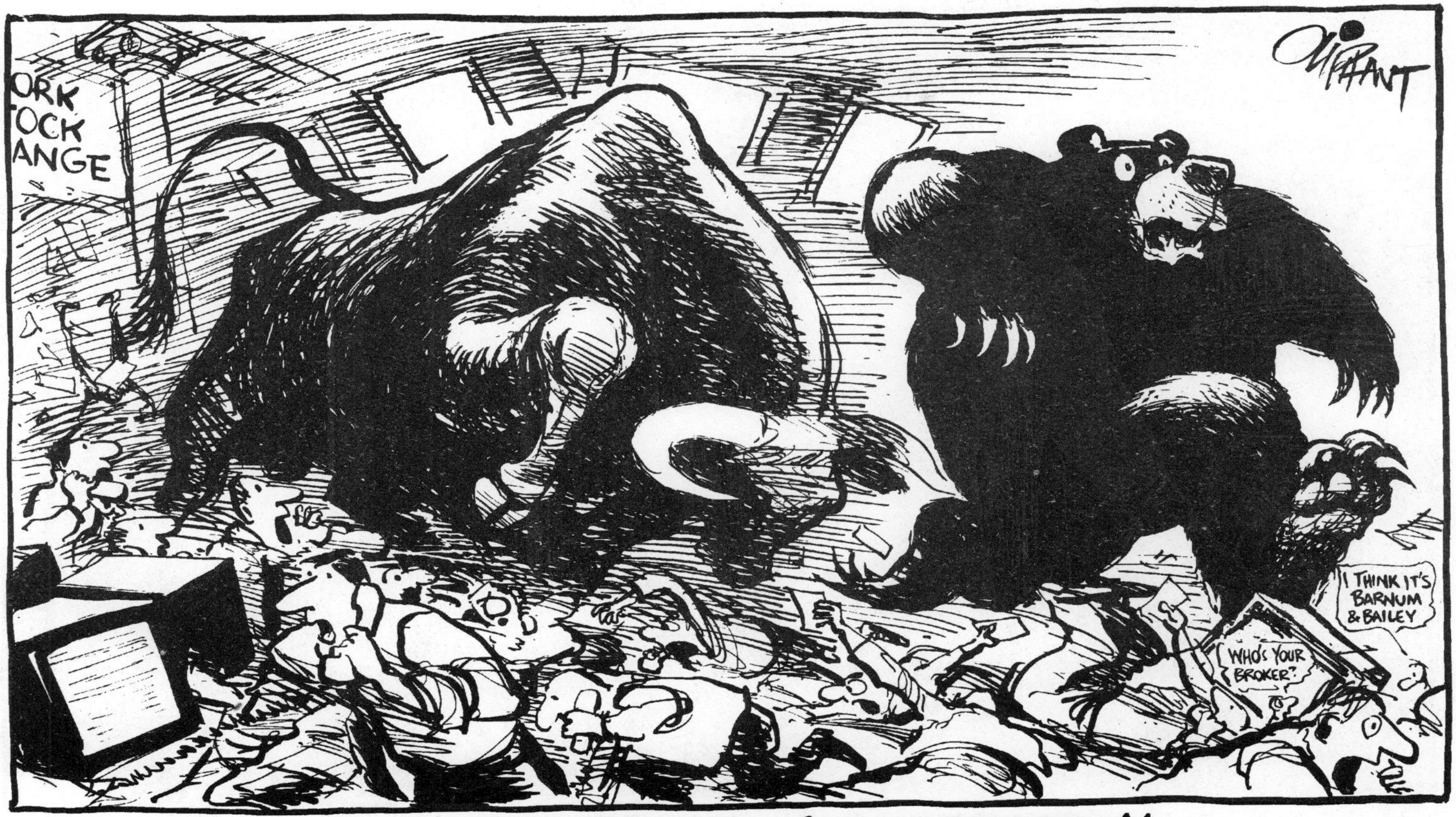

ORK
TOCK
ANGE
OLIPHANT
I THINK IT'S BARNUM & BAILEY
WHO'S YOUR BROKER?

'LIKE I SAID EARLIER— CATTLE FUTURES!'

April 1, 1994

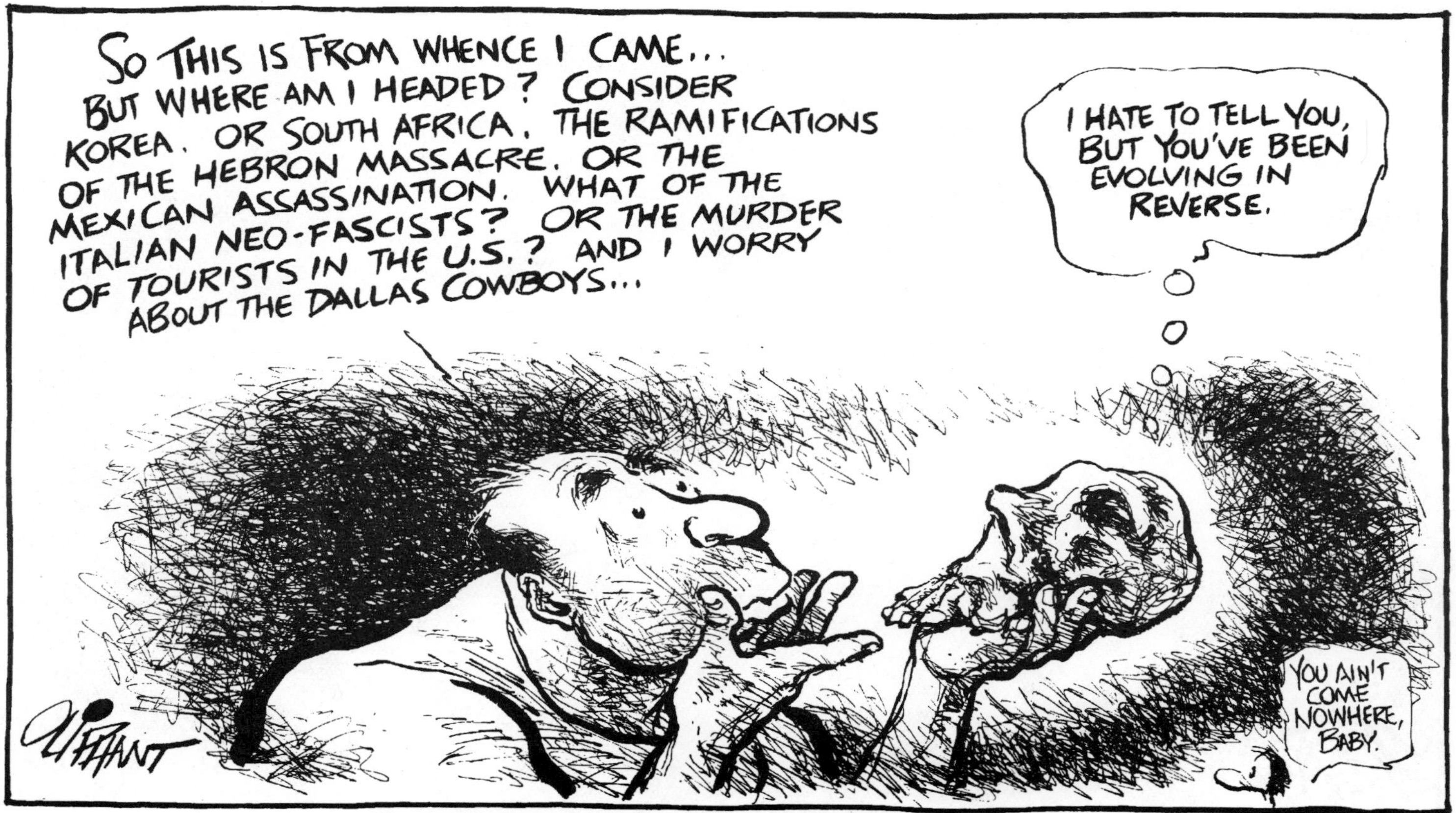

SO THIS IS FROM WHENCE I CAME... BUT WHERE AM I HEADED? CONSIDER KOREA. OR SOUTH AFRICA. THE RAMIFICATIONS OF THE HEBRON MASSACRE. OR THE MEXICAN ASSASSINATION. WHAT OF THE ITALIAN NEO-FASCISTS? OR THE MURDER OF TOURISTS IN THE U.S.? AND I WORRY ABOUT THE DALLAS COWBOYS...
I HATE TO TELL YOU, BUT YOU'VE BEEN EVOLVING IN REVERSE.
YOU AIN'T COME NOWHERE, BABY.

THE THREE-MILLION-YEAR-OLD MAN.

April 6, 1994

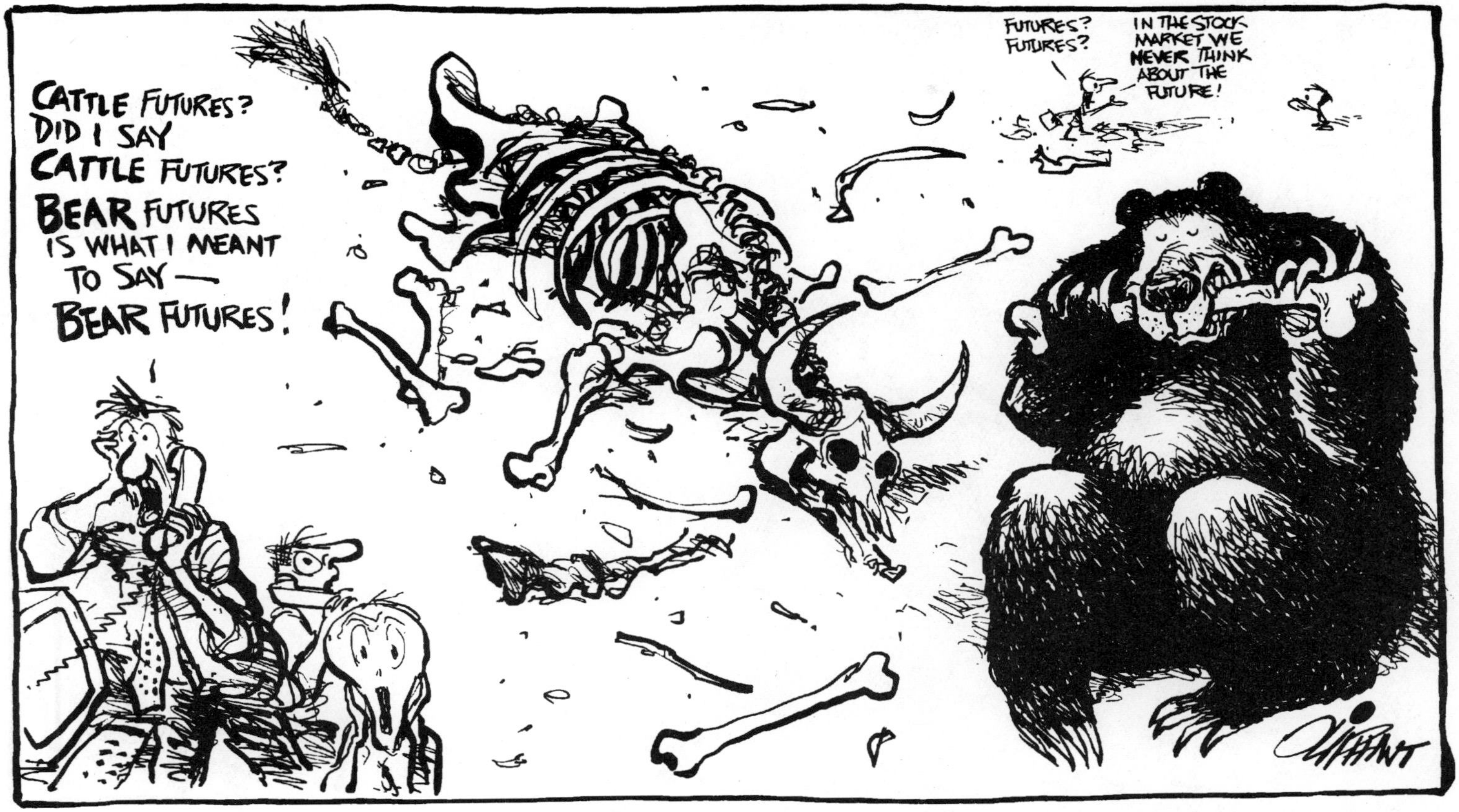
CATTLE FUTURES? DID I SAY CATTLE FUTURES? BEAR FUTURES IS WHAT I MEANT TO SAY — BEAR FUTURES!
FUTURES? FUTURES?
IN THE STOCK MARKET WE NEVER THINK ABOUT THE FUTURE!
OLIPHANT

April 7, 1994

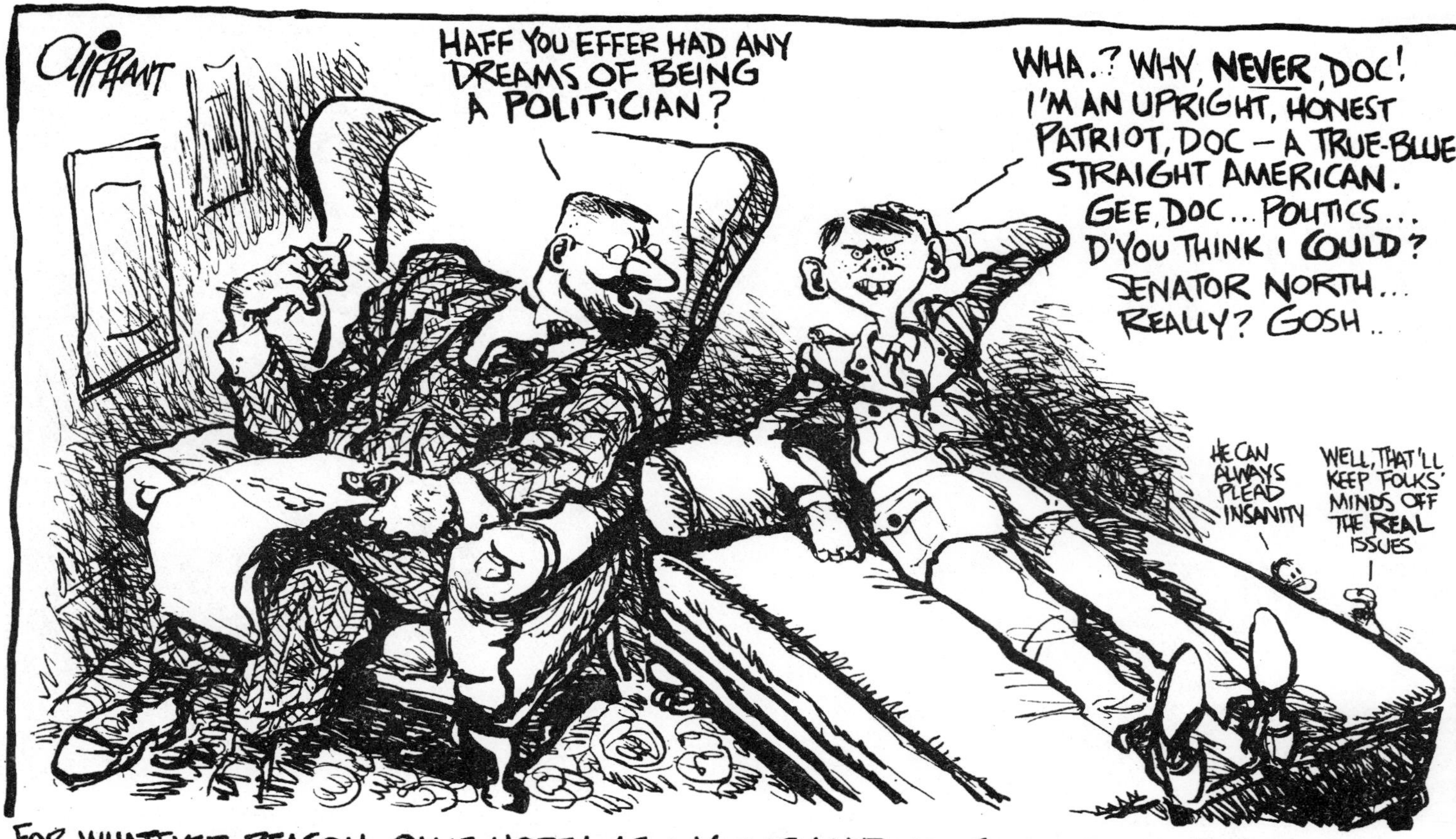
OLIPHANT
HAFF YOU EFFER HAD ANY DREAMS OF BEING A POLITICIAN?
WHA..? WHY, NEVER, DOC! I'M AN UPRIGHT, HONEST PATRIOT, DOC – A TRUE-BLUE, STRAIGHT AMERICAN. GEE, DOC... POLITICS... D'YOU THINK I COULD? SENATOR NORTH... REALLY? GOSH..
HE CAN ALWAYS PLEAD INSANITY
WELL, THAT'LL KEEP FOLKS' MINDS OFF THE REAL ISSUES

FOR WHATEVER REASON, OLLIE NORTH, AS A YOUNG MARINE, CONSULTED A PSYCHIATRIST. PERHAPS THAT IS WHERE IT ALL BEGAN...

April 8, 1994

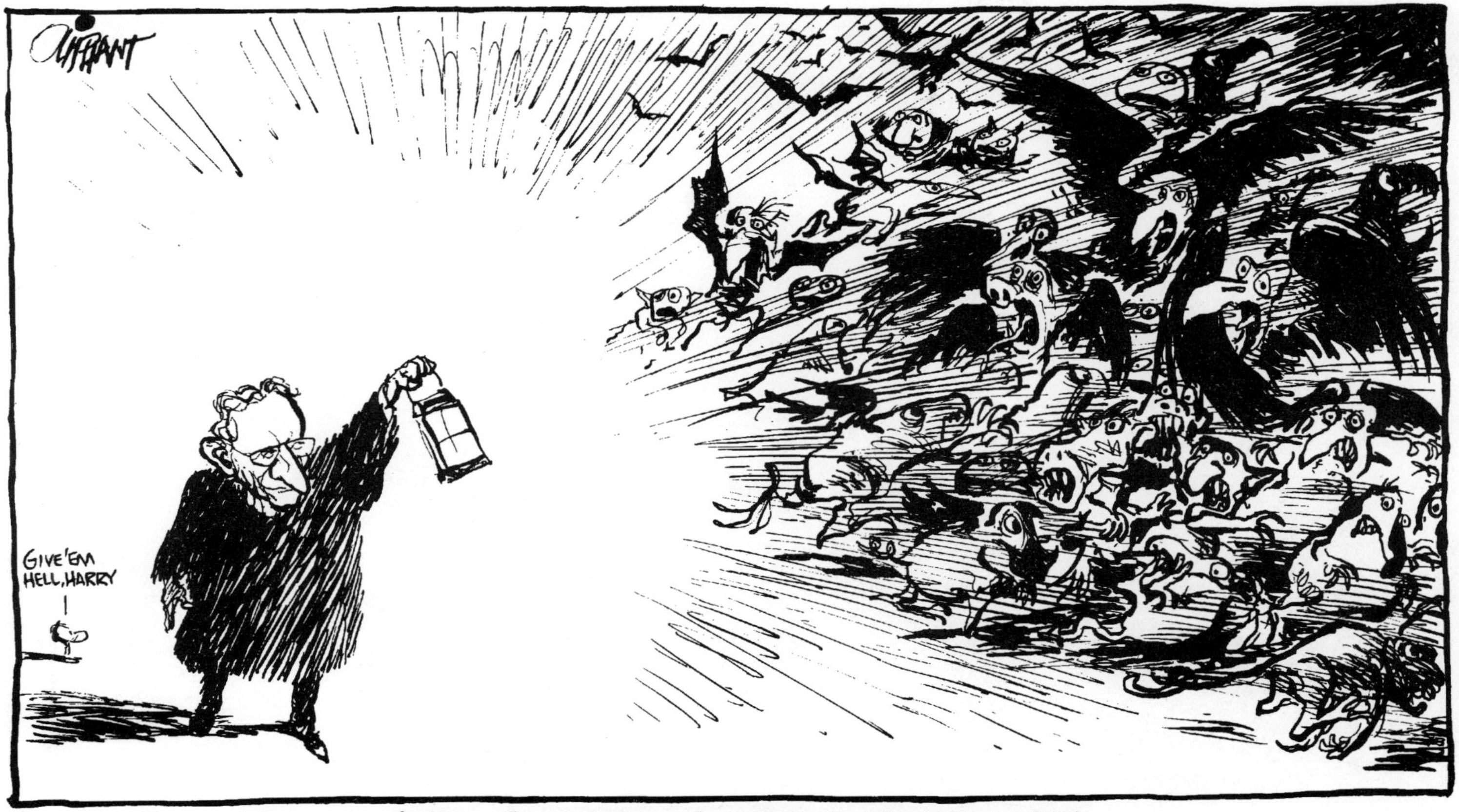
OLIPHANT
GIVE 'EM HELL, HARRY!

HARRY BLACKMUN, SUPREME COURT, 1970-1994.

April 9, 1994

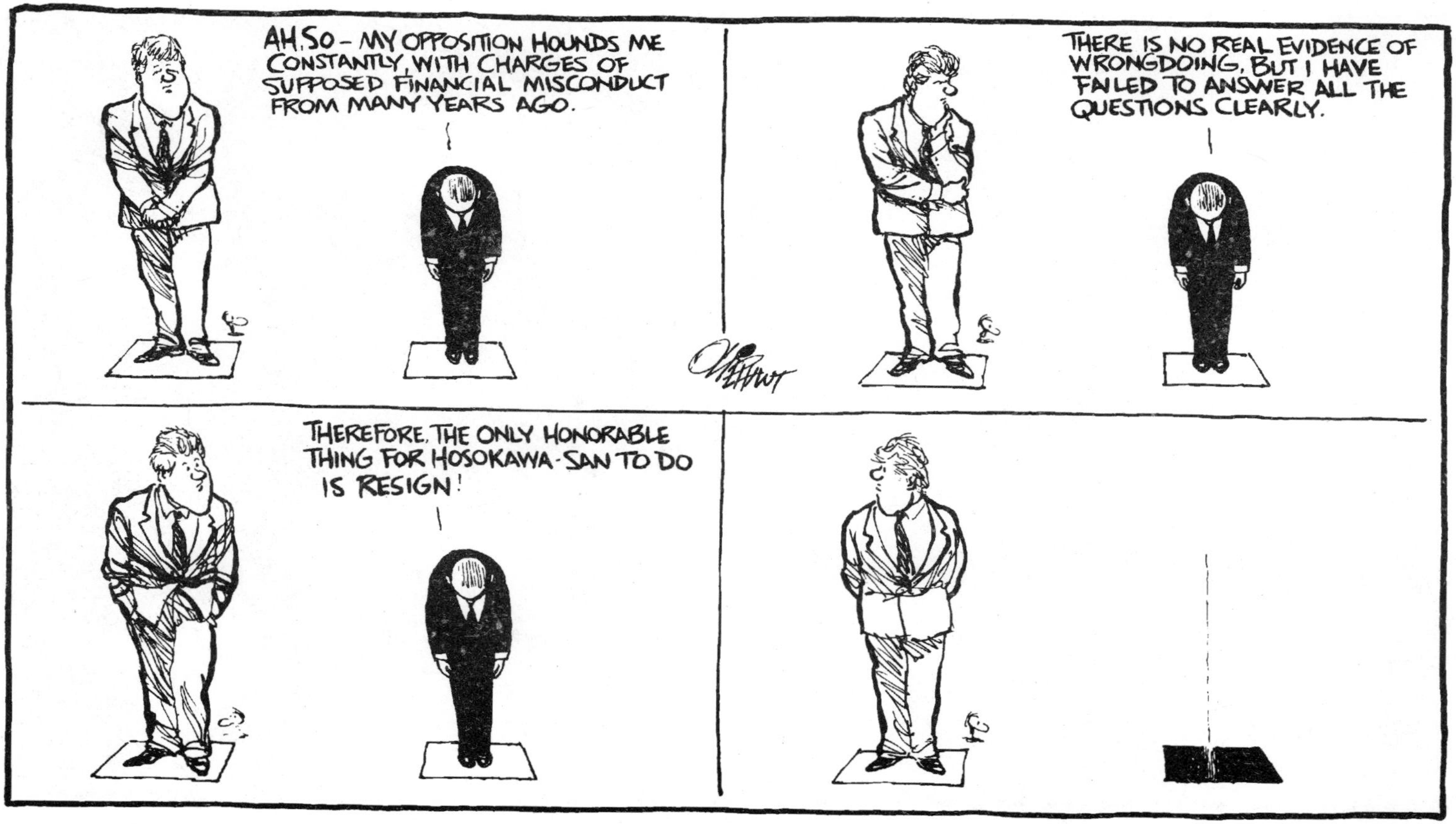
AH, SO - MY OPPOSITION HOUNDS ME CONSTANTLY, WITH CHARGES OF SUPPOSED FINANCIAL MISCONDUCT FROM MANY YEARS AGO.
THERE IS NO REAL EVIDENCE OF WRONGDOING, BUT I HAVE FAILED TO ANSWER ALL THE QUESTIONS CLEARLY.
THEREFORE, THE ONLY HONORABLE THING FOR HOSOKAWA-SAN TO DO IS RESIGN!

April 13, 1994

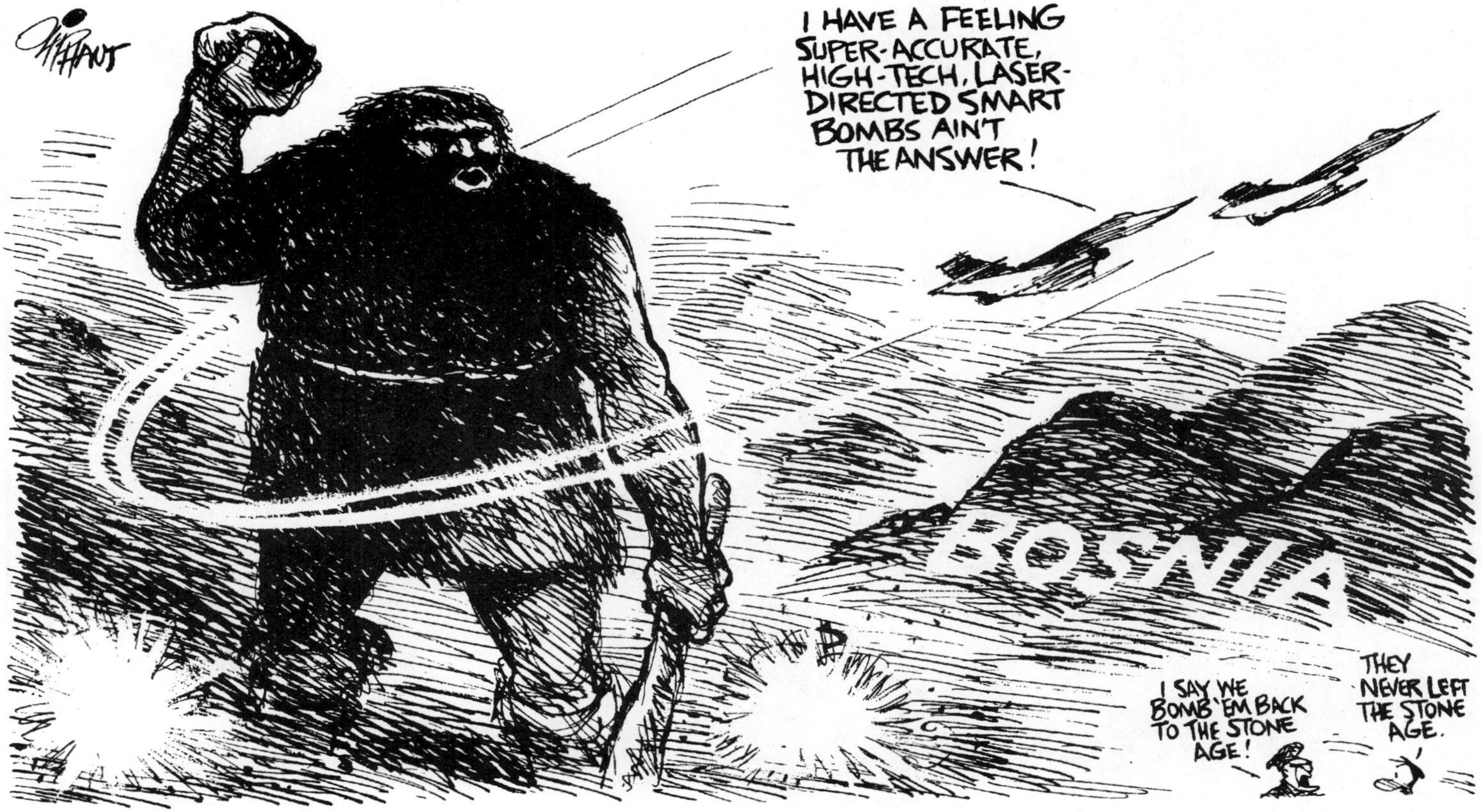
OLIPHANT
I HAVE A FEELING SUPER-ACCURATE, HIGH-TECH, LASER-DIRECTED SMART BOMBS AIN'T THE ANSWER!
BOSNIA
I SAY WE BOMB 'EM BACK TO THE STONE AGE!
THEY NEVER LEFT THE STONE AGE.

April 14, 1994

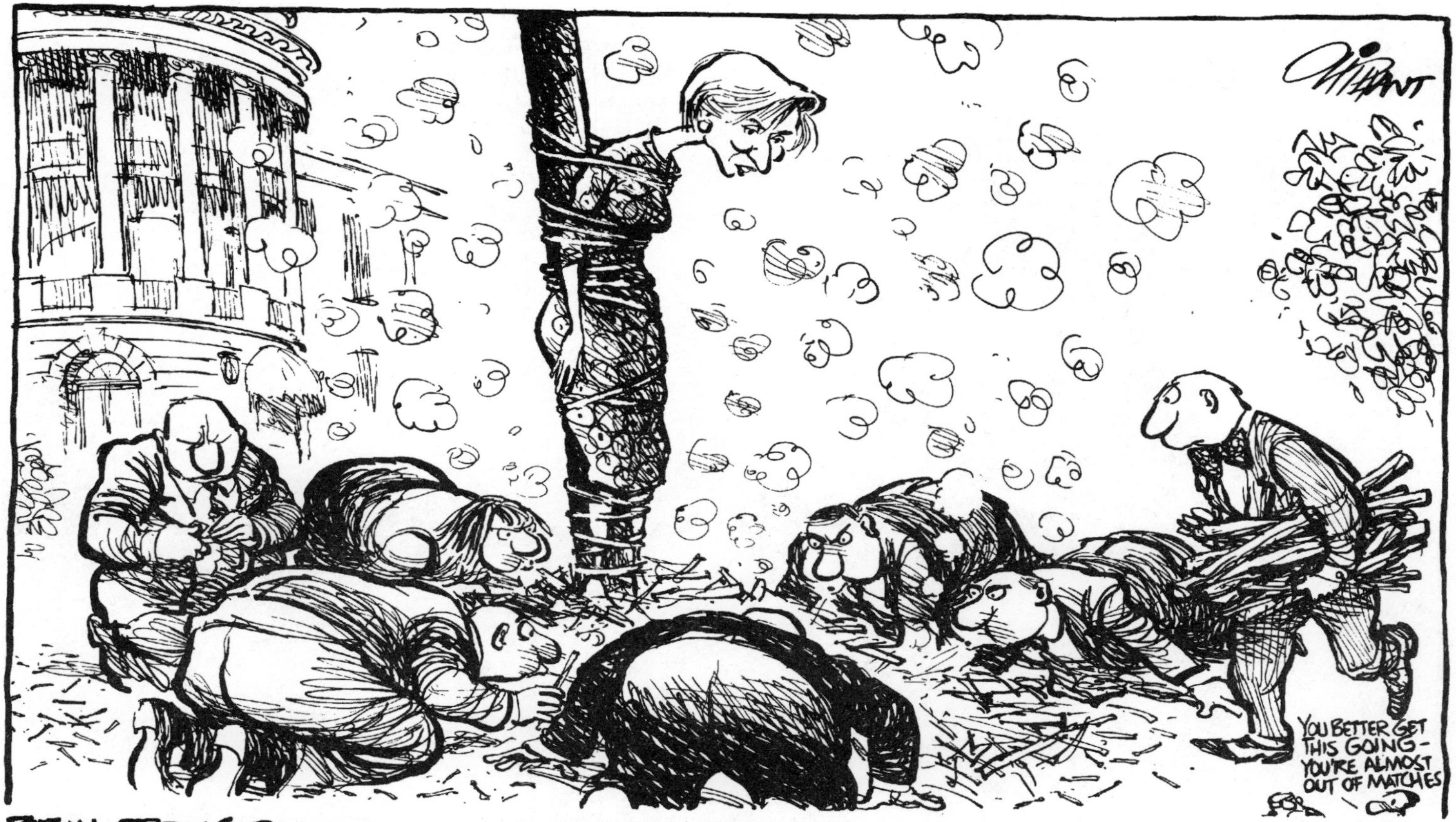
YOU BETTER GET THIS GOING - YOU'RE ALMOST OUT OF MATCHES

RITUAL SPRING BURNING BY THE WASHINGTON PRESS CORPS. ALL WELCOME. ADMISSION FREE.

April 16, 1994

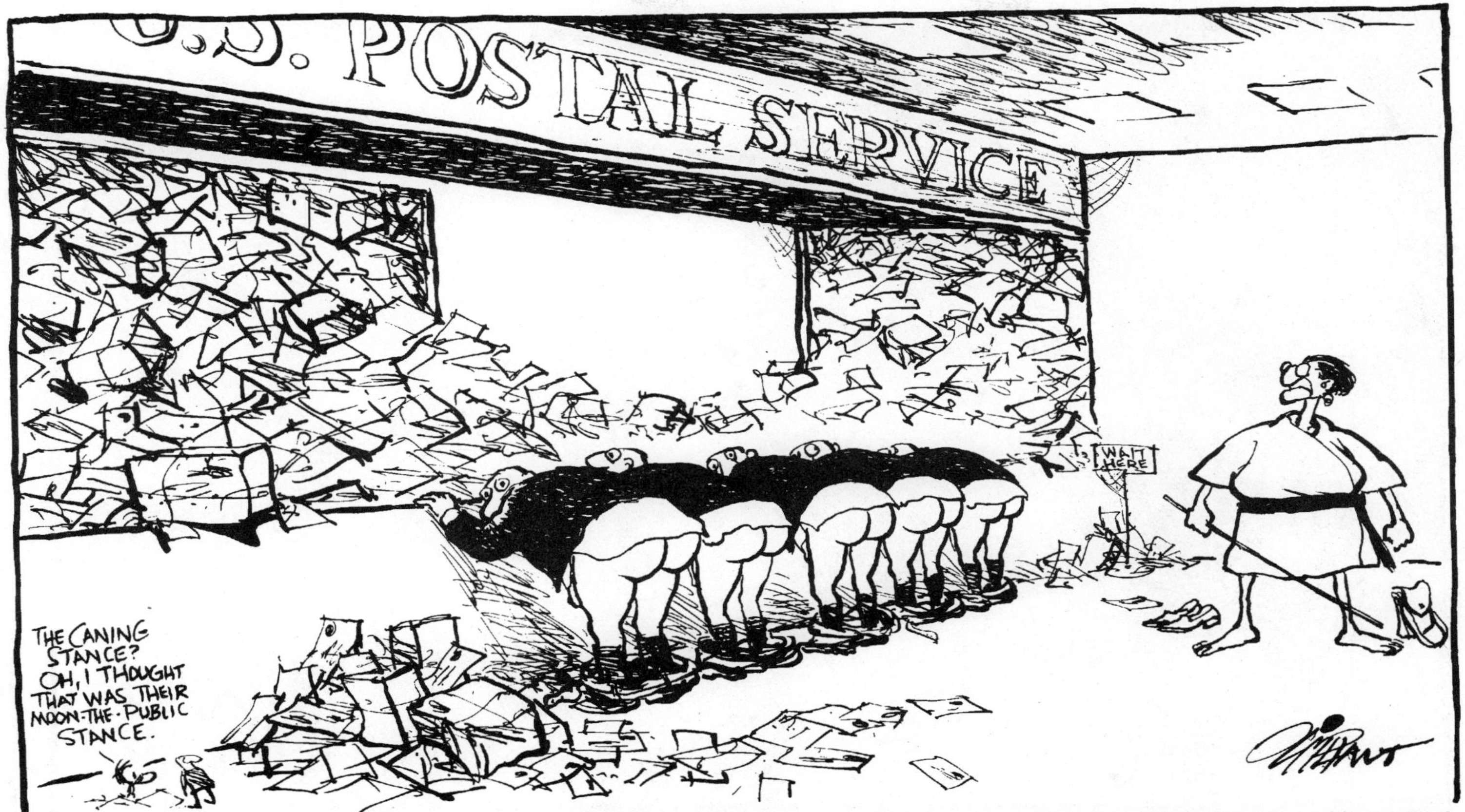
U.S. POSTAL SERVICE
WAIT HERE
THE CANING STANCE? OH, I THOUGHT THAT WAS THEIR MOON-THE-PUBLIC STANCE.

IMPROVING THE SERVICE: CANING OF POSTAL EXECUTIVES WILL BE ADMINISTERED BY A DISGUSTED POSTAL CUSTOMER HIGHLY SKILLED IN THE MARTIAL ARTS.

April 20, 1994

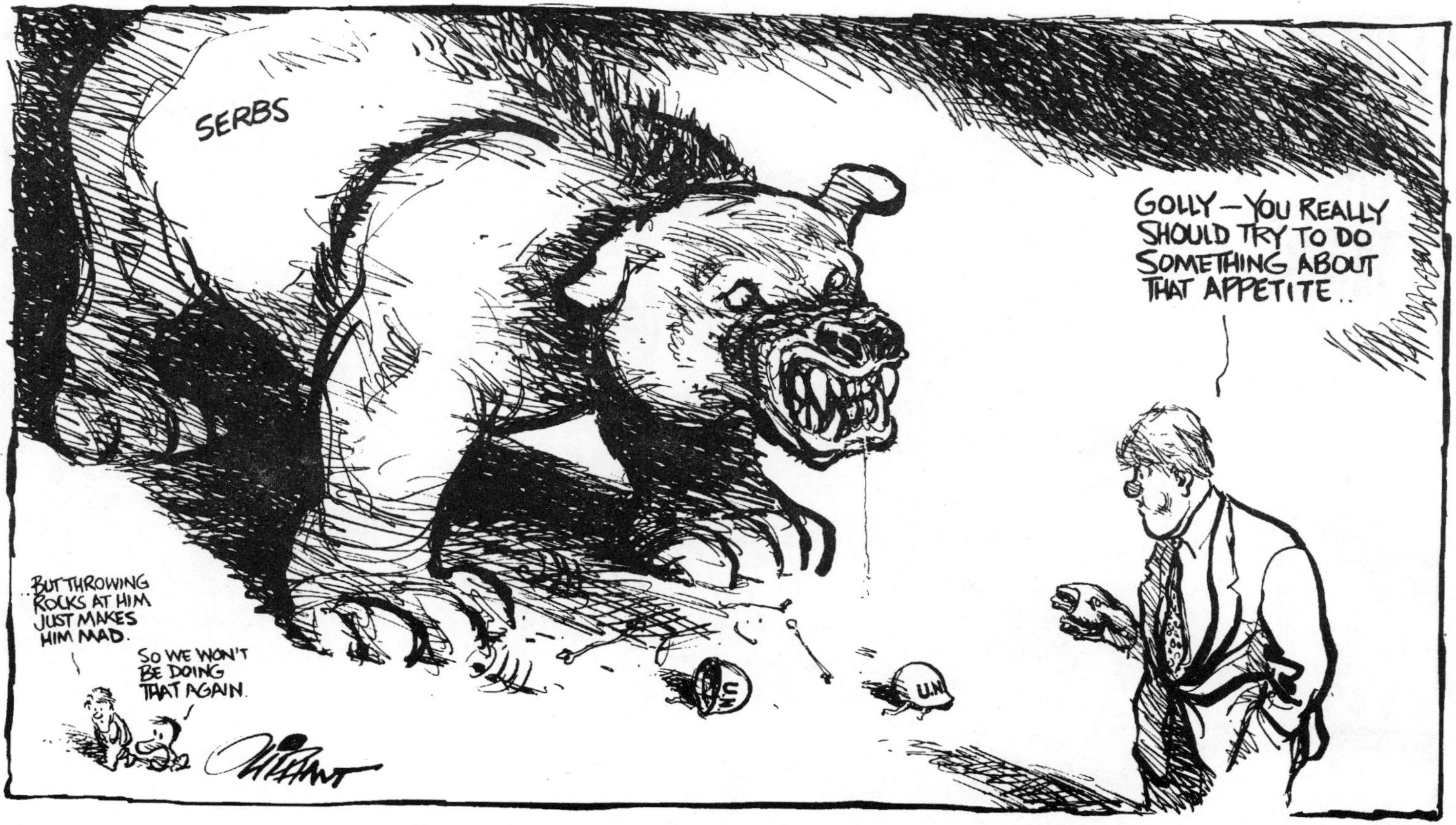
SERBS
GOLLY — YOU REALLY SHOULD TRY TO DO SOMETHING ABOUT THAT APPETITE..
U.N.
U.N.
..BUT THROWING ROCKS AT HIM JUST MAKES HIM MAD.
SO WE WON'T BE DOING THAT AGAIN.

April 21, 1994

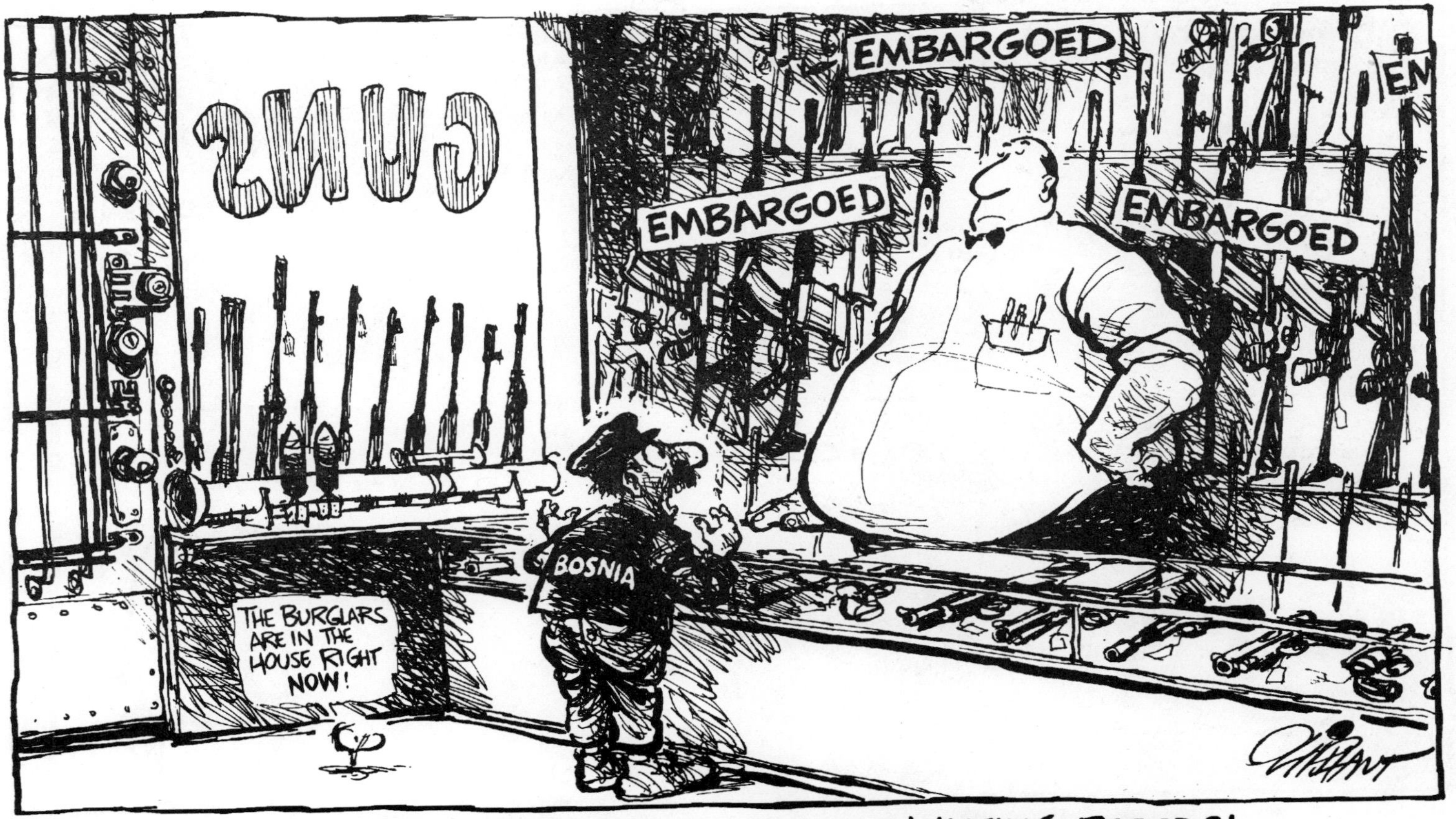
GUNS
EMBARGOED
EMBARGOED
EMBARGOED
BOSNIA
THE BURGLARS ARE IN THE HOUSE RIGHT NOW!

'WAITING PERIOD?? HOW LONG IS WAITING PERIOD?'

April 22, 1994

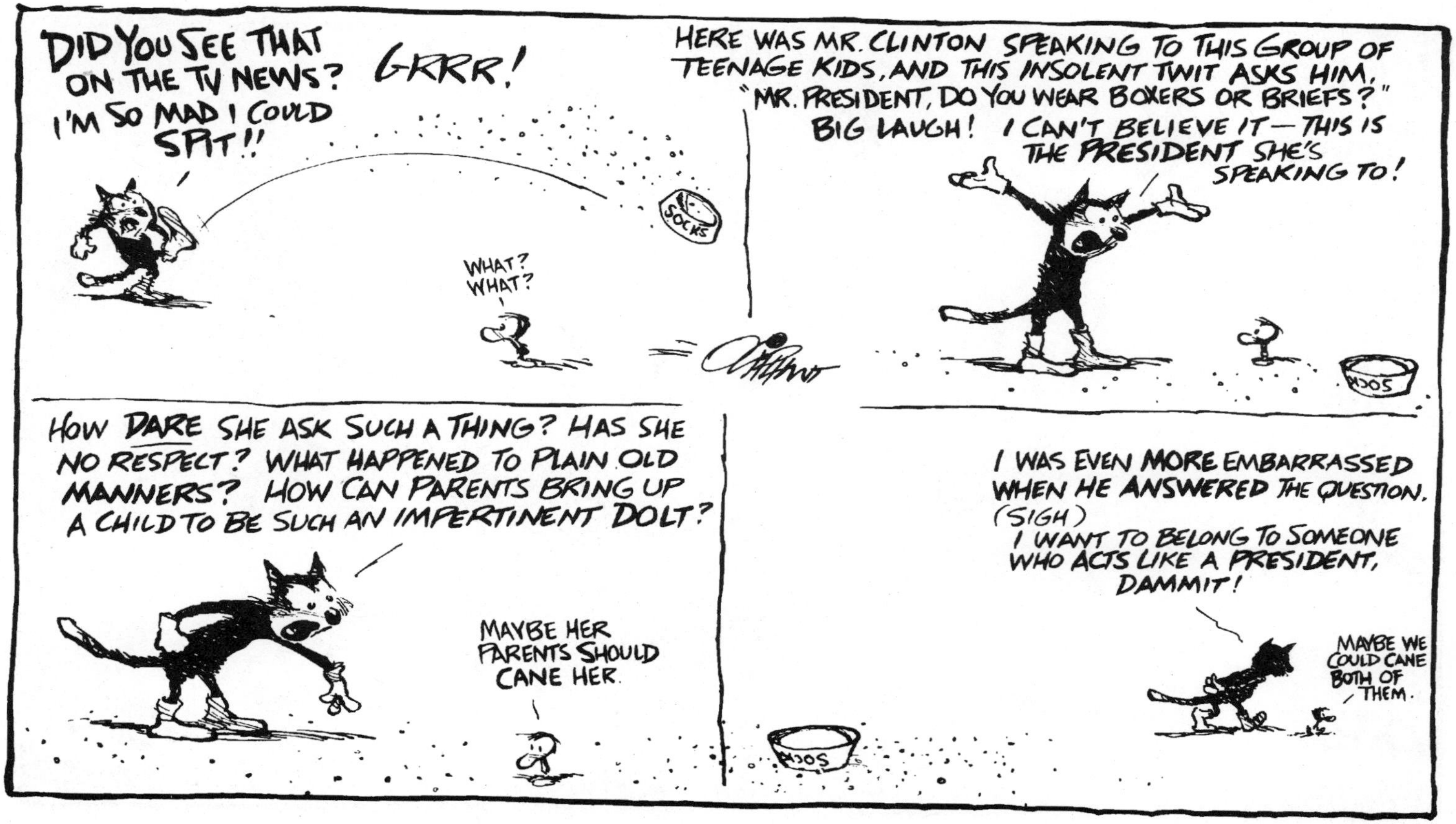

DID YOU SEE THAT ON THE TV NEWS? I'M SO MAD I COULD SPIT!!
GRRR!
SOCKS
WHAT? WHAT?
HERE WAS MR. CLINTON SPEAKING TO THIS GROUP OF TEENAGE KIDS, AND THIS INSOLENT TWIT ASKS HIM, "MR. PRESIDENT, DO YOU WEAR BOXERS OR BRIEFS?" BIG LAUGH! I CAN'T BELIEVE IT — THIS IS THE PRESIDENT SHE'S SPEAKING TO!
SOCK
HOW DARE SHE ASK SUCH A THING? HAS SHE NO RESPECT? WHAT HAPPENED TO PLAIN OLD MANNERS? HOW CAN PARENTS BRING UP A CHILD TO BE SUCH AN IMPERTINENT DOLT?
MAYBE HER PARENTS SHOULD CANE HER.
I WAS EVEN MORE EMBARRASSED WHEN HE ANSWERED THE QUESTION. (SIGH) I WANT TO BELONG TO SOMEONE WHO ACTS LIKE A PRESIDENT, DAMMIT!
MAYBE WE COULD CANE BOTH OF THEM.
SOCKS

April 23, 1994

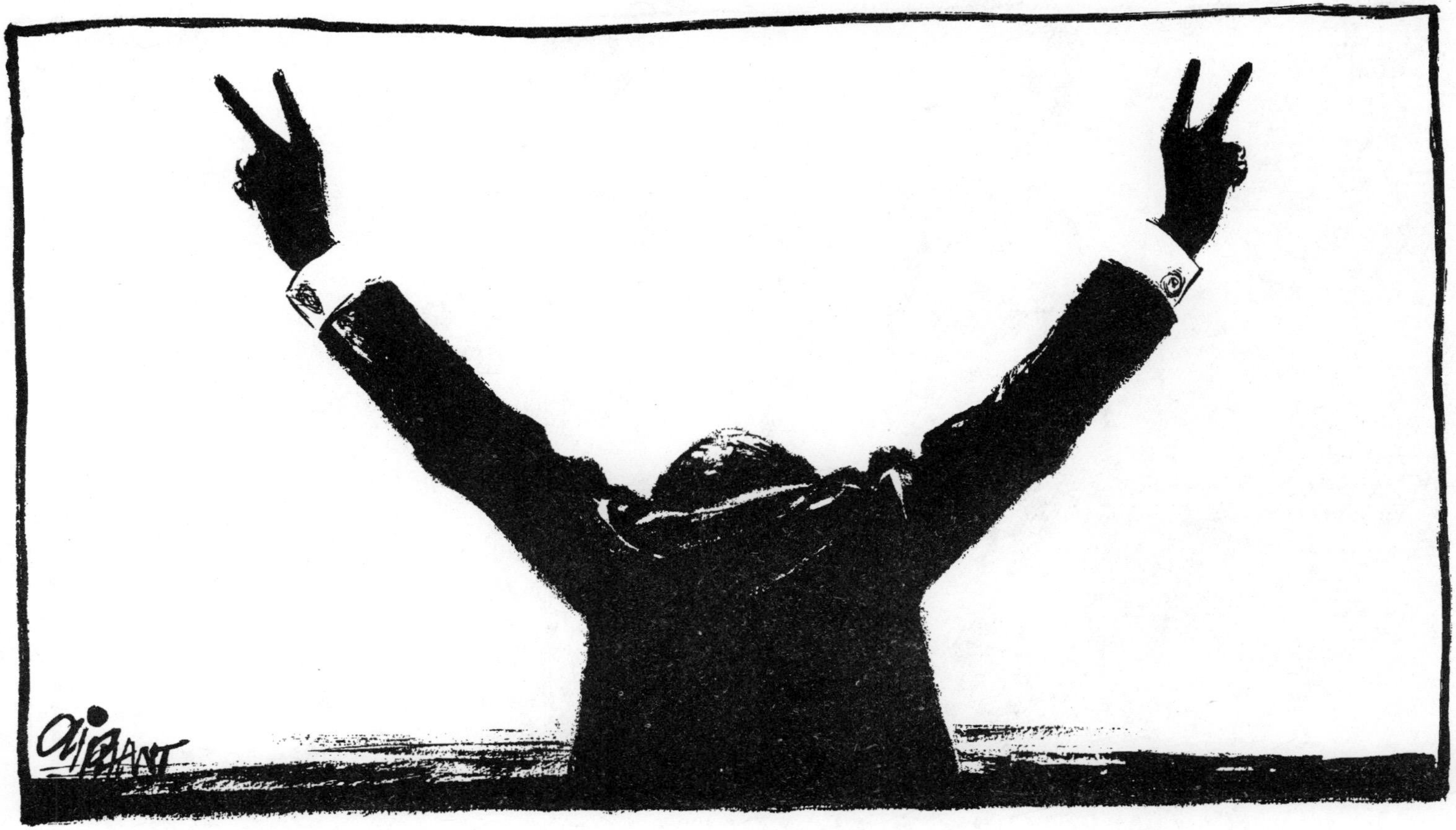

April 27, 1994

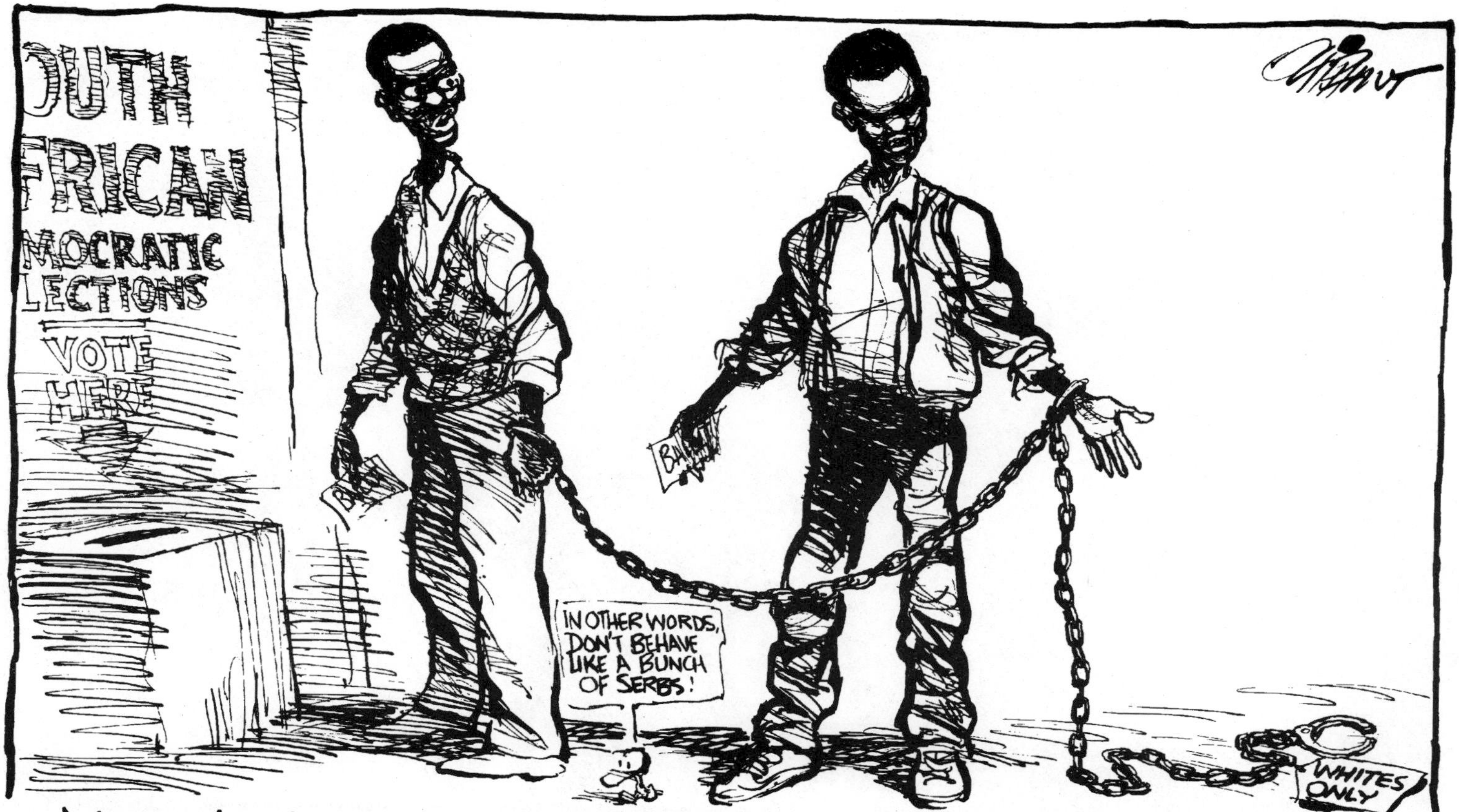
OUTH
FRICAN
MOCRATIC
LECTIONS
VOTE
HERE
IN OTHER WORDS, DON'T BEHAVE LIKE A BUNCH OF SERBS!
WHITES ONLY

'NOW WE'RE CHAINED ONLY TO EACH OTHER, I HOPE WE CAN KEEP IT CIVIL.'

April 28, 1994

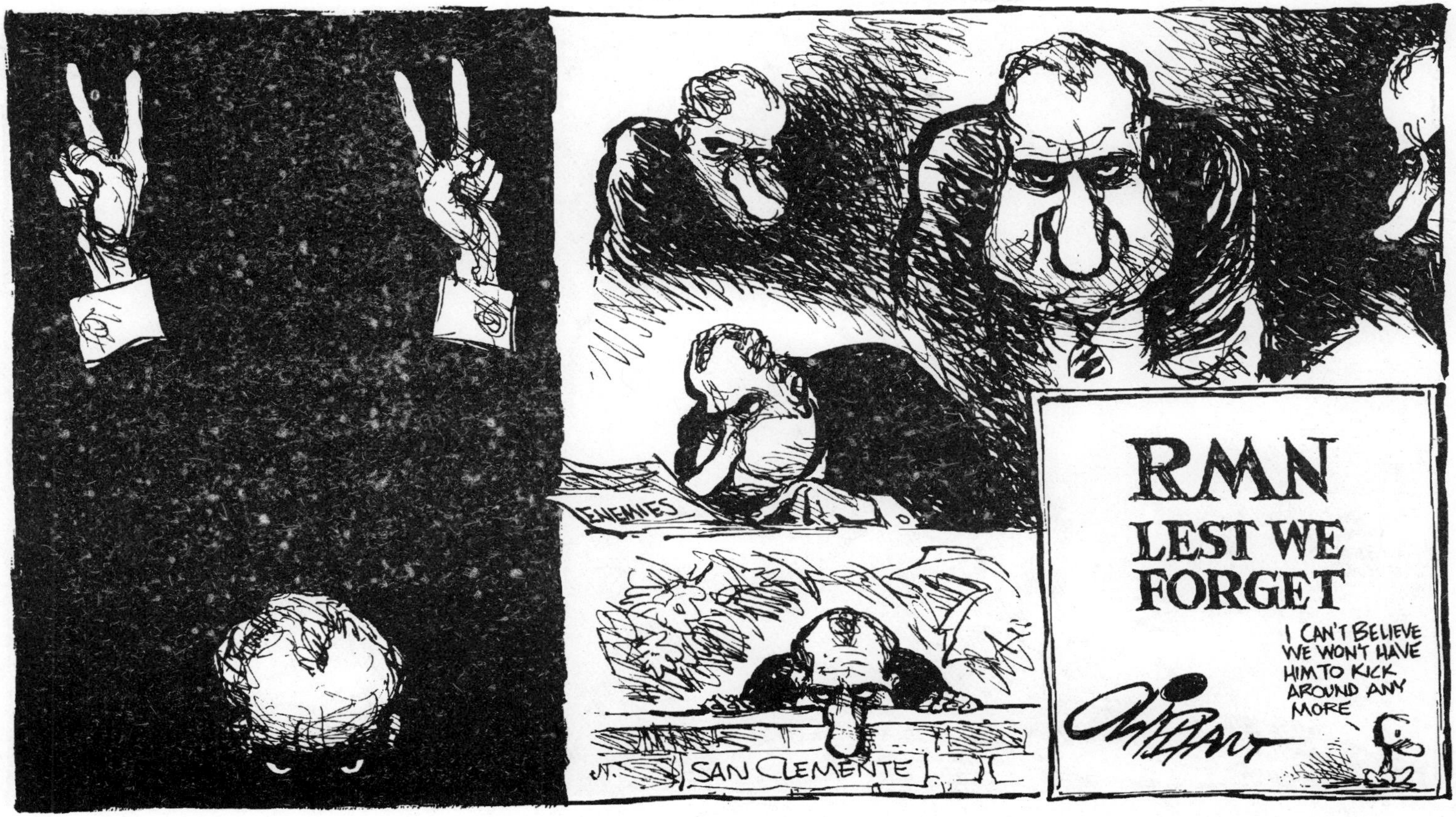
ENEMIES
SAN CLEMENTE
RMN
LEST WE FORGET
I CAN'T BELIEVE WE WON'T HAVE HIM TO KICK AROUND ANY MORE

April 29, 1994

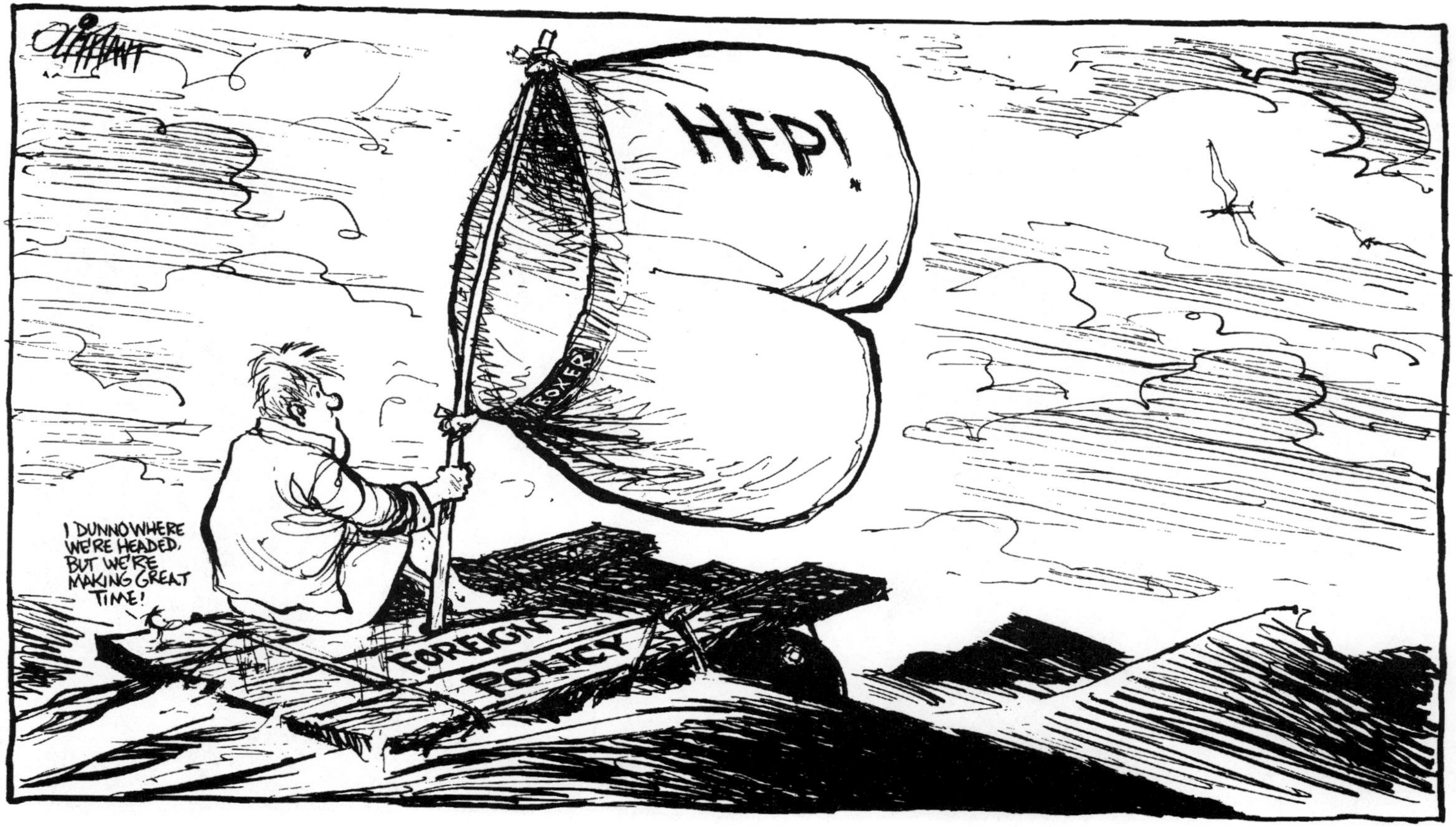
HEP!
BOXER
I DUNNO WHERE WE'RE HEADED, BUT WE'RE MAKING GREAT TIME!
FOREIGN POLICY

May 1, 1994

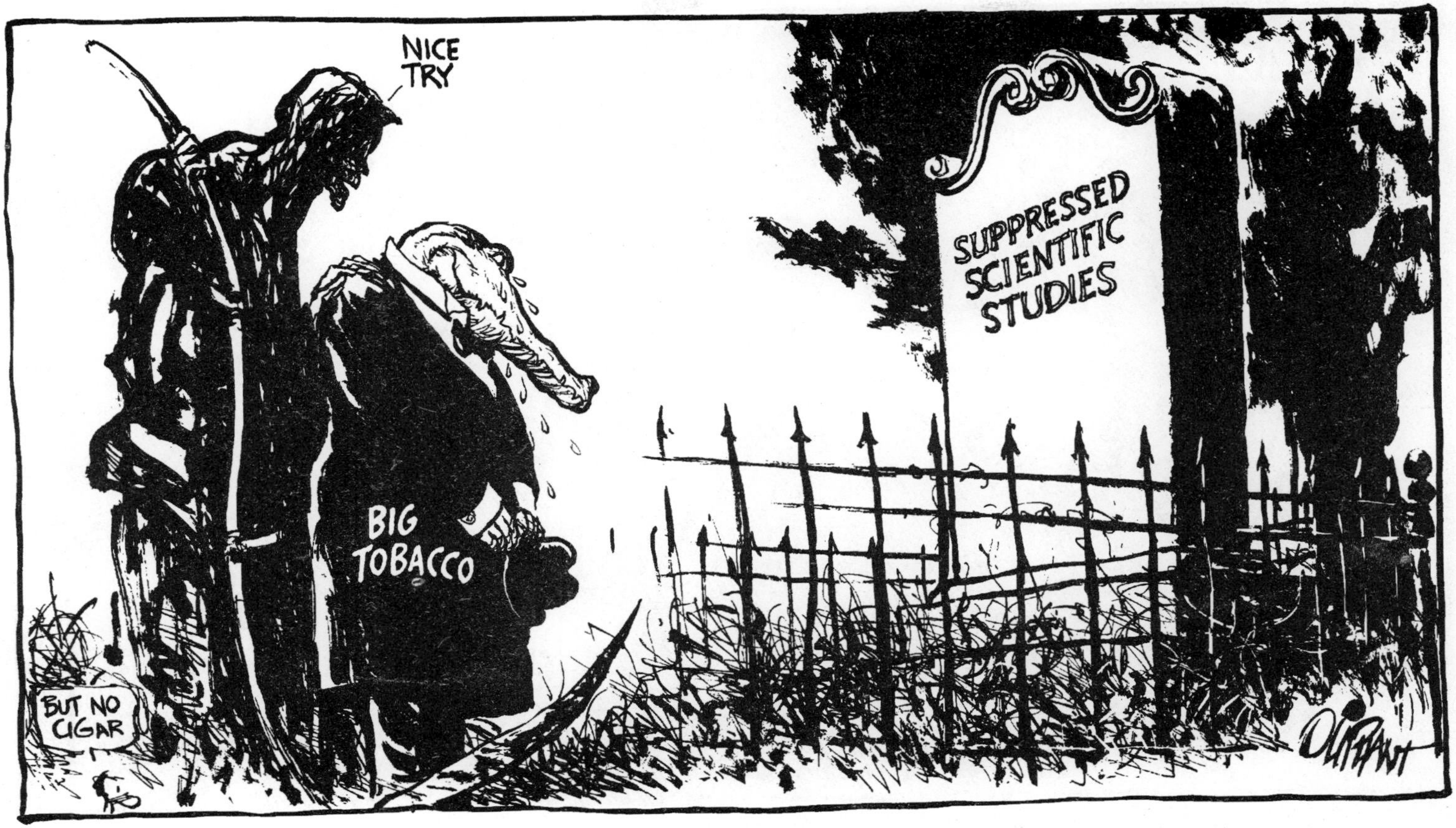
NICE TRY
BIG TOBACCO
SUPPRESSED SCIENTIFIC STUDIES
BUT NO CIGAR
OLIPHANT

May 4, 1994

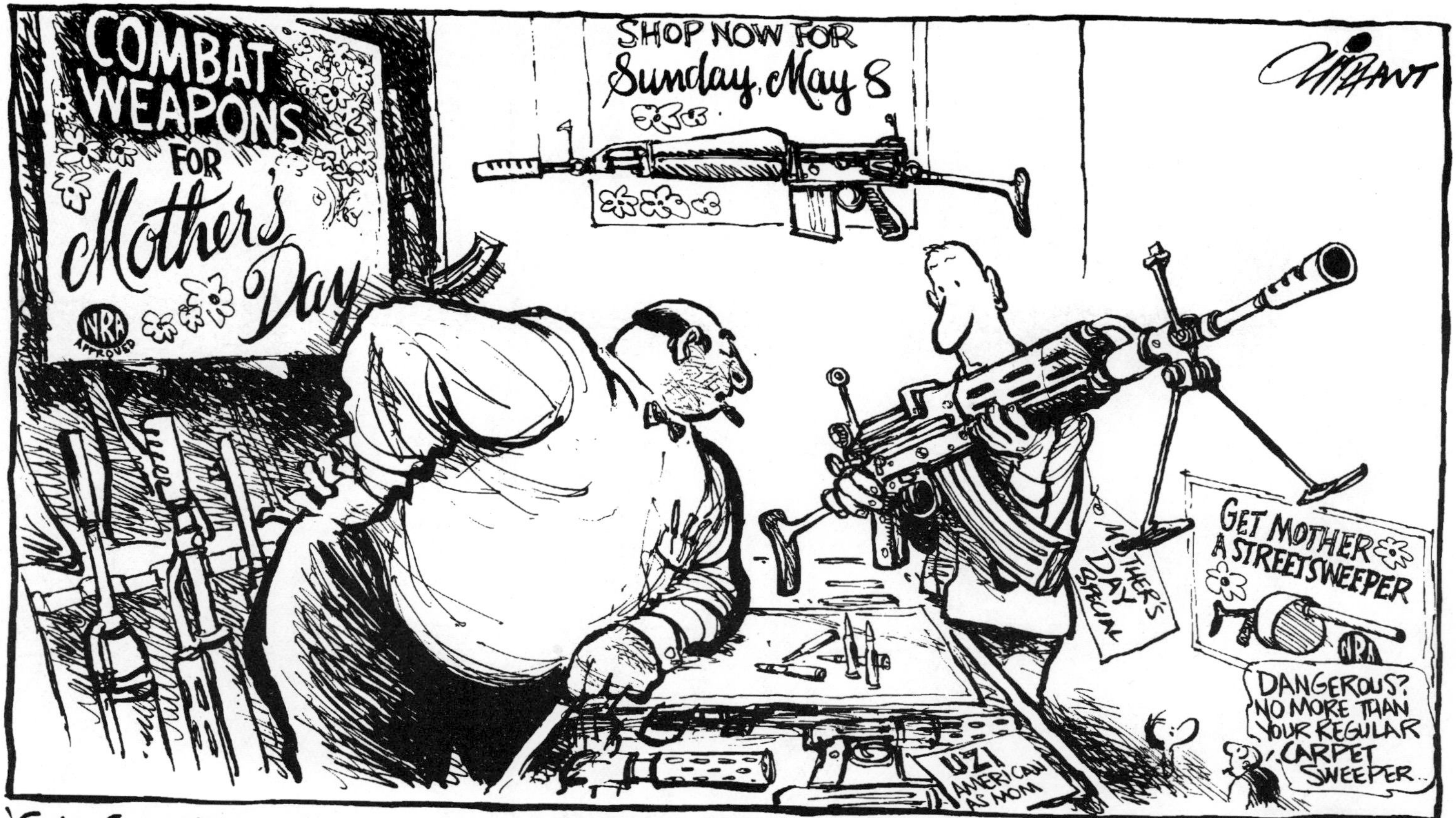
COMBAT WEAPONS FOR Mother's Day
NRA APPROVED
SHOP NOW FOR Sunday, May 8
MOTHER'S DAY SPECIAL
GET MOTHER A STREETSWEEPER
NRA
DANGEROUS? NO MORE THAN YOUR REGULAR CARPET SWEEPER
UZI AMERICAN AS MOM

'SHE CAN HUNT WITH IT, SHE CAN TARGET SHOOT WITH IT, ..'COURSE SHE'LL LIKE IT.'

May 5, 1994

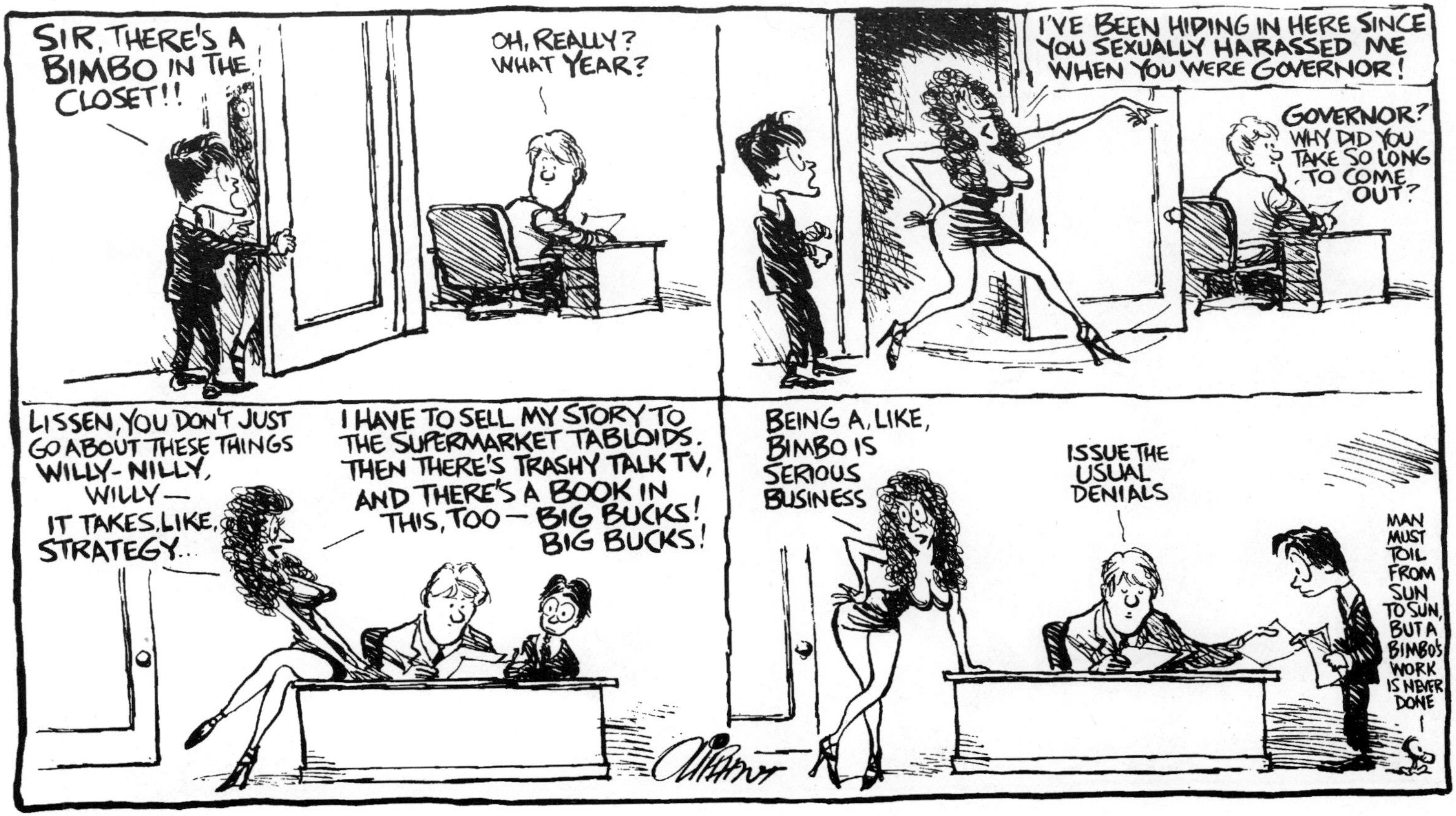

SIR, THERE'S A BIMBO IN THE CLOSET!!
OH, REALLY? WHAT YEAR?
I'VE BEEN HIDING IN HERE SINCE YOU SEXUALLY HARASSED ME WHEN YOU WERE GOVERNOR!
GOVERNOR? WHY DID YOU TAKE SO LONG TO COME OUT?
LISSEN, YOU DON'T JUST GO ABOUT THESE THINGS WILLY-NILLY, WILLY— IT TAKES, LIKE, STRATEGY...
I HAVE TO SELL MY STORY TO THE SUPERMARKET TABLOIDS. THEN THERE'S TRASHY TALK TV, AND THERE'S A BOOK IN THIS, TOO— BIG BUCKS! BIG BUCKS!
BEING A, LIKE, BIMBO IS SERIOUS BUSINESS
ISSUE THE USUAL DENIALS
MAN MUST TOIL FROM SUN TO SUN, BUT A BIMBO'S WORK IS NEVER DONE

May 6, 1994

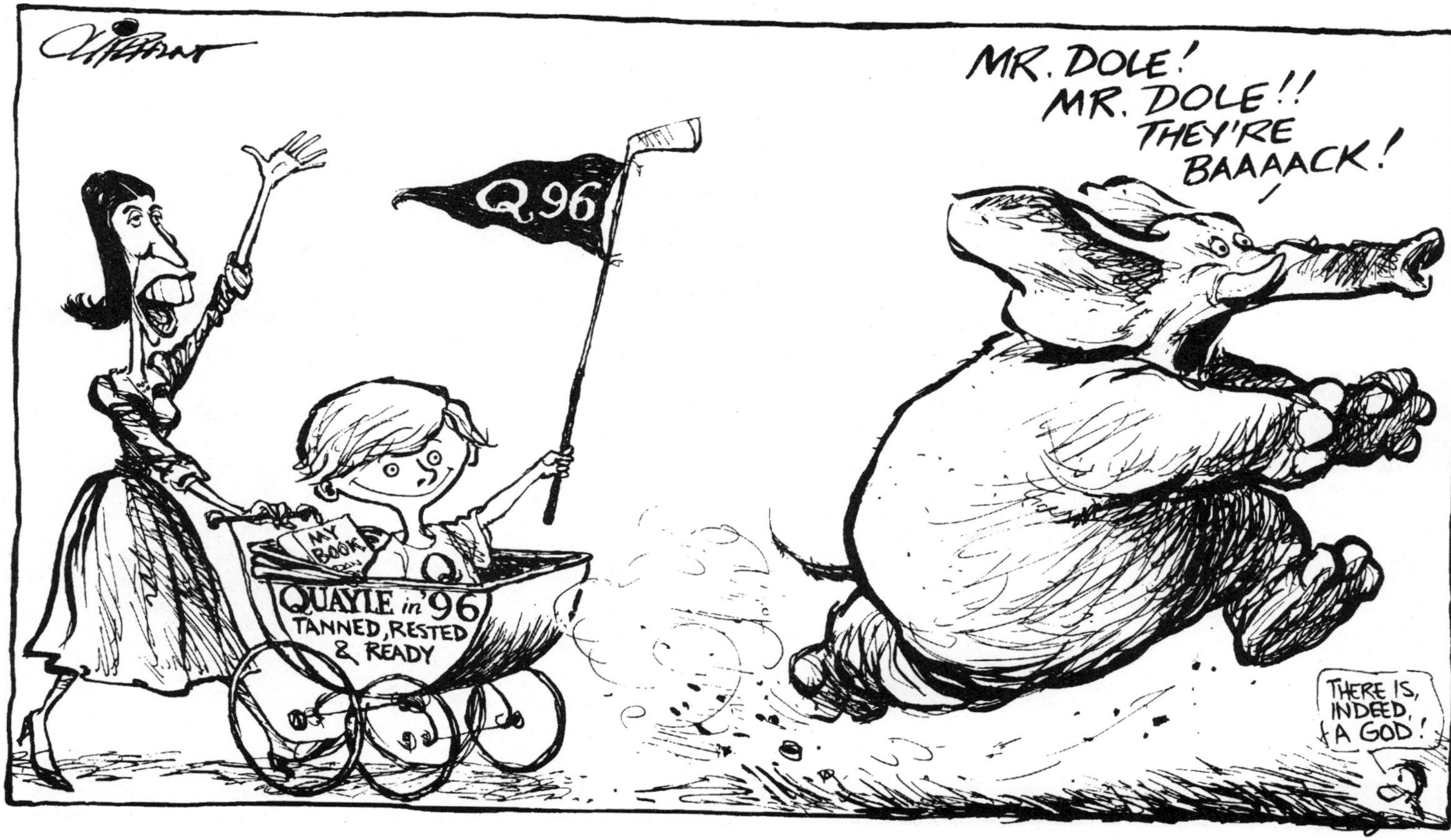
MR. DOLE! MR. DOLE!! THEY'RE BAAAACK!
Q96
MY BOOK
QUAYLE in '96 TANNED, RESTED & READY
THERE IS, INDEED, A GOD!

May 7, 1994

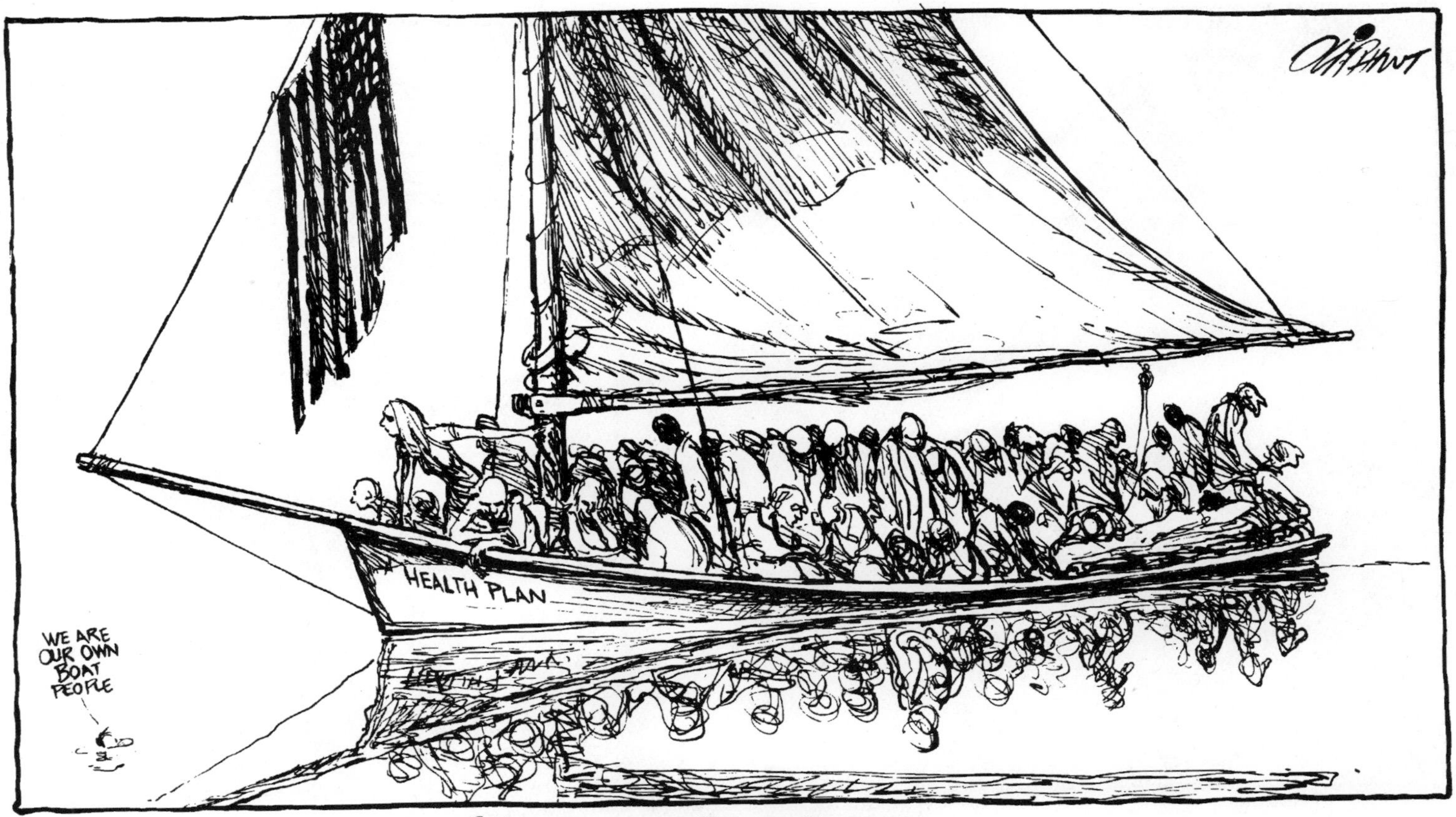

OLIPHANT
HEALTH PLAN
WE ARE OUR OWN BOAT PEOPLE

SPEAKING OF BOAT PEOPLE...

May 11, 1994

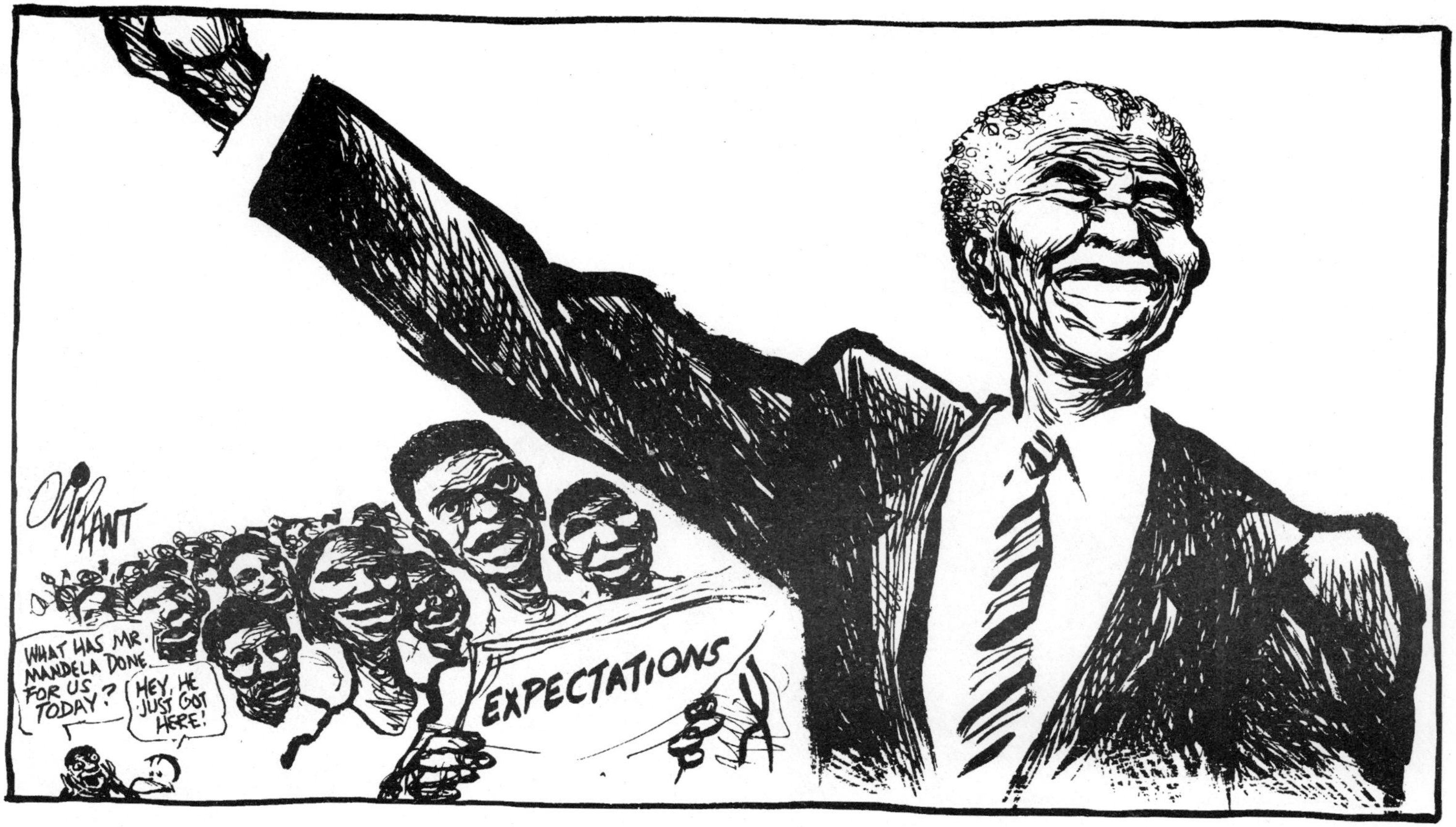
OLIPHANT
EXPECTATIONS
WHAT HAS MR. MANDELA DONE FOR US TODAY?
HEY, HE JUST GOT HERE!

May 12, 1994

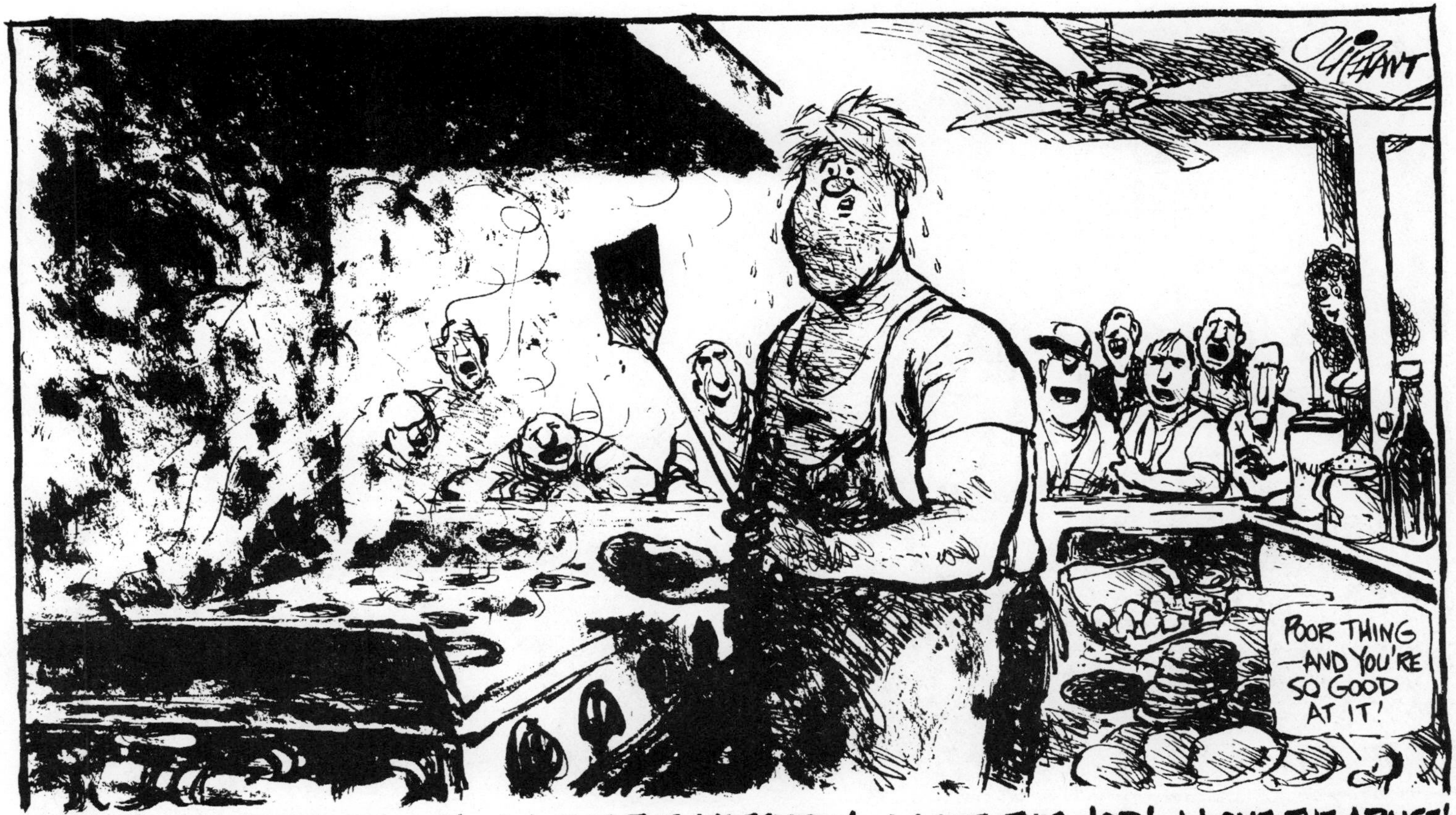
OLIPHANT
POOR THING —AND YOU'RE SO GOOD AT IT!

'HEAT? I LOVE THE HEAT! I LOVE THE KITCHEN! I LOVE THIS JOB! I LOVE THE ABUSE! I LOVE EVERYONE PICKING ON ME! I LOVE HOW I CAN NEVER DO ANYTHING RIGHT!..'

May 13, 1994

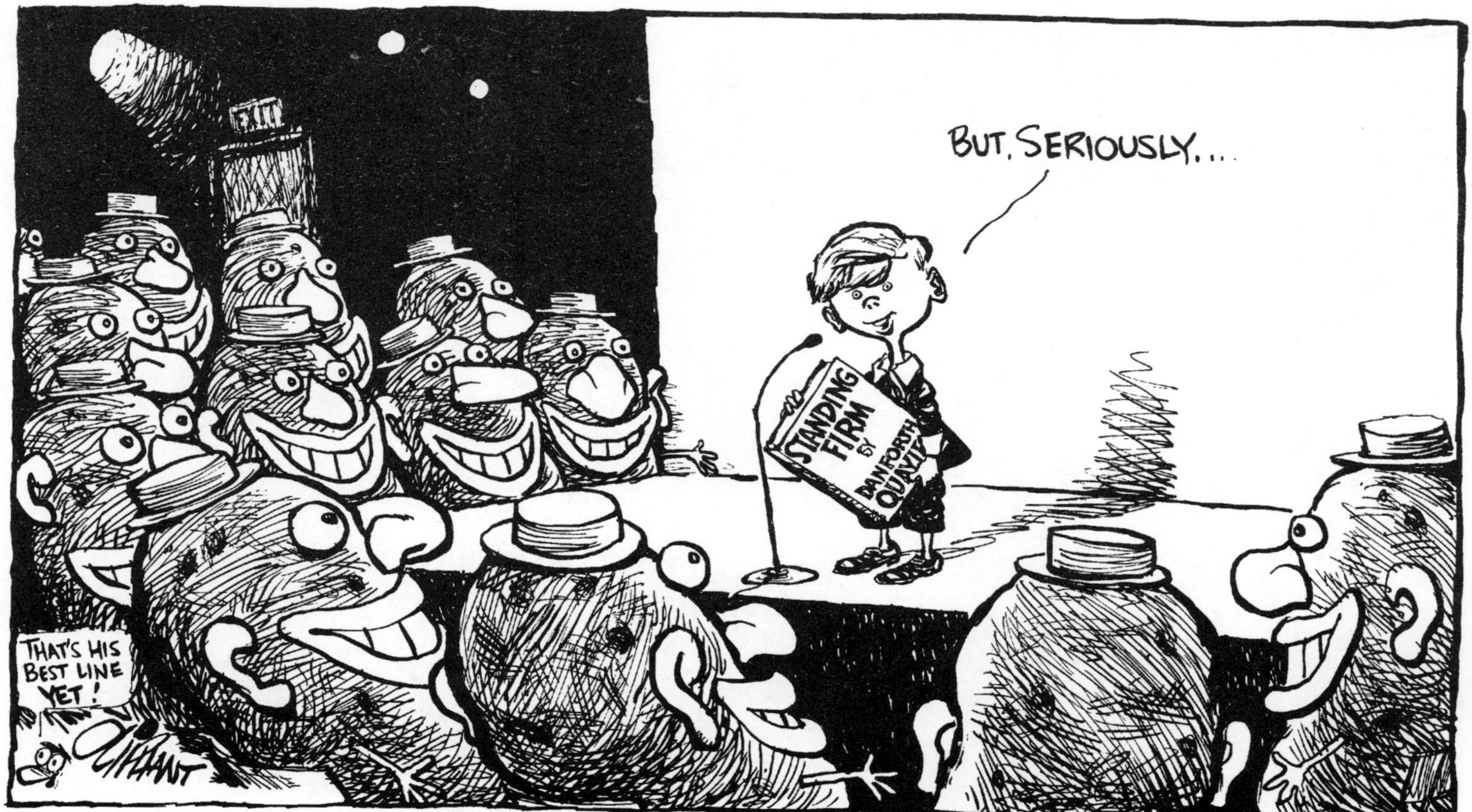
BUT, SERIOUSLY....
STANDING FIRM BY DANFORTH QUAYLE
THAT'S HIS BEST LINE YET!
OLIPHANT

NEW ACT AT THE POTATOE ROOM.

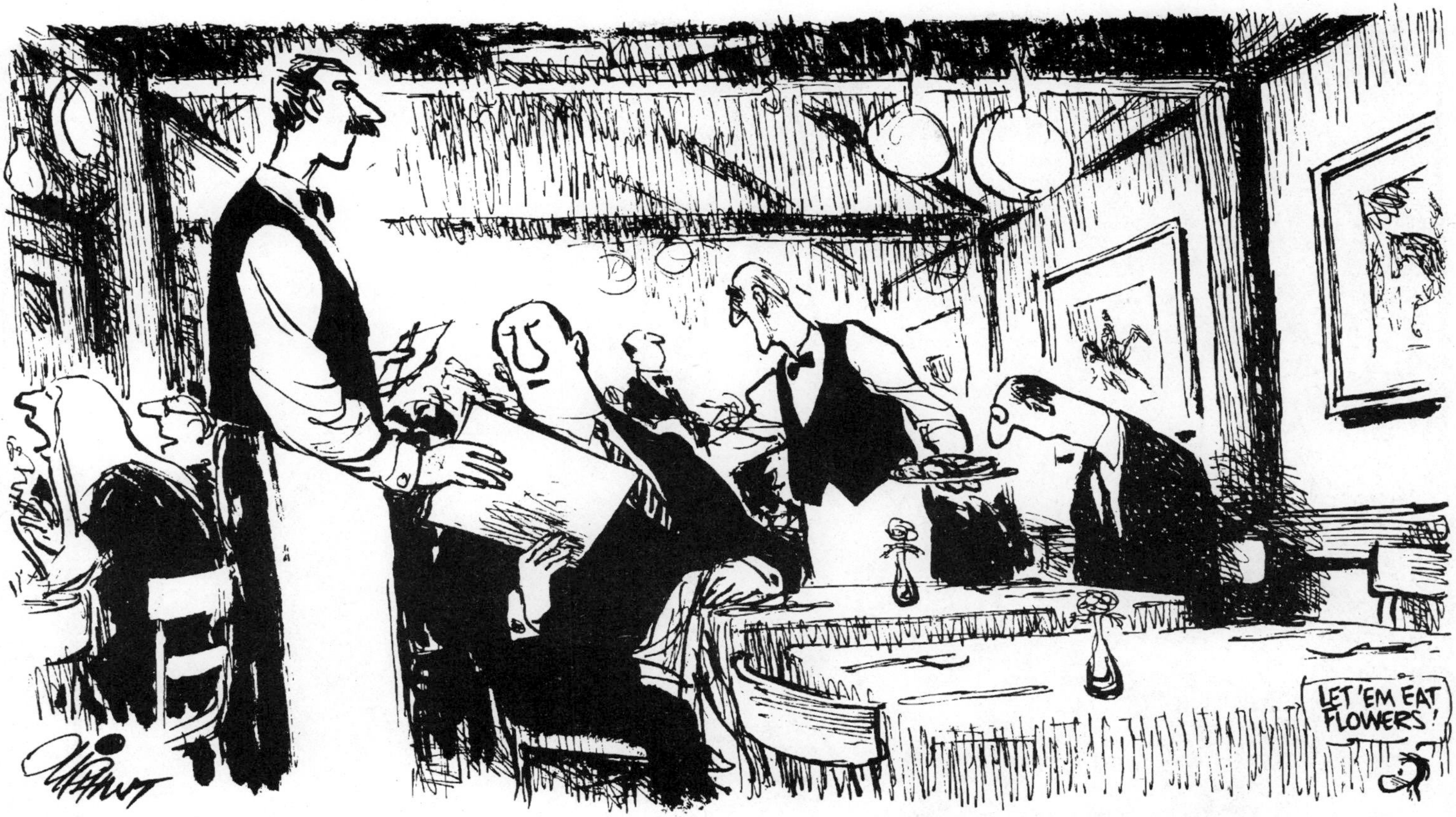
LET 'EM EAT FLOWERS!

'I'LL HAVE THE LOBBYIST'S CHATEAUBRIAND AND MY CONGRESSMAN BUDDY WILL EAT THE TABLE DECORATION . . . AND SEPARATE CHECKS, PLEASE.'

May 17, 1994

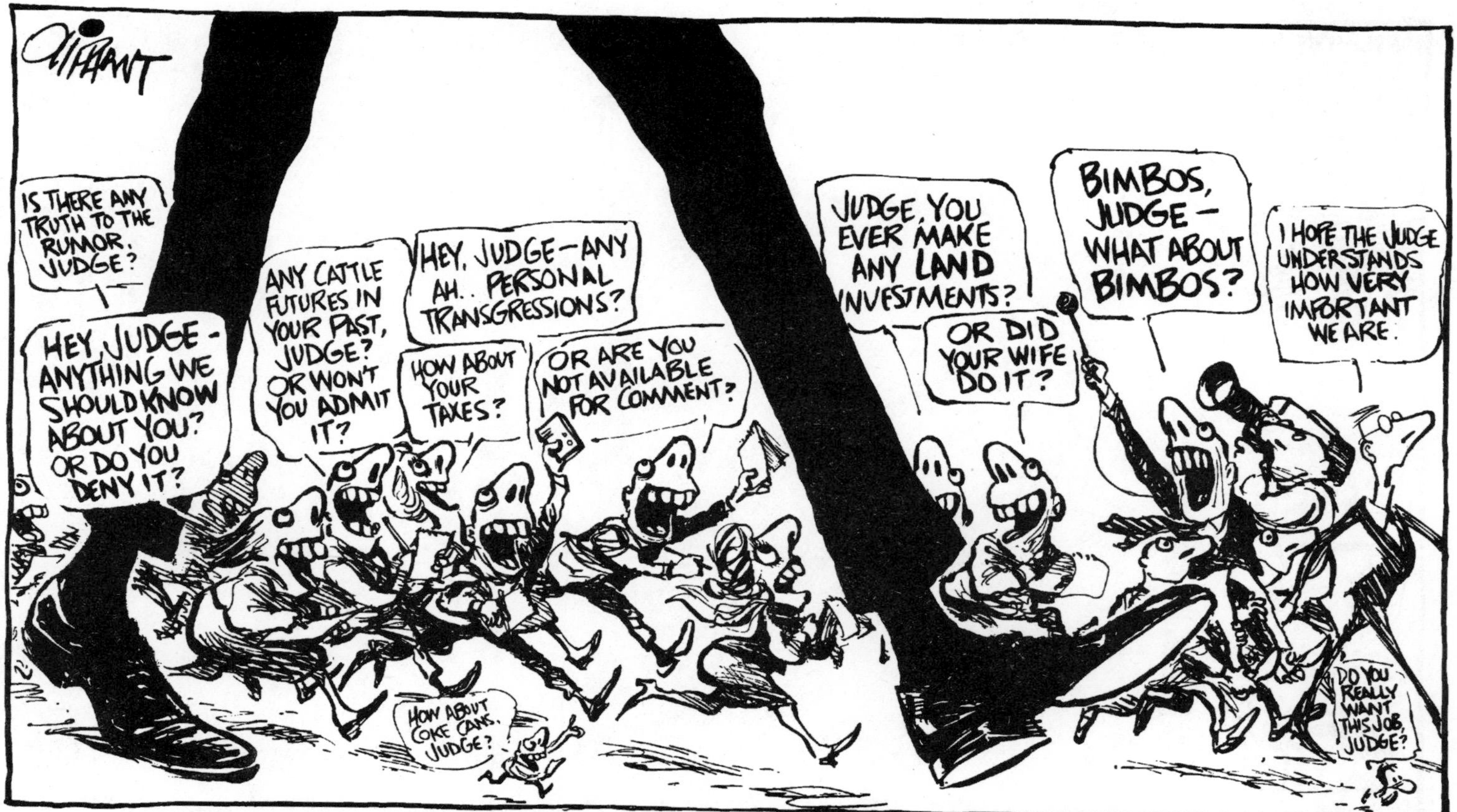
IS THERE ANY TRUTH TO THE RUMOR, JUDGE?
HEY, JUDGE - ANYTHING WE SHOULD KNOW ABOUT YOU? OR DO YOU DENY IT?
ANY CATTLE FUTURES IN YOUR PAST, JUDGE? OR WON'T YOU ADMIT IT?
HEY, JUDGE—ANY AH.. PERSONAL TRANSGRESSIONS?
HOW ABOUT YOUR TAXES?
OR ARE YOU NOT AVAILABLE FOR COMMENT?
HOW ABOUT COKE CANS, JUDGE?
JUDGE, YOU EVER MAKE ANY LAND INVESTMENTS?
OR DID YOUR WIFE DO IT?
BIMBOS, JUDGE - WHAT ABOUT BIMBOS?
I HOPE THE JUDGE UNDERSTANDS HOW VERY IMPORTANT WE ARE.
DO YOU REALLY WANT THIS JOB, JUDGE?

WELCOME, JUDGE BREYER... MEET THE WASHINGTON PRESS CORPS.

May 18, 1994

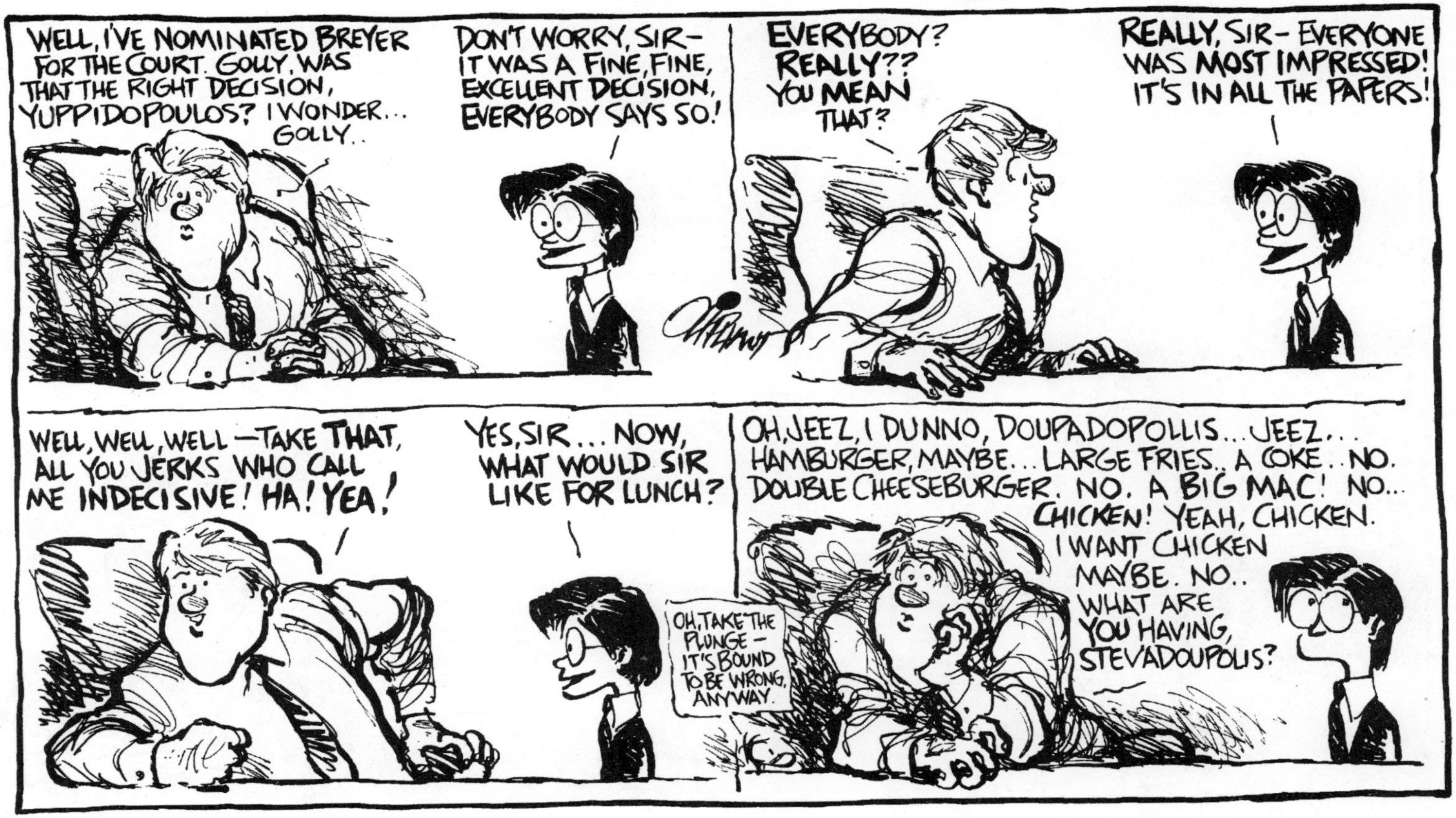
WELL, I'VE NOMINATED BREYER FOR THE COURT. GOLLY, WAS THAT THE RIGHT DECISION, YUPPIDOPOULOS? I WONDER... GOLLY..
DON'T WORRY, SIR- IT WAS A FINE, FINE, EXCELLENT DECISION, EVERYBODY SAYS SO!
EVERYBODY? REALLY?? YOU MEAN THAT?
REALLY, SIR- EVERYONE WAS MOST IMPRESSED! IT'S IN ALL THE PAPERS!
WELL, WELL, WELL—TAKE THAT, ALL YOU JERKS WHO CALL ME INDECISIVE! HA! YEA!
YES, SIR... NOW, WHAT WOULD SIR LIKE FOR LUNCH?
OH, TAKE THE PLUNGE— IT'S BOUND TO BE WRONG ANYWAY.
OH, JEEZ, I DUNNO, DOUPADOPOLLIS... JEEZ... HAMBURGER, MAYBE... LARGE FRIES.. A COKE.. NO. DOUBLE CHEESEBURGER. NO. A BIG MAC! NO... CHICKEN! YEAH, CHICKEN. I WANT CHICKEN MAYBE. NO.. WHAT ARE YOU HAVING, STEVADOUPOLIS?

May 19, 1994

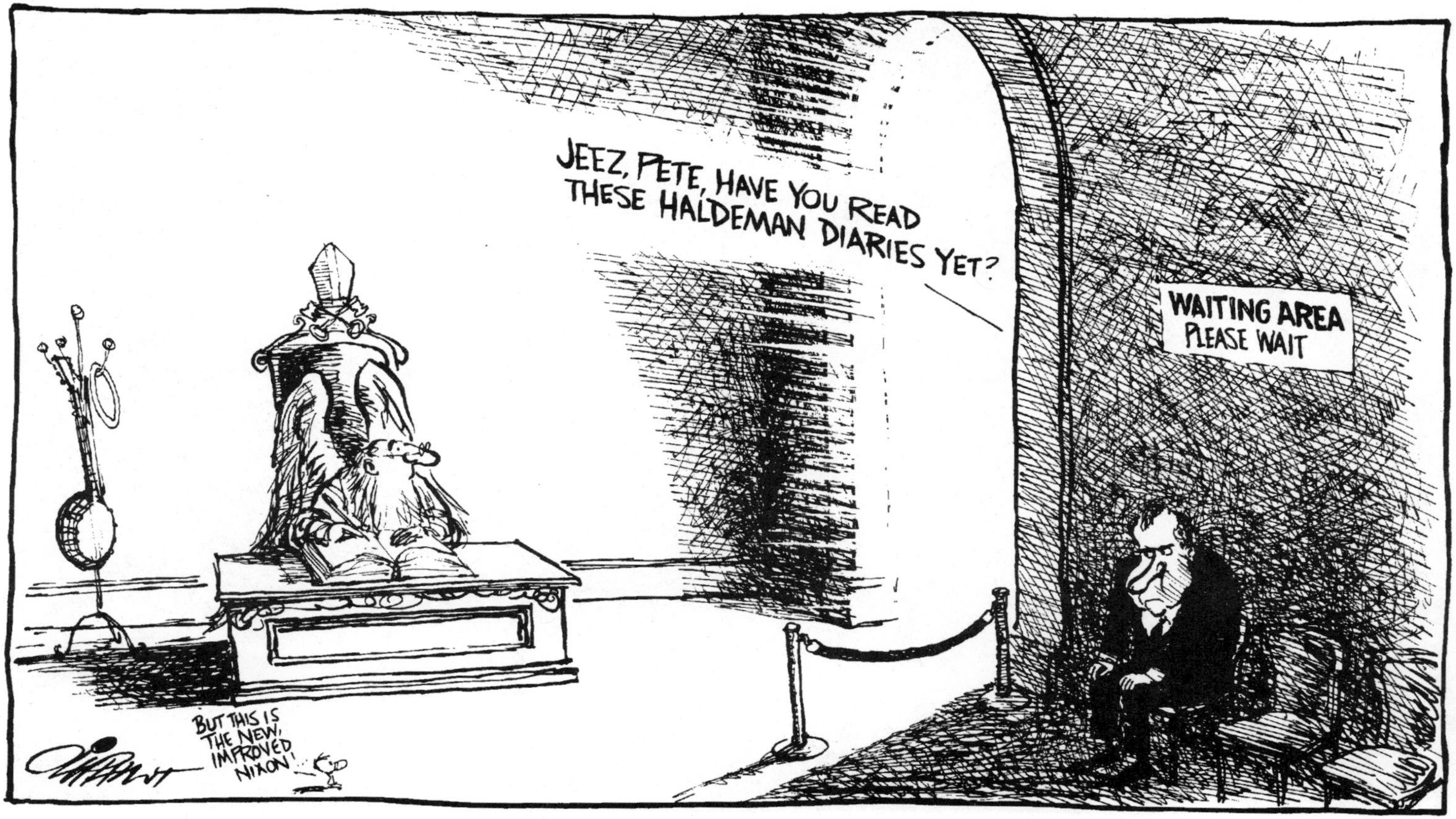
JEEZ, PETE, HAVE YOU READ THESE HALDEMAN DIARIES YET?
WAITING AREA
PLEASE WAIT
BUT THIS IS THE NEW, IMPROVED NIXON!

May 20, 1994

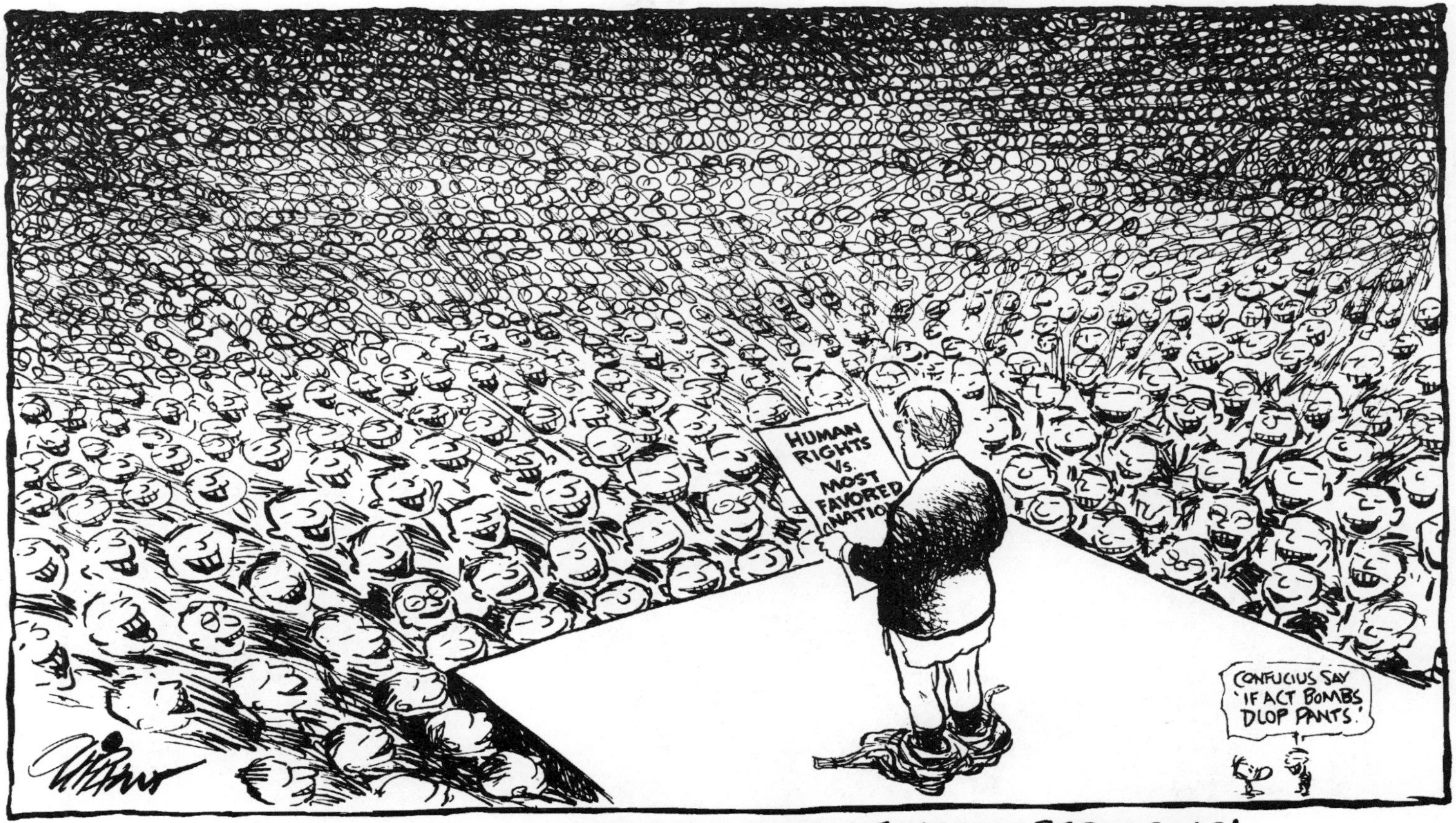
HUMAN RIGHTS Vs. MOST FAVORED NATION
CONFUCIUS SAY 'IF ACT BOMBS DLOP PANTS.'

'WHY DO I GET THE FEELING NOBODY TAKES ME SERIOUSLY?'

May 25, 1994

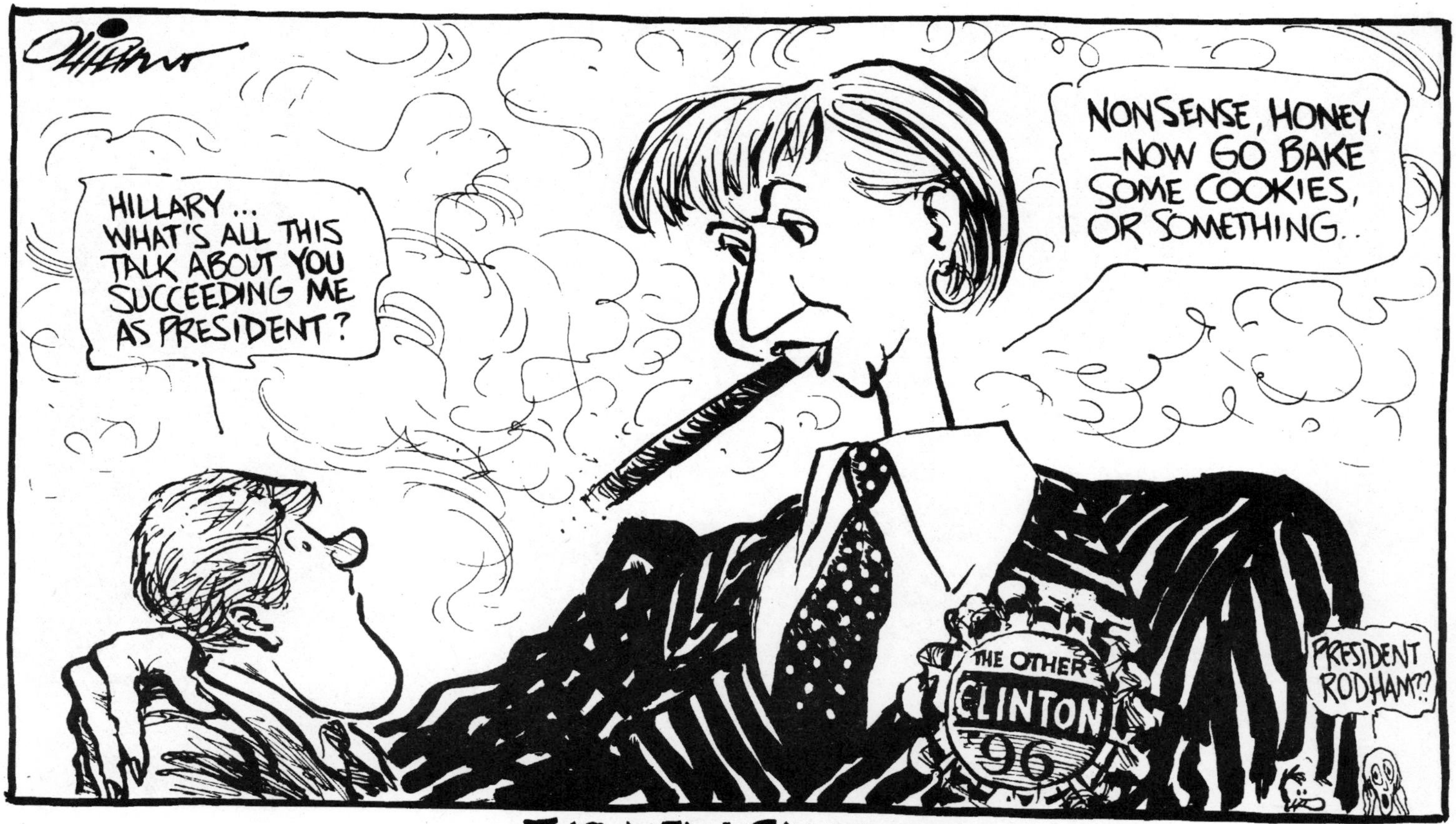

HILLARY... WHAT'S ALL THIS TALK ABOUT YOU SUCCEEDING ME AS PRESIDENT?
NONSENSE, HONEY. —NOW GO BAKE SOME COOKIES, OR SOMETHING..
THE OTHER CLINTON '96
PRESIDENT RODHAM??

THE NEW CAMELOT.

May 26, 1994

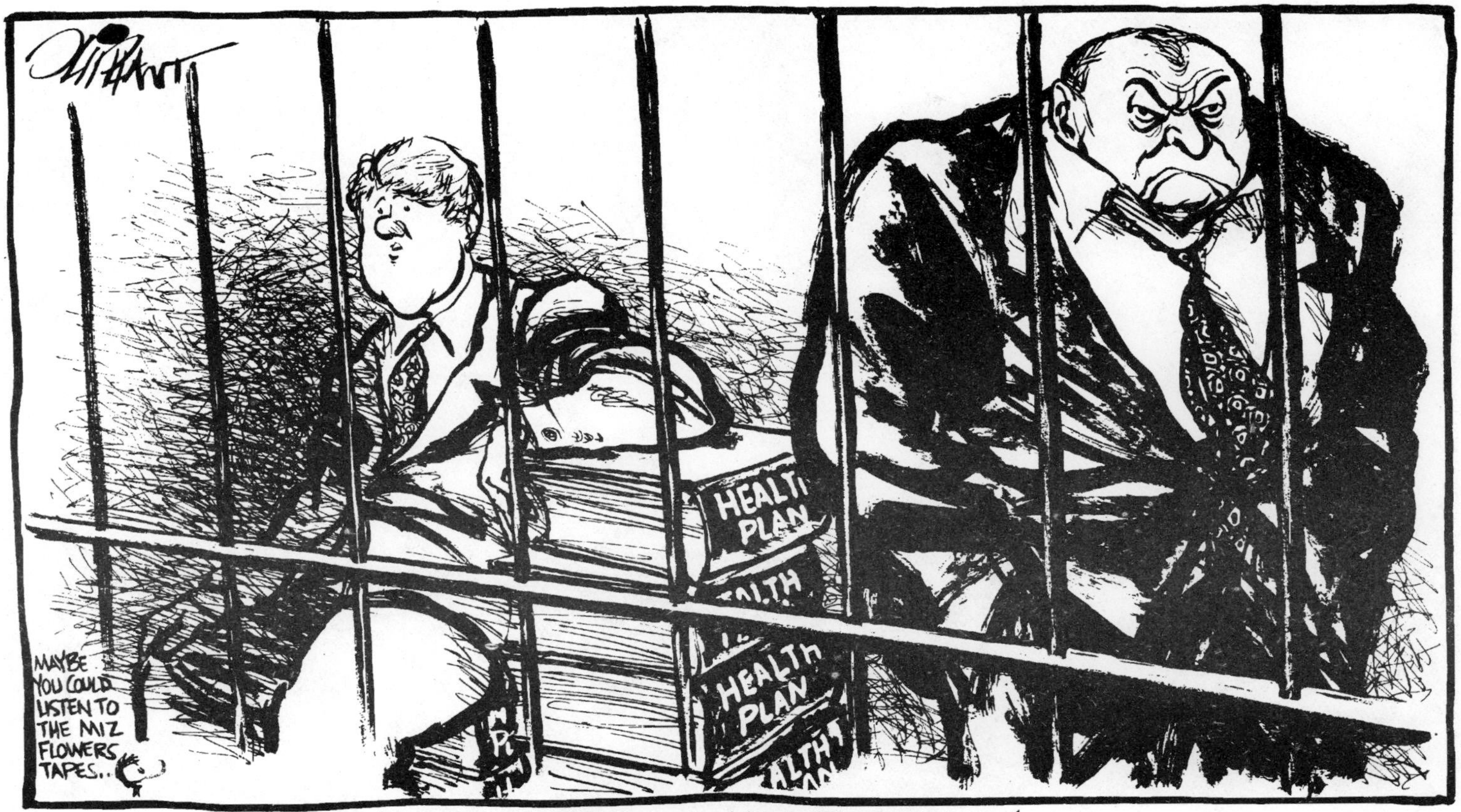
HEALTH PLAN
HEALTH PLAN
MAYBE YOU COULD LISTEN TO THE MIZ FLOWERS TAPES..

'WELL, HERE WE ARE, ROSTY...'

May 27, 1994

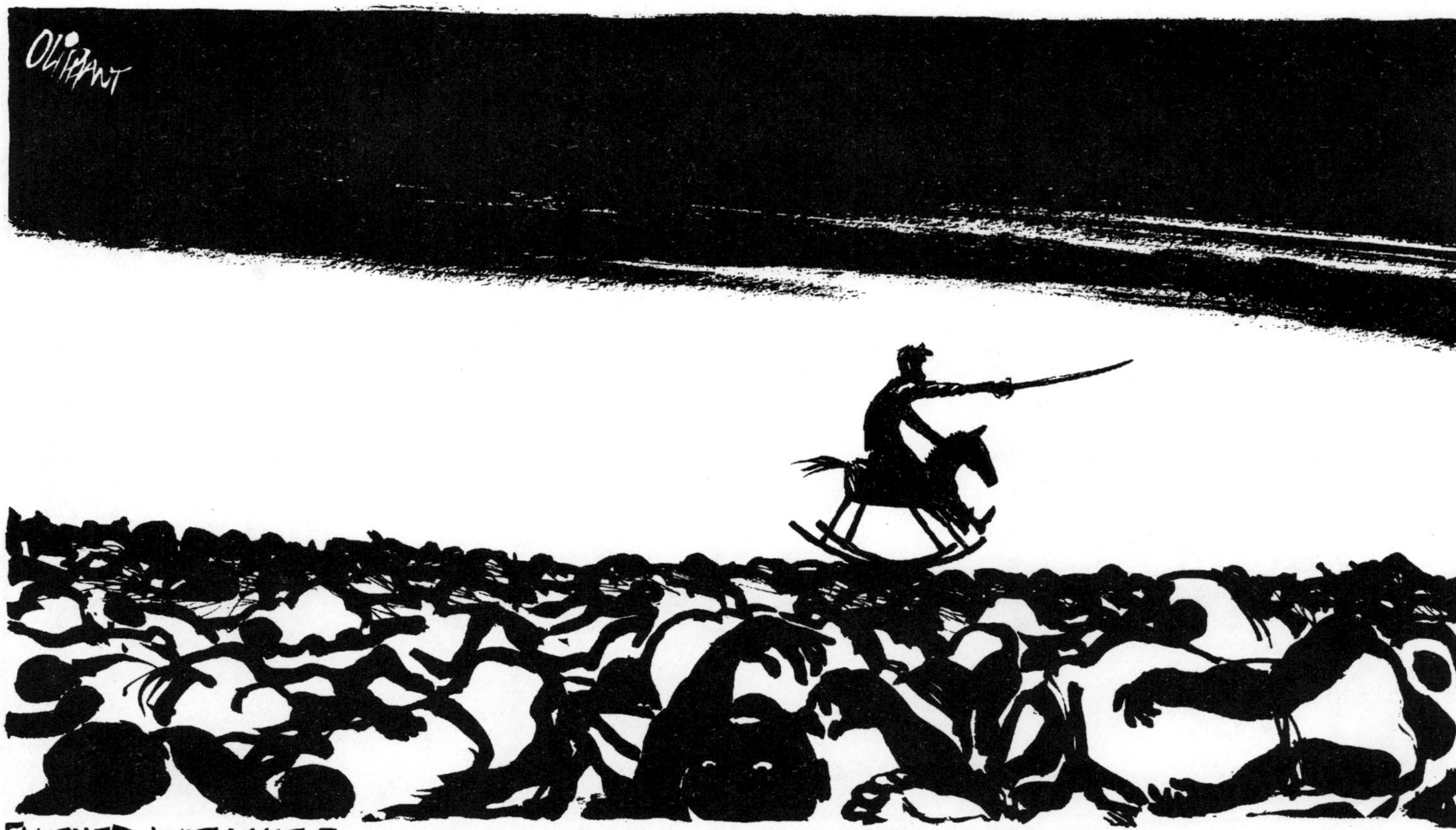
OLIPHANT

FLUSHED WITH HIS SUCCESSES IN SOMALIA AND BOSNIA, GENERAL BOUTROS-GHALI LEADS HIS VICTORIOUS U.N. TROOPS IN THE RELIEF OF RWANDA.

May 27, 1994

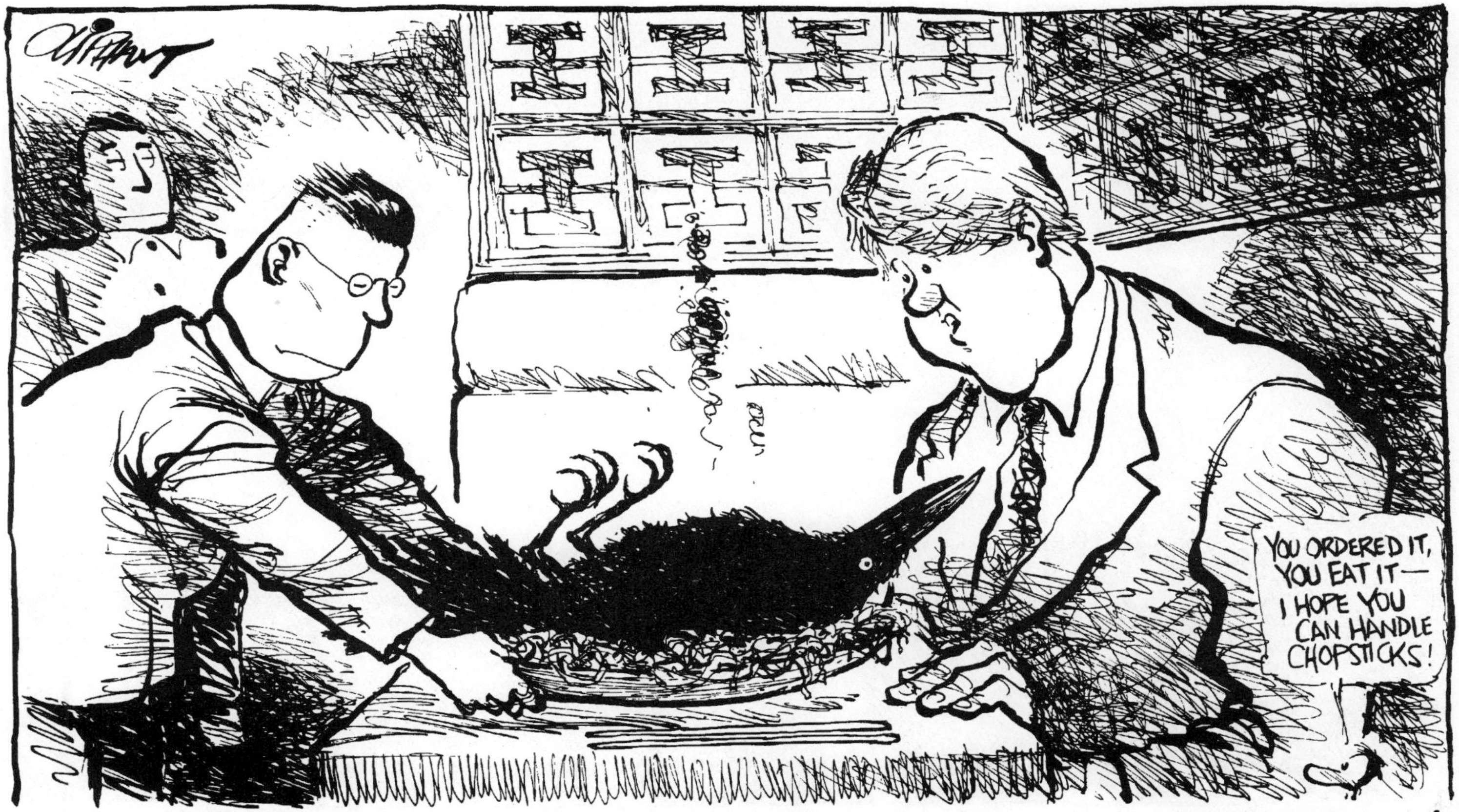
YOU ORDERED IT, YOU EAT IT— I HOPE YOU CAN HANDLE CHOPSTICKS!

'CRISPY CROW WITH MOST FAVORED NOODLES—GOD, I LOVE CHINESE FOOD!'

June 1, 1994

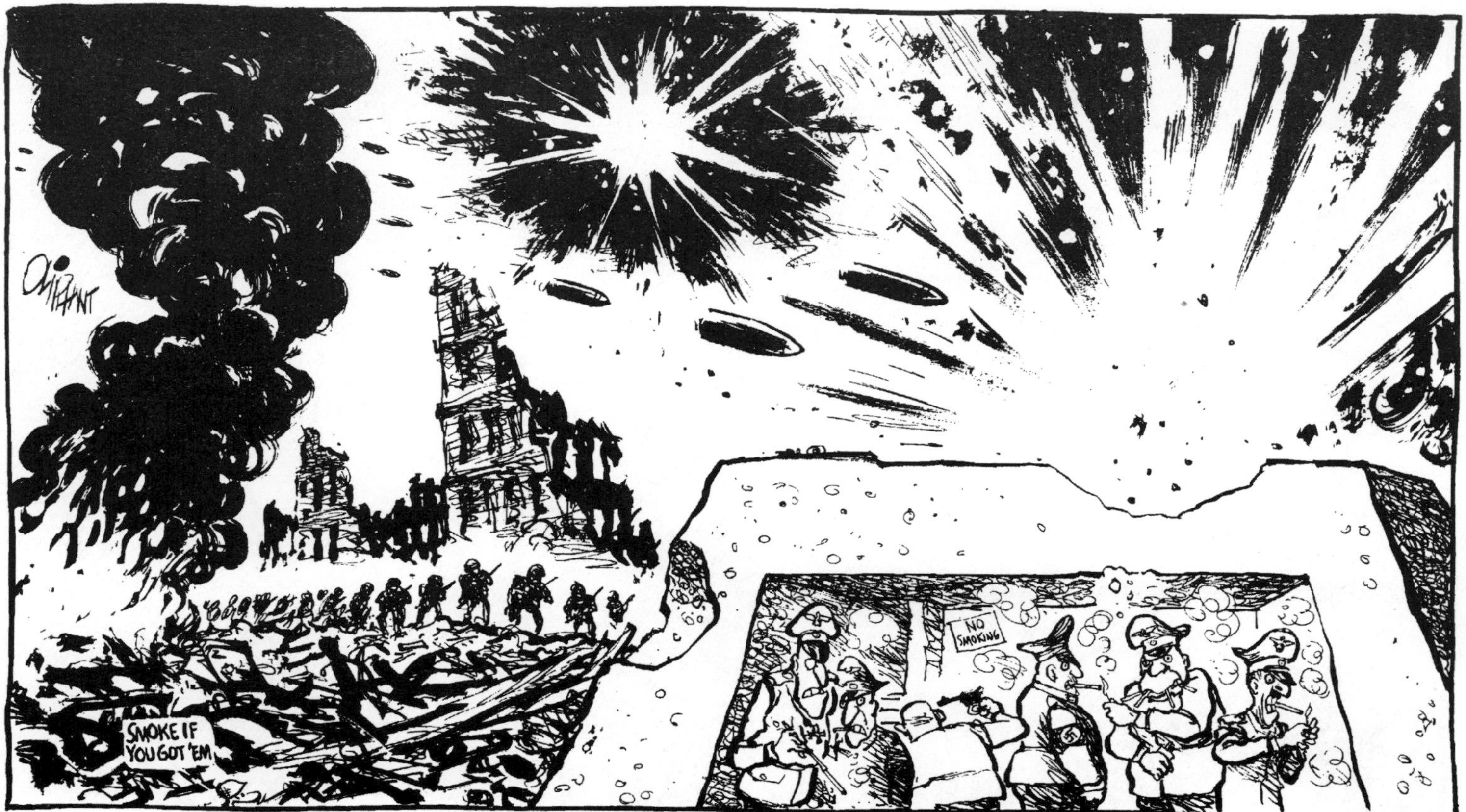
OLIPHANT
NO SMOKING
SMOKE IF YOU GOT 'EM

IN THE TOBACCO INDUSTRY BUNKER.

June 2, 1994

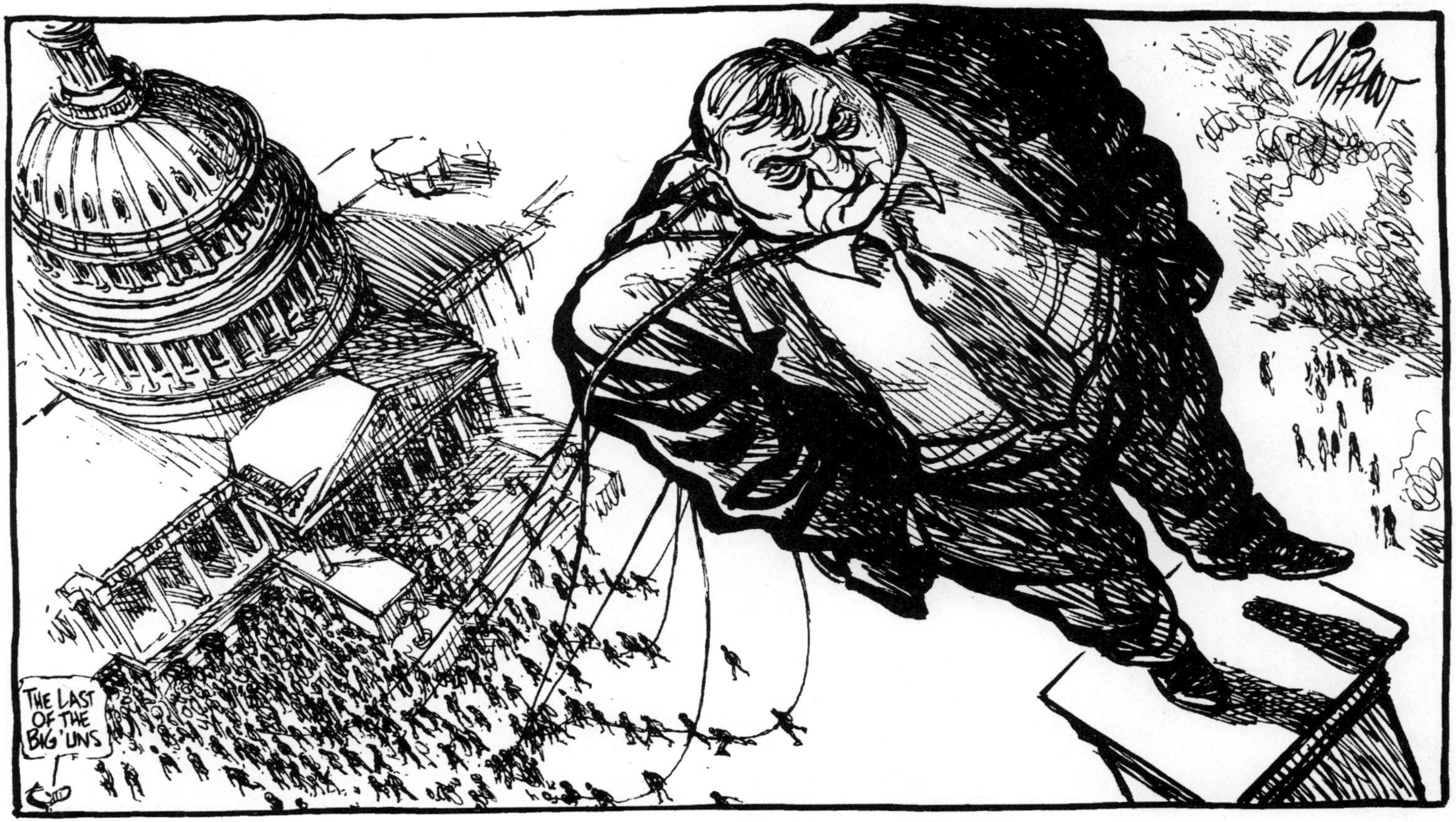
THE LAST OF THE BIG 'UNS

June 3, 1994

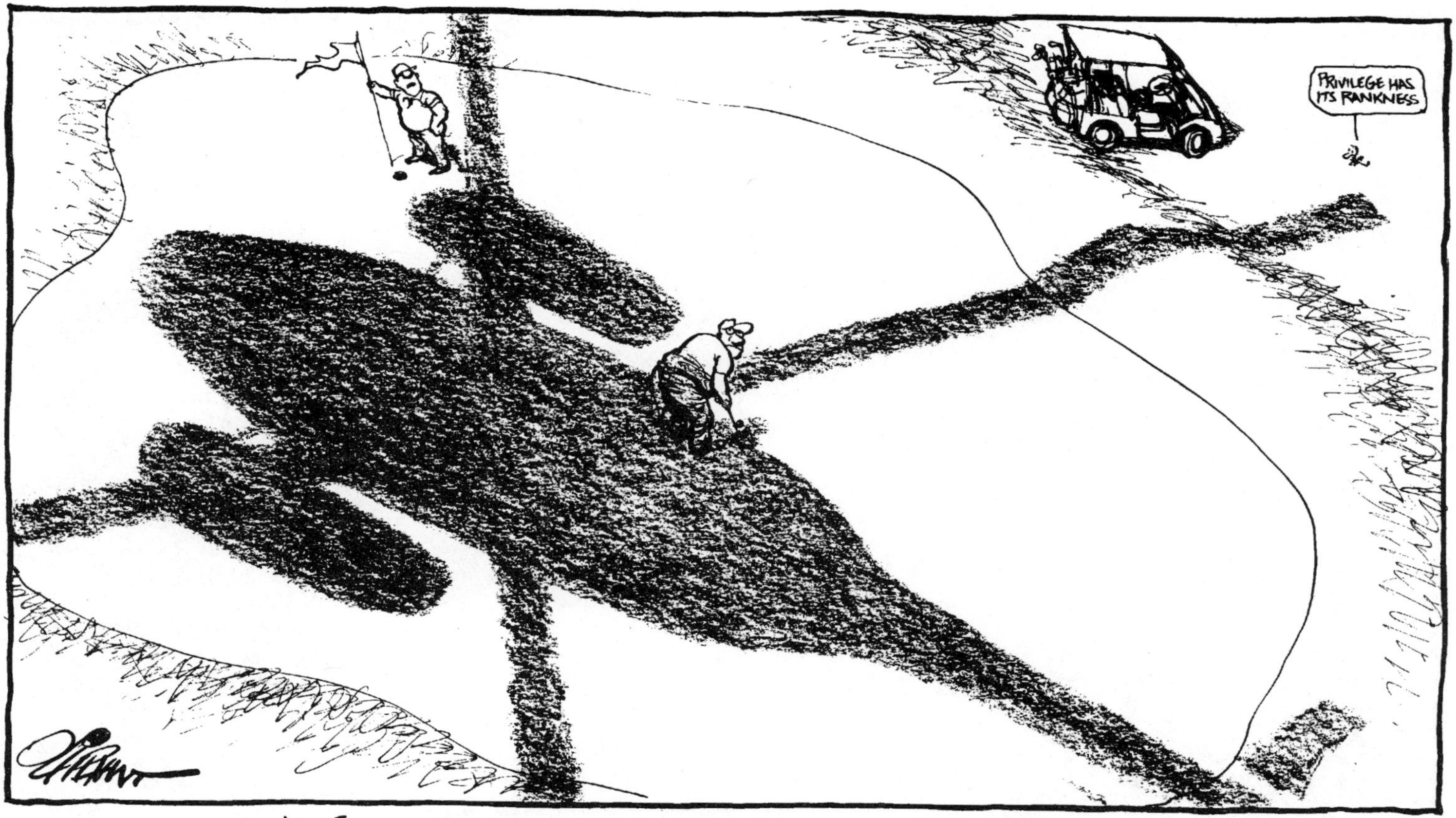
PRIVILEGE HAS
ITS RANKNESS

'I GUESS THE WHITE HOUSE CROWD WANTS TO PLAY THROUGH.'

June 5, 1994

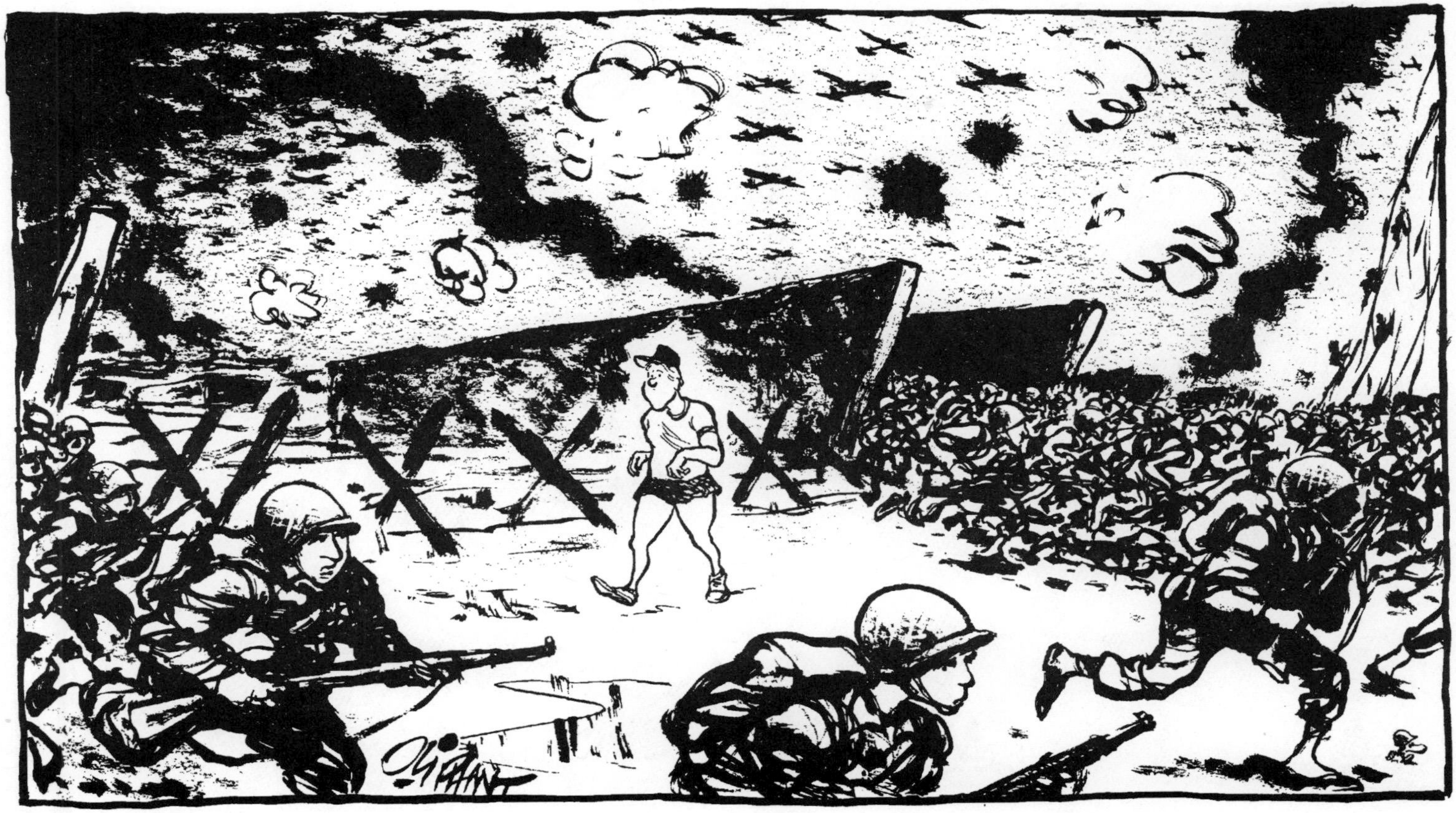
OLIPHANT

June 8, 1994

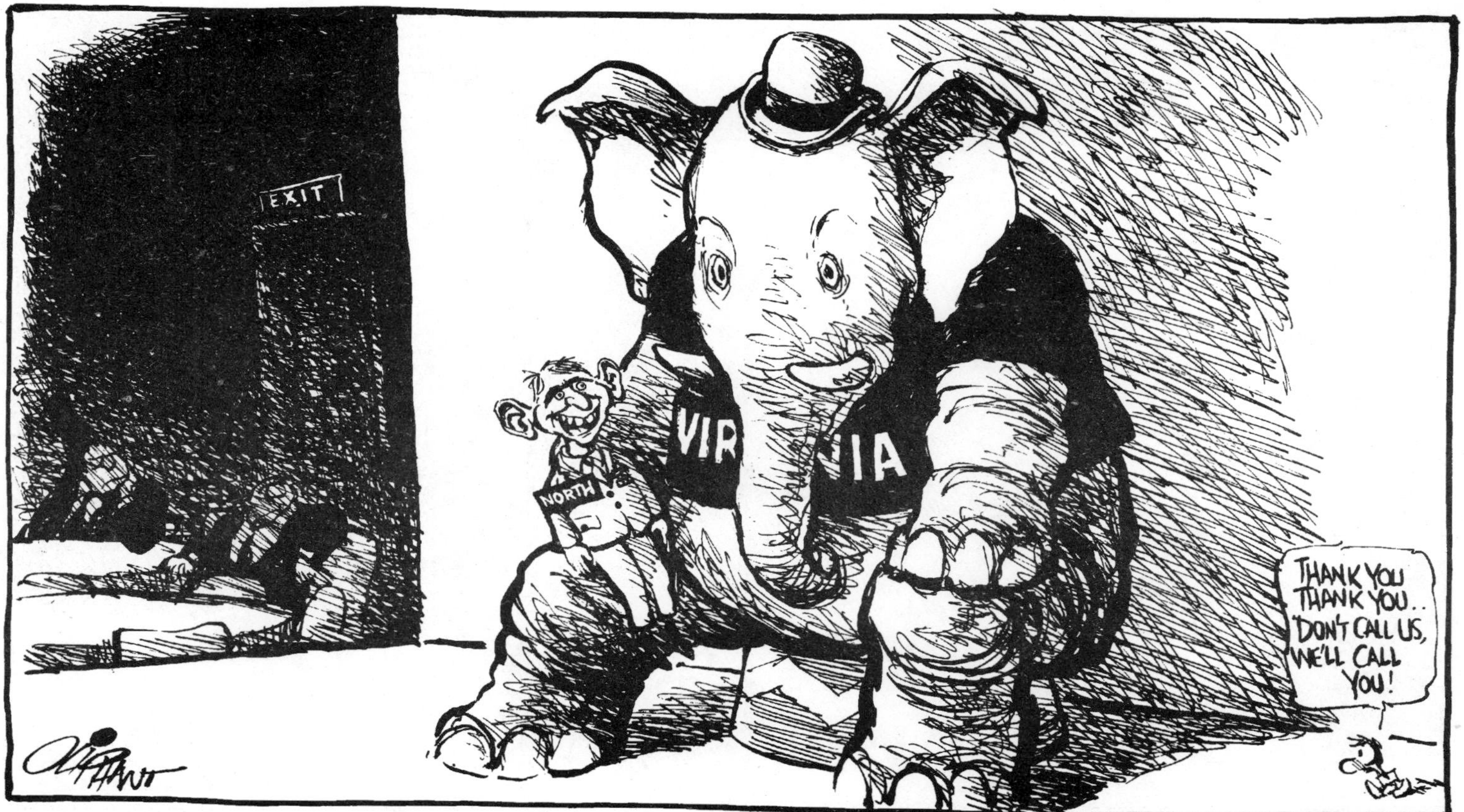
EXIT
VIR NIA
NORTH
THANK YOU THANK YOU.. 'DON'T CALL US, WE'LL CALL YOU!

THANKS FOR AUDITIONING, ANYWAY.

June 9, 1994

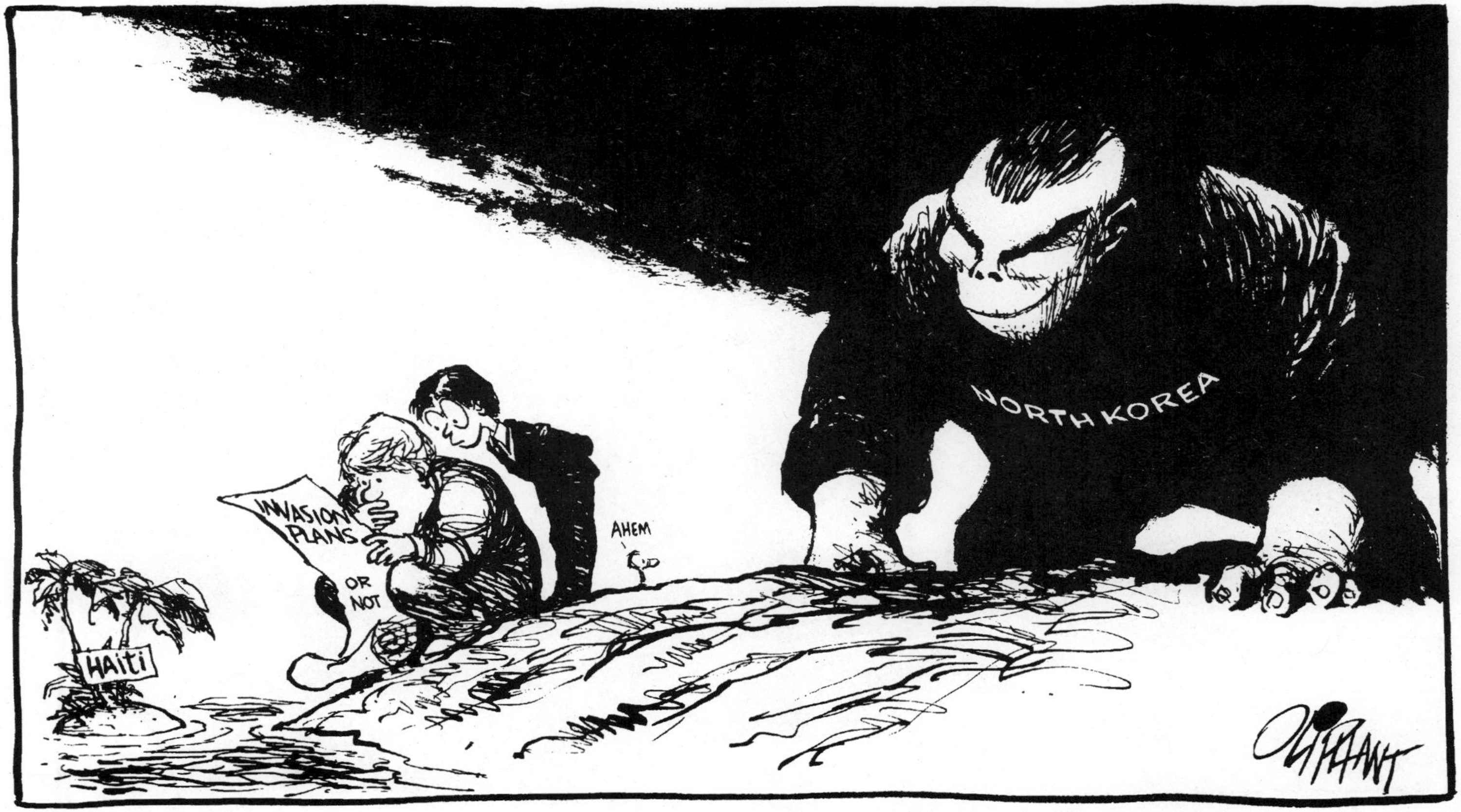
INVASION PLANS
OR NOT
AHEM
NORTH KOREA
HAITI
OLIPHANT

June 10, 1994

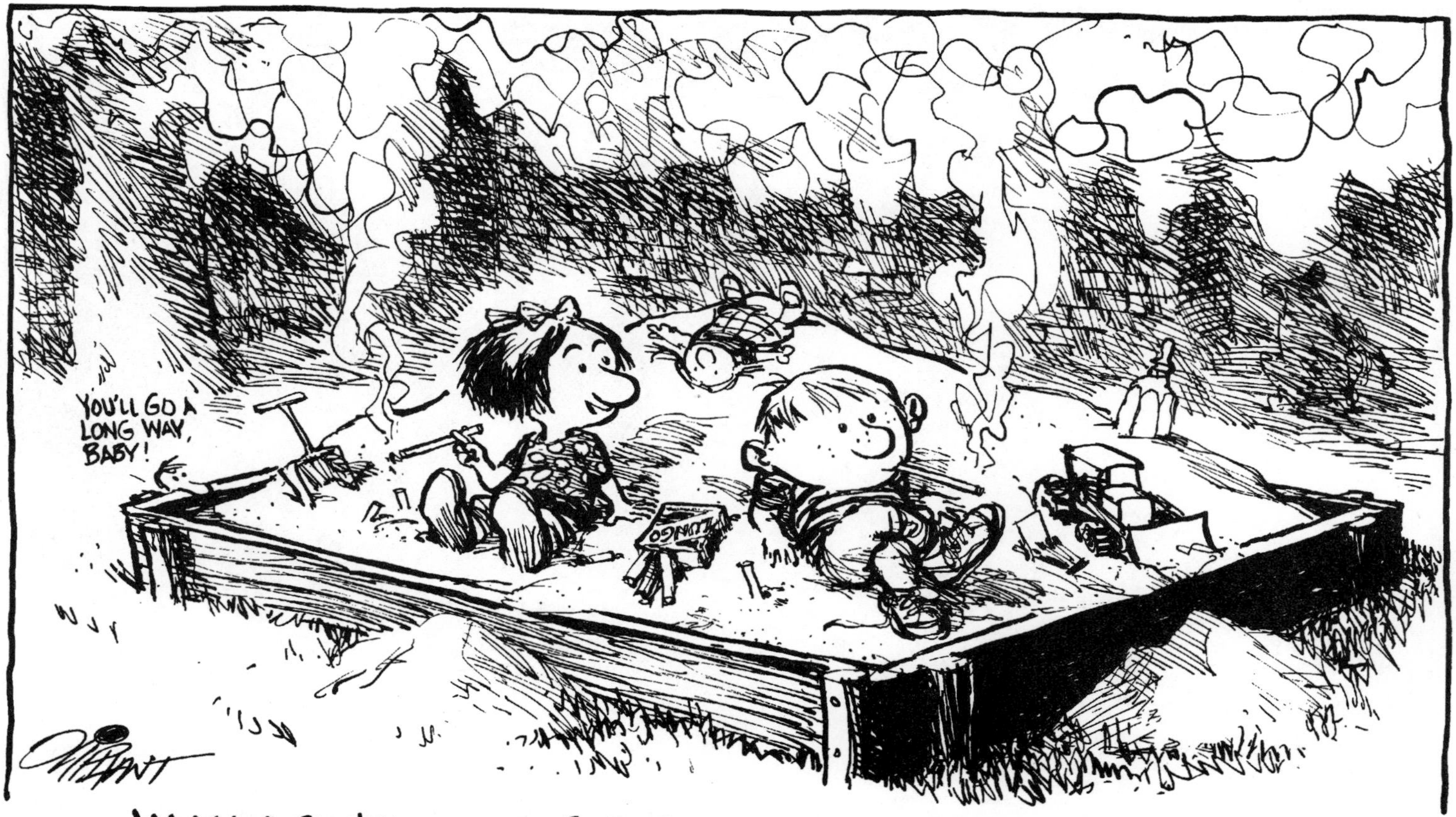
YOU'LL GO A
LONG WAY,
BABY!

'MAN, I CAN'T WAIT TO GET TO COLLEGE AND START DRINKING.'

June 11, 1994

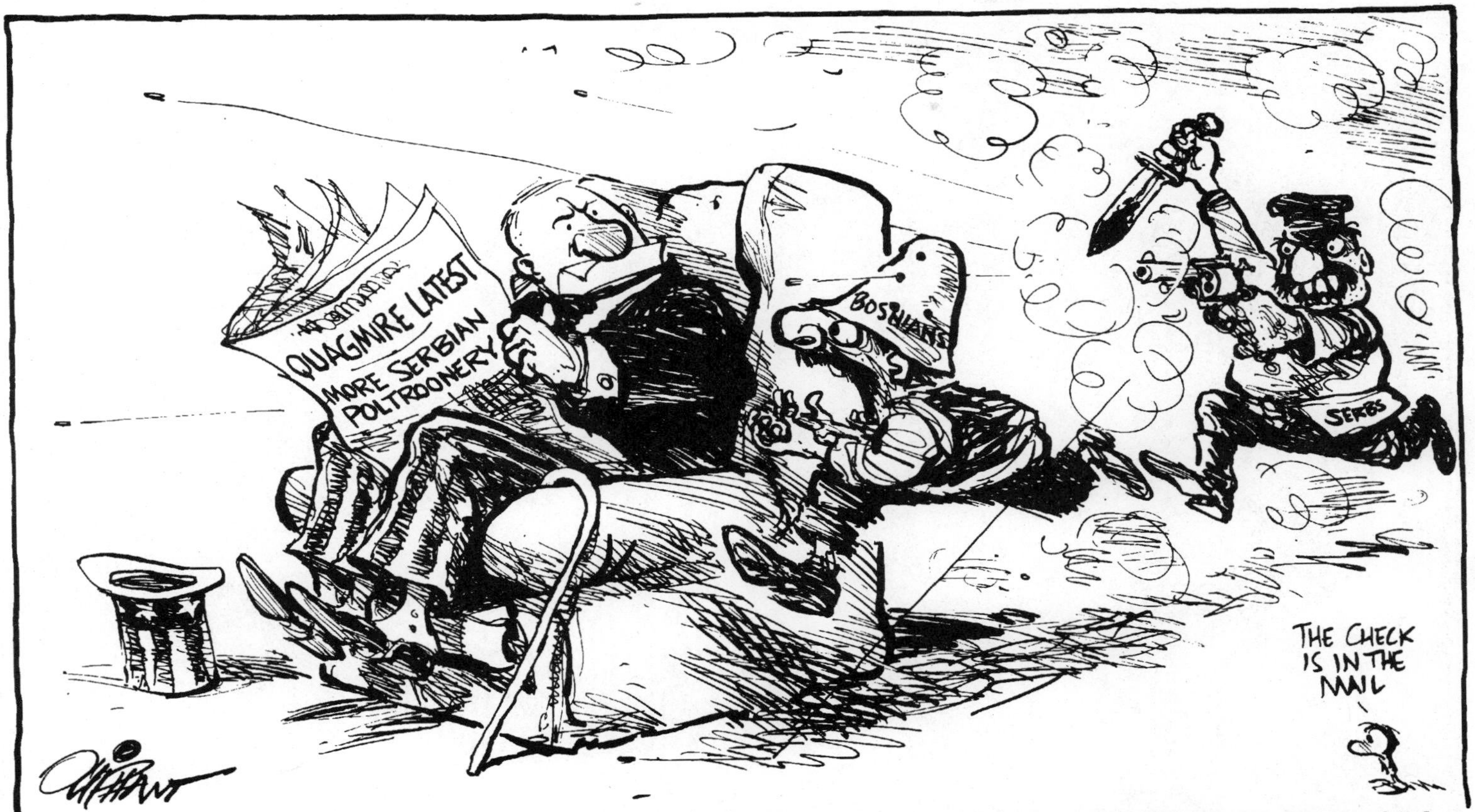
QUAGMIRE LATEST
MORE SERBIAN POLTROONERY
BOSNIANS
SERBS
THE CHECK IS IN THE MAIL

'A GUN! I PROMISE YOU WON'T BE INVOLVED, HONEST—GIMME A GUN!!'

June 15, 1994

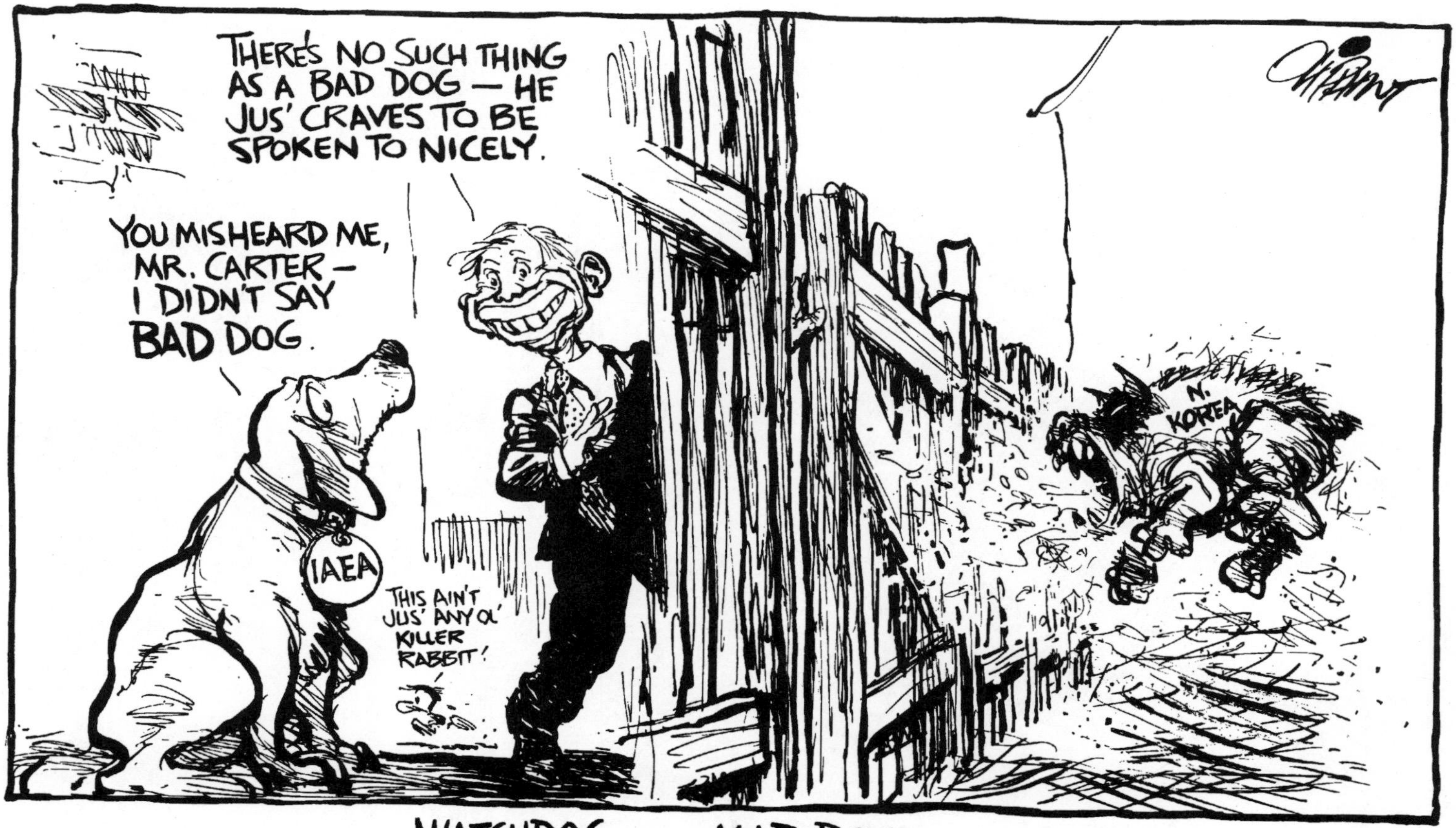
THERE'S NO SUCH THING AS A BAD DOG — HE JUS' CRAVES TO BE SPOKEN TO NICELY.
YOU MISHEARD ME, MR. CARTER — I DIDN'T SAY BAD DOG.
IAEA
THIS AIN'T JUS' ANY OL' KILLER RABBIT!
N. KOREA

WATCHDOG . . . MAD DOG.

June 16, 1994

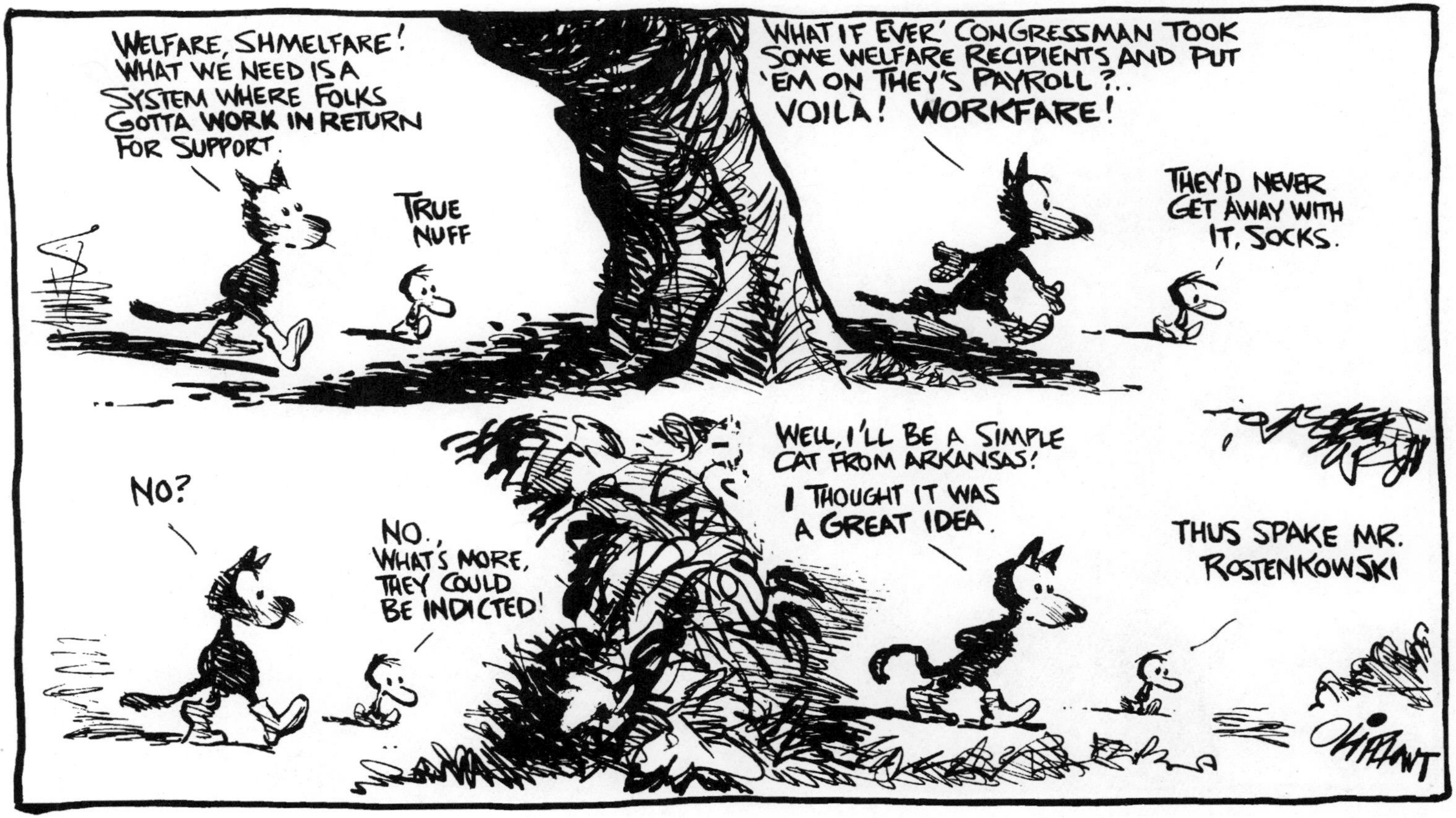
WELFARE, SHMELFARE! WHAT WE NEED IS A SYSTEM WHERE FOLKS GOTTA WORK IN RETURN FOR SUPPORT.
TRUE NUFF
WHAT IF EVER' CONGRESSMAN TOOK SOME WELFARE RECIPIENTS AND PUT 'EM ON THEY'S PAYROLL?.. VOILÀ! WORKFARE!
THEY'D NEVER GET AWAY WITH IT, SOCKS.
NO?
NO., WHAT'S MORE, THEY COULD BE INDICTED!
WELL, I'LL BE A SIMPLE CAT FROM ARKANSAS! I THOUGHT IT WAS A GREAT IDEA.
THUS SPAKE MR. ROSTENKOWSKI
OLIPHANT

June 17, 1994

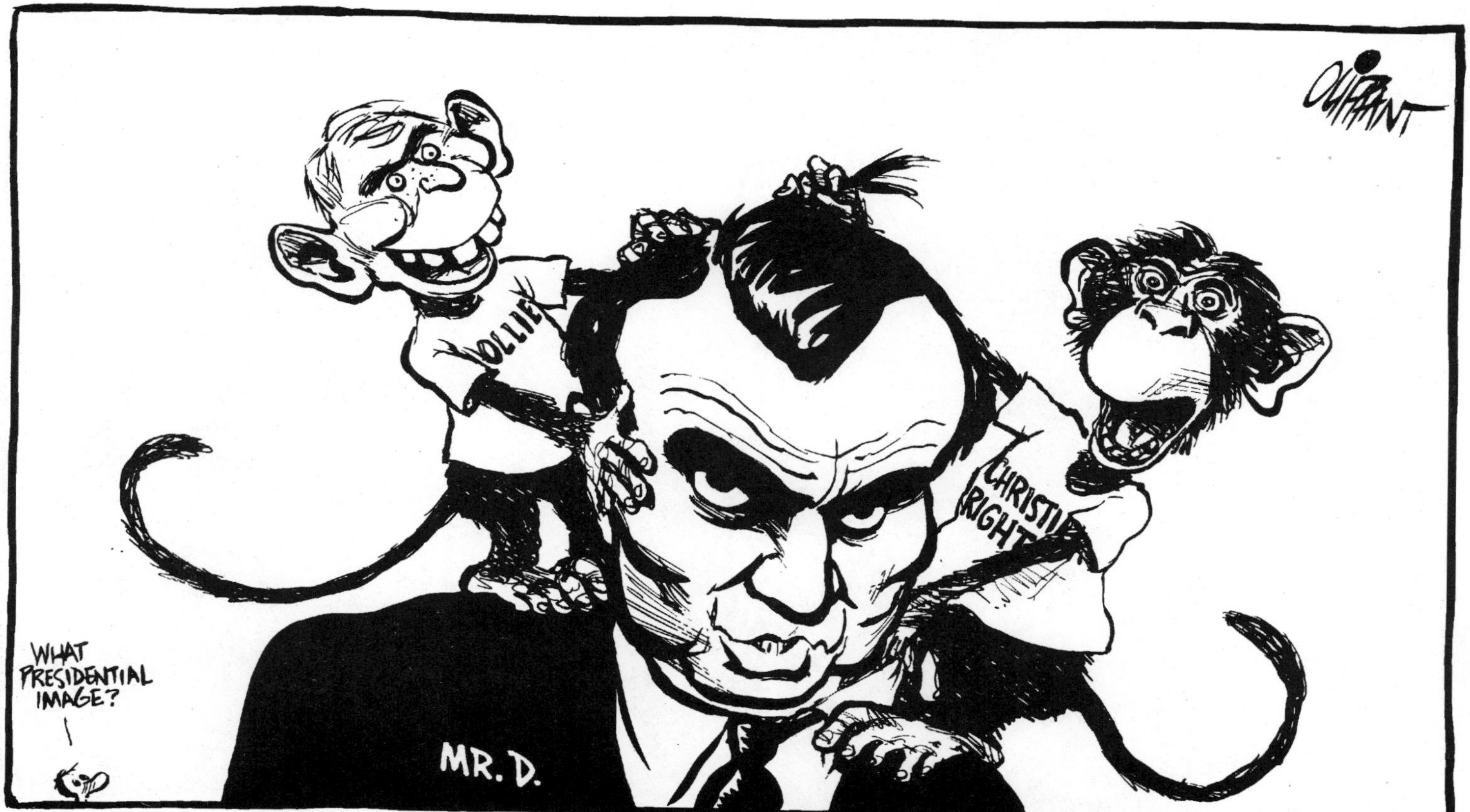
OLLIE
CHRISTI
RIGHT
WHAT PRESIDENTIAL IMAGE?
MR. D.

'WHAT MONKEYS?'

June 18, 1994

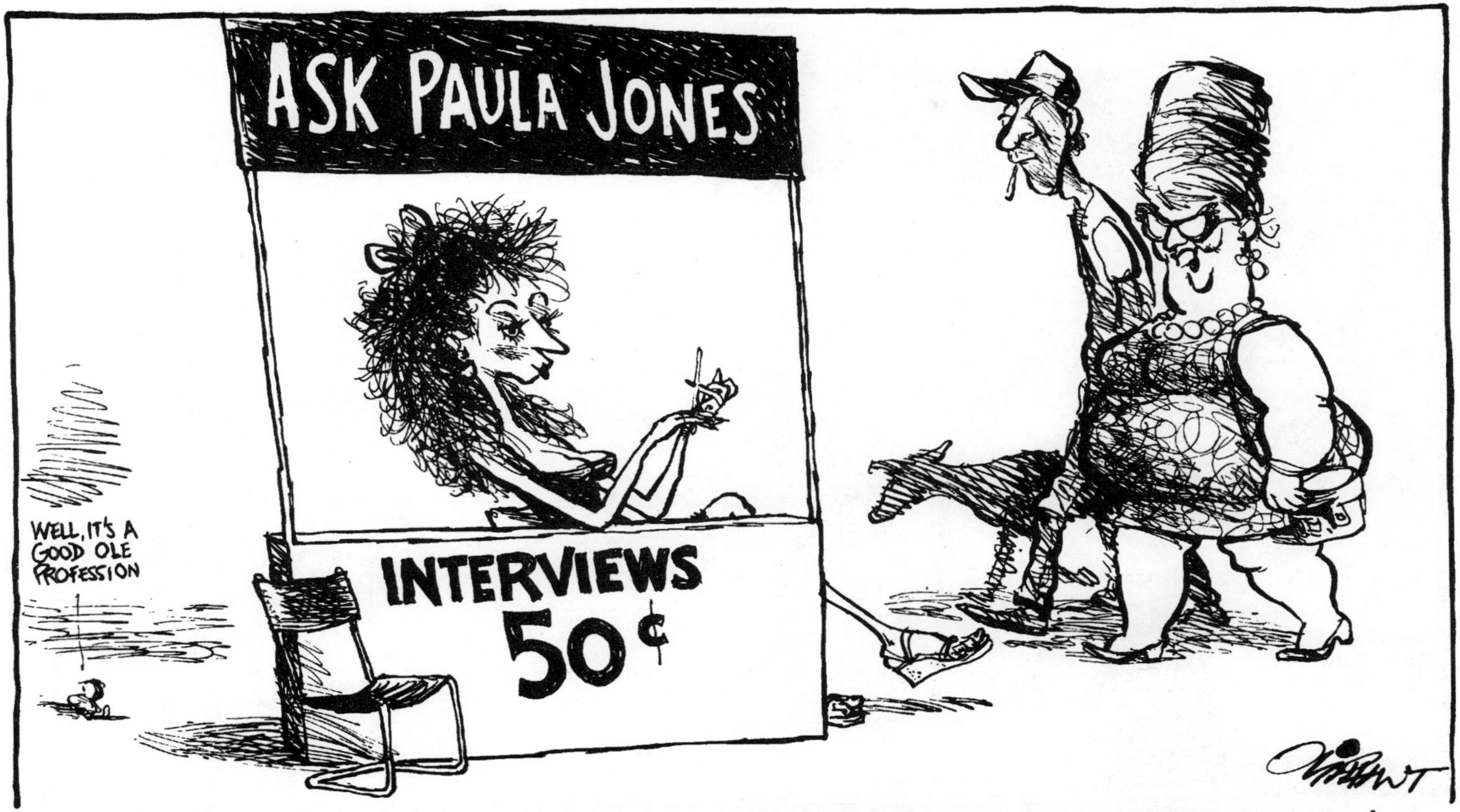
ASK PAULA JONES
INTERVIEWS
50¢
WELL, IT'S A GOOD OLE PROFESSION

'I ALWAYS KNEW PAULA WAS GONNA MAKE IT BIG ONE DAY AS A PROFESSIONAL WOMAN.'

June 22, 1994

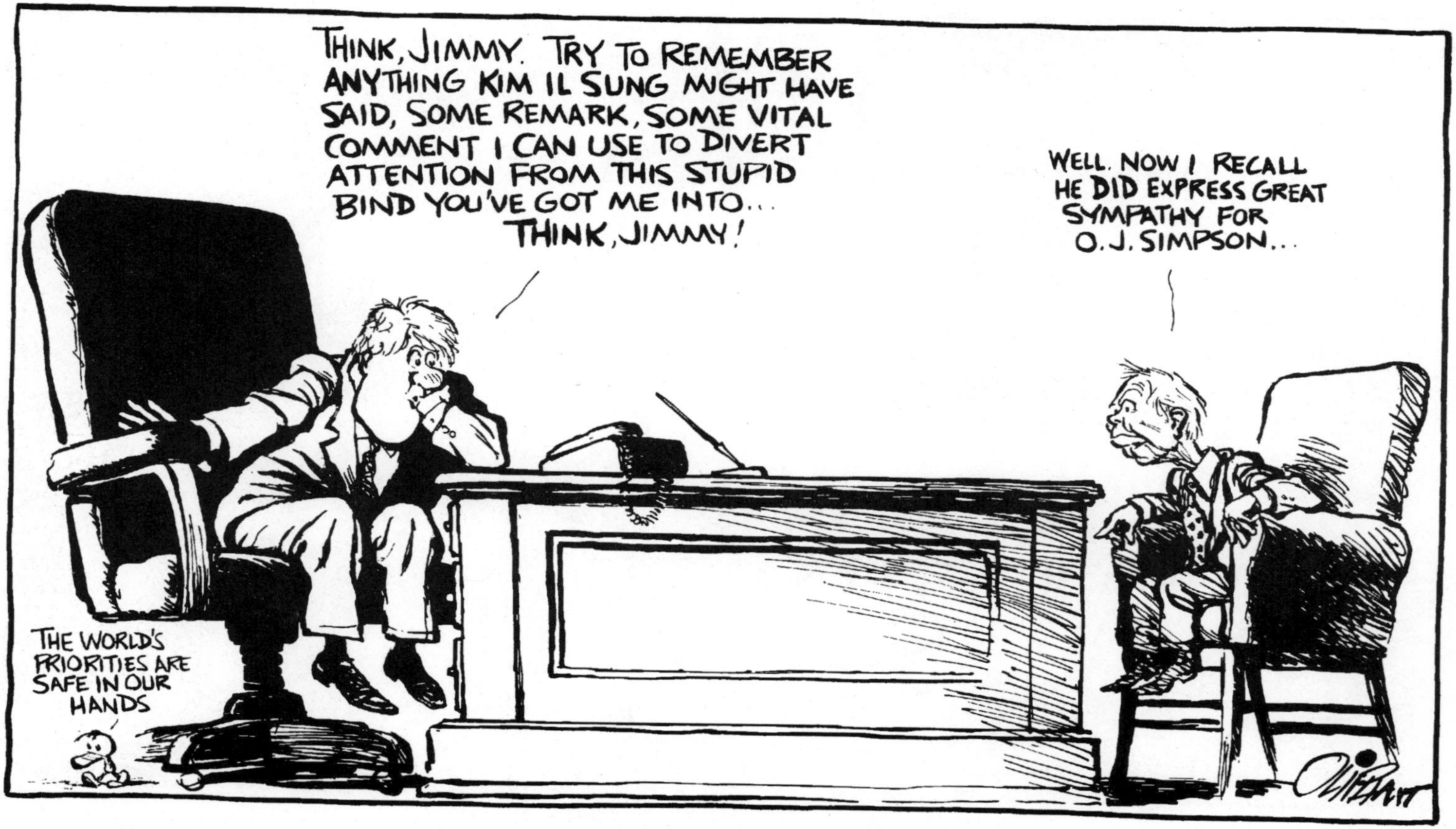
THINK, JIMMY. TRY TO REMEMBER ANYTHING KIM IL SUNG MIGHT HAVE SAID, SOME REMARK, SOME VITAL COMMENT I CAN USE TO DIVERT ATTENTION FROM THIS STUPID BIND YOU'VE GOT ME INTO... THINK, JIMMY!
WELL, NOW I RECALL HE DID EXPRESS GREAT SYMPATHY FOR O.J. SIMPSON...
THE WORLD'S PRIORITIES ARE SAFE IN OUR HANDS
OLIPHANT

June 23, 1994

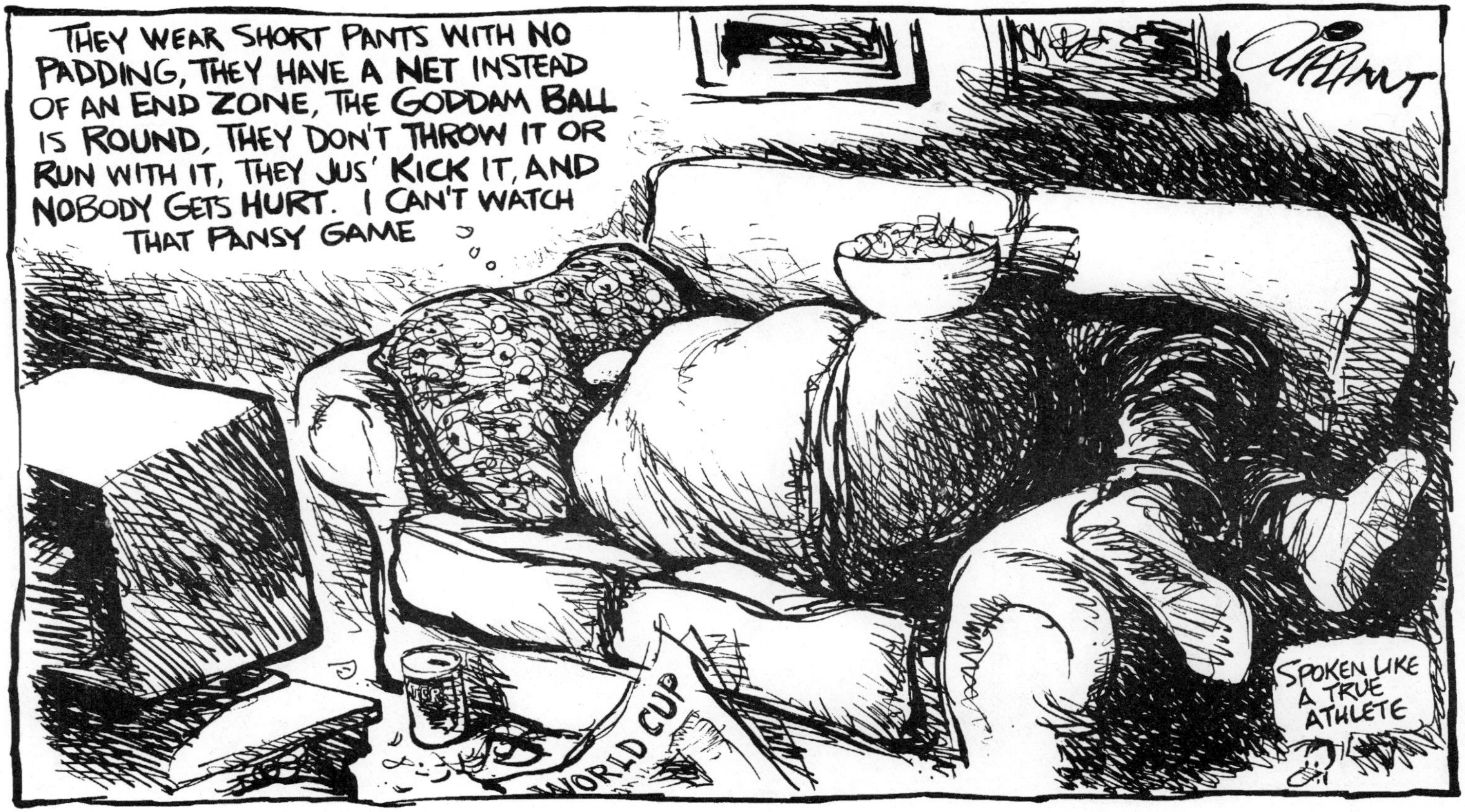
THEY WEAR SHORT PANTS WITH NO PADDING, THEY HAVE A NET INSTEAD OF AN END ZONE, THE GODDAM BALL IS ROUND, THEY DON'T THROW IT OR RUN WITH IT, THEY JUS' KICK IT, AND NOBODY GETS HURT. I CAN'T WATCH THAT PANSY GAME
WORLD CUP
SPOKEN LIKE A TRUE ATHLETE

June 24, 1994

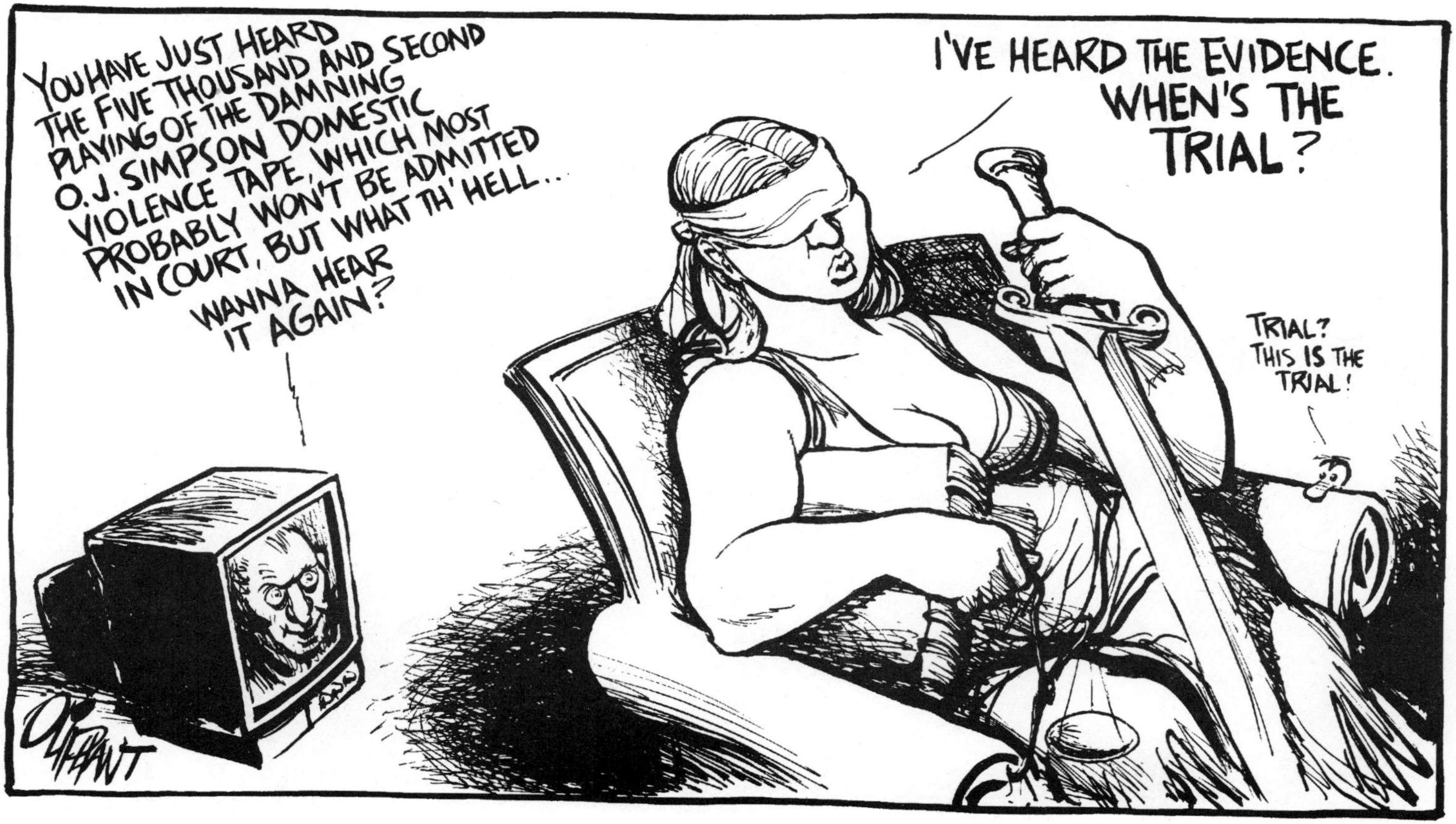
YOU HAVE JUST HEARD THE FIVE THOUSAND AND SECOND PLAYING OF THE DAMNING O.J. SIMPSON DOMESTIC VIOLENCE TAPE, WHICH MOST PROBABLY WON'T BE ADMITTED IN COURT, BUT WHAT TH' HELL...
WANNA HEAR IT AGAIN?
I'VE HEARD THE EVIDENCE. WHEN'S THE TRIAL?
TRIAL? THIS IS THE TRIAL!
OLIPHANT

June 25, 1994

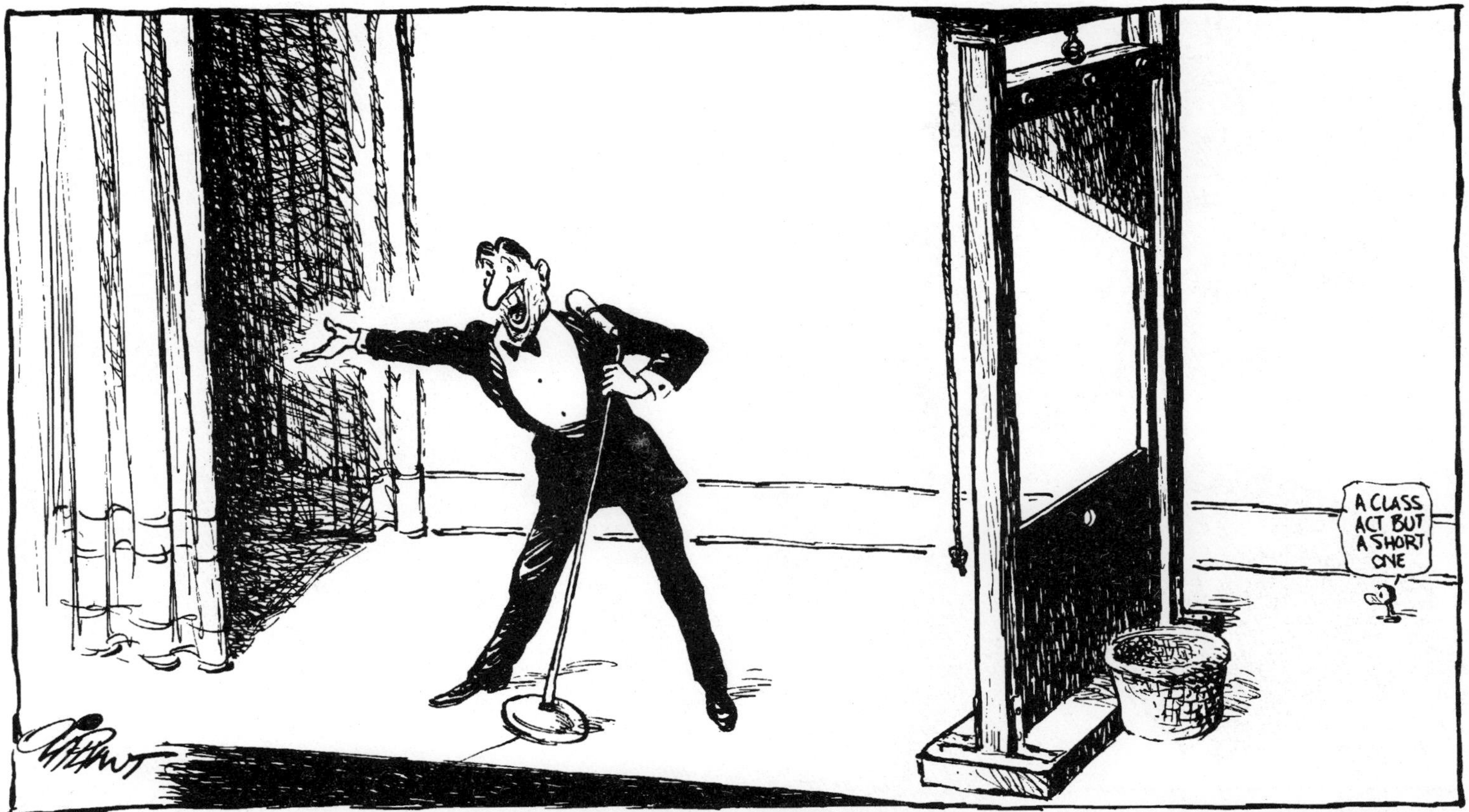
A CLASS ACT BUT A SHORT ONE

'AND NOW, ON STAGE FOR THE FIRST TIME, A SWELL GUY WITH HIS OWN UNIQUE ACT, TAKING HIS FIRST CRACK AT SHOW BIZ, LADIES AND GENTLEMEN A BIG HAND FOR JOOOHHN BOBBITT!'